CHECHE

Reminiscences of a Radical Magazine

CHECHE

Reminiscences of a Radical Magazine

Karim F Hirji (Editor)

MKUKI NA NYOTA
DAR—ES—SALAAM

Published by:

Mkuki na Nyota Publishers Ltd.

Nyerere Road, Quality Plaza Building

P. O. Box 4246

Dar es Salaam, Tanzania

www.mkukinanyota.com

ISBN 978 9987 08 098 4

Contents

Acronyms

ANC	African National Congress
DUSO	Dar es Salaam University Students Organization
FRELIMO	Frente de Libertacao de Mocambique
MPLA	Movimento Popular de Libertacao de Angola
OAU	Organization of African Unity
PAC	Pan Africanist Congress
SWAPO	South West African People's Organization
TANU	Tanganyika African National Union
TShs	Tanzania Shillings
TYL	TANU Youth League
UCD	University College, Dar es Salaam
UDSM	University of Dar es Salaam
USARF	University Students African Revolutionary Front
USUD	University Students Union of Dar es Salaam
ZANU	Zimbabwe African National Union
ZAPU	Zimbabwe African Peoples Union

Preface

The rationale for this book emerges from contrasting one event of the past with one of the present. In October 1967, the general meeting of the TANU Youth League in Arusha passed many radical resolutions which, among other things, called for the expulsion of all American Peace Corps volunteers from Tanzania (The Nationalist 1967e). The US at that time backed the Apartheid regime and Portuguese colonial rule in Africa, and stood behind numerous brutal dictatorships across the world. The Peace Corps was seen as a device to mask the imperial character of its foreign policy. This call was not an isolated event, but a sign of the times. In particular, university student groups across Africa in those days tended to adopt a militant anti-imperialist, Pan-African, and, in some cases, a socialist stand (Legum 1972; The Nationalist 1967h; 1969m; 1969n).

Four decades later, a prominent paper in Tanzania carried the headline: "Peace Corps set for duty in 19 districts" (The Citizen 2009). It pictured thirty-eight joyous American volunteers at their swearing-in ceremony presided over by their ambassador. The story glossed over the history of these volunteers in Tanzania and the world, mentioned their 38 years of service, and focused on the alleged common interests and strong bond between Tanzania and the US. There were no words on why, almost five decades after attaining self-rule, our nation should not be self-reliant on a simple matter like secondary school teachers. Was our continued reliance on charity not a matter of shame? No, the story was predicated on being grateful to the peace- loving nations like the US for most generous assistance they provide to the poor people of this planet. It read more like a verbatim reproduction of an embassy press release than the work of an independent, knowledgeable local reporter.

Today, the youth in Tanzania and Africa mostly, if not solely, hear such biased versions of events. Accurate renditions of what happened in the past and why that happened have been expunged from the media and commonly accessed sources, and thus from memory. It is hardly in the interest of those who dominate this planet today that the person in the street acquires a comprehensive understanding of history. Yet, if Africa is to rescue itself from its current predicaments, that is an essential requirement.

The main aim of this book is to remedy a part of that gap in knowledge. In particular, it narrates the turbulent life and times of a radical, socialist student magazine published at the University of Dar es Salaam (UDSM) from 1969 to 1970. *Cheche* -- Swahili for Spark -- was the organ of the University Students African Revolutionary Front (USARF). Four issues in all saw the light of the day (Appendix A shows their tables of contents). Though socialism was the official policy of Tanzania, the Marxist orientation and editorial independence of this magazine drew the ire of the university and state authorities. Matters increasingly came to a head, and in November 1970, USARF and *Cheche* were banned by the government.

The student activists were now constrained to operate under the umbrella of the ruling party. Nevertheless, the following year, they managed to bring out a successor magazine, *MajiMaji*. The radical orientation laid down earlier continued, and forty-six issues came out over the next fifteen years. To promote wider local access, some of them were in Swahili. A number of the later issues were of compromised quality. Publication became sporadic during the 1980s, and it died a natural death in 1986. The two magazines bore Swahili names; their origin and significance were also matters of controversy, forming one pillar of the story we unveil.

Cheche was the first anti-imperialist, socialist magazine originating from East Africa. It presented serious social, historical and economic analyses of Tanzania, Africa and the world at large. Poems, satire, cartoons, reviews and letters enlivened its pages. Its signature hallmark was the combination of novel analyses with militant anti-imperialism, a solid commitment to socialism, and uncompromising independence from the state and external powers. Over its short life, *Cheche* gained national and international prominence. Progressive students, academics and activists -- at home and abroad -- and the African liberation movements commended it. *MajiMaji* also garnered a similar reputation.

These magazines played a pivotal role in the emergence of a new incisive radical scholarship from and about Africa. Established radical authors and some who later became leading lights contributed articles. Yet, apart from short notes in a few papers and book chapters, the history of these student-run progressive journalistic endeavors is largely unknown. The shortfall needs to be remedied. This book, a first step in that direction, describes how *Cheche* came into being, the social context under which it was produced, the type of material it carried, and the reactions it elicited. It also reflects on the relevance of the student activism of yesterday to the current times.

This project has brewed in the editor's mind for a long time. A panel discussion chaired by Professor Issa Shivji on USARF and *Cheche* at the UDSM in April 2008 catalyzed the process. Several meetings with former comrades followed. The first outcome is this book, with contributions by seven erstwhile student activists. A second book on the successor magazine, *MajiMaji*, has been planned as well.

All contributors to this book were eye-witnesses to, and participants in, the events they narrate. In addition to the entire editorial board of *Cheche* -- Karim Hirji, Henry Mapolu and Zakia Hamdani Meghji -- they are George Hajivayanis, poet and all round activist; Ramadhan Meghji, artistic designer; and Christopher Liundi, the ruling party contact person for the university activists who later worked closely with *MajiMaji*. A relevant article from *Cheche* by Yoweri Museveni, the founding chairman of USARF, is reproduced here as well.

Content and Style
What the contributors say and how they say it reflects who they were. First hand knowledge enables them to combine personal, in-the-trenches stories with analyses of the local and global situations. Chapter 1 gives a summary of the social and political context of the times. Chapters 2 to 10 constitute the central portion in which the contributors describe their student experiences, editorial work and activism. Chapter 11 has three relevant poems, two of which have been previously published. Chapter 12 places the ban on USARF and *Cheche* in the context of the socialist experience of Tanzania; Chapter 13 compares and contrasts the current global situation with that of the 1970s; and Chapter 14 critiques the student activism of the past and reflects on its relevance to the present times.

The records preserved by the present editor and the discussions we held helped us to pin down dates and reconstruct events with a reasonable degree of accuracy. Yet, memories fade, events are obscured and many details are lost. Further, we remember some past events in different, even contradictory ways. The context and trends of that era, the main roles of the actors and the nature of key events, though, are consistently etched in our minds. In editing this book, vagueness and contradictions in recall were reconciled as follows. Say, comrade X is mentioned as a participant in a visit to an *Ujamaa* village or a student demonstration. In some cases, that is precisely known. In other cases, we know that X participated in several events of this type, but he or she may not have been present in that particular event. To faithfully portray the general situation and reconstruct events to a good degree of accuracy, literary license was combined with documented fact and personal recall to craft a cohesive tale. The basic aim is to accurately represent the spirit of a turbulent period in the form of a smoothly flowing narrative.

When a person first appears in a chapter, his or her full name is used; later, only the first or last name may be used, although exceptions do occur. While USARF, the parent organization of *Cheche*, is mentioned frequently in this book, this is not a history of USARF. The life span of *Cheche* was a year; that of USARF was three years. A complete history of USARF has yet to be produced.

Sources

Several sources were used for this book. Besides the copies of *Cheche*, the present editor has the original manuscripts, correspondence, financial records, and other administrative matters kept by the editorial board. Further, he has three batches of newspaper cuttings, papers and cyclostyled documents, and his personal diaries for 1969 and 1970. These were valuable for establishing timelines and recalling details. Personal recall was enhanced by discussions among ourselves, and with other comrades. Naijuka Kasihwaki, Nizar Visram, Issa Shivji, Lionel Cliffe, and Henry Mapolu were particularly helpful. Issa Shivji provided the inaugural issue of *MajiMaji* and two old letters from the present editor. Ed Ferguson gave copies of thirty-four relevant reports and articles from *The Nationalist*. All quotes used in this book fall within the fair use provision of copyright laws. We could not locate the publisher of Castillo (1984) which has the poem by O.R. Castillo reproduced in Chapter 11. However, this poem has appeared in several publications. When the copyright holder contacts us, we will gladly pay the requisite permission fees.

Eleven previous publications relate to the history we cover. In alphabetic order, these are Hirji (1971a; 1990; 2009a), Kamenju (1973), Legum (1972), Othman (2010), Peter and Mvungi (1986), Saul (1973; 2009), Shivji (1993a; 1993b). But none of these works contains more than one or two paragraphs about *Cheche*. They were used to cross check what we have written. Overall, what we present complements the historic record, and gives a richer day-to-day account that acknowledges the efforts of a large group of activists who, in their unique ways, furthered the socialist and anti-imperialist struggles at the UDSM.

Chapter 2 deserves a special note. It is an edited version of the article by Yoweri Museveni entitled My Three Years in Tanzania: Glimpses of the Struggle between Revolution and Reaction which appeared in *Cheche* No. 2 in July 1970. At the present time, Mr. Yoweri K Museveni is the President of the Republic of Uganda. This chapter should not be taken to reflect, in any way, the current views of President Museveni, or of the government of Uganda. Moreover, its inclusion here does not in any shape, degree or form signal our agreement or disagreement with the policies or actions of his government. It has been produced, without any attempt to seek permission, as a historic document of special relevance to this book. Its author is Yoweri Museveni, a radical student leader who studied at the University College, Dar es Salaam from 1967 to 1970. It was not submitted for this book by His Excellency, Mr. Yoweri K Museveni.

It was the explicit editorial policy of *Cheche* and *MajiMaji* not to subscribe to "bourgeois copyright laws." As editors, we stated in writing that our material could be reproduced without permission by anyone and for any purpose. All issues of *Cheche* are in the public domain. Our reproduction of historic material from this magazine subscribes to that philosophy and fact.

Acknowledgments

The guiding spirit of this book derives from the editorial work we did forty years ago. Namely, that it has been produced with our own efforts and resources. I make this point especially because these days "nothing of consequence" happens in Tanzania or Africa without external donor funds. Even the erstwhile progressive intellectuals are now engulfed by donor dollars. It is therefore a real pleasure to report that no donor funds or support of any sort have been used to plan, write, edit, or produce this book.

The comrades named above helped this effort. Henry Mapolu, Rosa Hirji and Laurel Ackerson assisted with archival research. Rosa Hirji also xii

gave comments that improved the presentation. Ed Ferguson deserves
a special mention for pointing out key sources, copying useful material
and giving extensive comments on all the chapters. Warren Reed, my
editor at Mkuki na Nyota, carefully read the manuscript and gave useful
suggestions. I extend many radical thanks to them all.

Each contributor to this work is responsible only for that which
appears under his or her name. As the editor, I take the additional
responsibility for the book as a whole, and for errors that persist.

Karim F Hirji
Dar es Salaam
August 2010

In Memory of

Abdulrahaman M Babu,
Ahmed Gora Ebrahim,
Jonathan M Kamala, Charles Kileo,
Ramadhan N Meghji, A S Namama,
Haroub Othman, Walter Rodney
and Andrew Shija

1

An Era of Global Turbulence

Karim F Hirji

"We, the people of Tanzania, would like to light a candle and put it on top of Mount Kilimanjaro which would shine beyond our borders, giving hope where there was despair, love where there was hate and dignity where before there was only humiliation."

- Mwalimu Julius K Nyerere -

Two Systems

The world in 1970 was divided into three political camps. The USA led the capitalist camp (the Western camp) that also contained Canada, Western Europe, Japan, Israel, Australia and New Zealand. The USSR, Eastern Europe, China, North Vietnam, North Korea, Laos and Cuba made up the communist camp (the Eastern bloc). The other nations of Africa, the Middle East, Asia, Latin America and the Caribbean constituted the Third World. Many of them had discarded the shackles of colonial rule barely a decade or so previously. A few, mostly in Africa, were still under colonial or settler rule. Communist nations outside of Europe at times participated in the forums that brought Third World nations together.

There were, though, only two economic systems, the (international) capitalist system and the socialist system. The former system had two segments; the industrialized states (the West) formed the dominant segment and the underdeveloped nations (the Third World), the dominated segment. While sharply divided internally along class lines, the two segments were at the same time linked by a complex web of economic ties that favored the rich nations. Accordingly, the poor nations supplied agricultural and mineral commodities and cheap labor to the rich nations, and formed captive markets for their manufactures. Under capitalism the economic surplus (new wealth) was appropriated by small internal and external business classes and was invested to maximize the profits of its members (Baran and Sweezy 1968; Cox 1964; Frank 1969; Jalee 1968; Leys 1975; Prashad 2008; Rodney 1972a; Woddis 1968).

The communist nations functioned under the socialist economic system. Under socialism, the surplus accrued into public coffers and was directed to promote general welfare. In broad terms, and with many variations, this was the main distinction between these systems. Earlier, the communist nations had been dominated by capitalism but through varied revolutionary processes and war, they had managed to disengage themselves from that system. Trade and other ties with capitalist nations did not cease completely but their economies were no longer governed by the rules and dictates of capitalism (Dobb 1970; Donahue 1986; Hinton 1970; Hinton and Magdoff 2008; Raby 2009; Rosendahl 1998).

Throughout this era, neither capitalism nor socialism was a static system with uniform component parts. Internal class struggles and external conflicts propelled nations in different directions. Fierce competition for global resources between major capitalist nations produced two world wars. The colonized nations fought for, and won their freedom, to one degree or another. The USA strove to replace Britain and France as the major actor in their former colonies while the USSR and China parted ways in the 1960s. The latter event generated a deep schism within the socialist camp, especially as each party tried to get more political allies in the Third World.

The long term aim of the West was to monopolize the wealth of this planet for the benefit of their multinational corporations. The dual objectives of maintaining decisive economic control over poor nations and recapturing the nations that had broken away were pursued on several fronts. Military violence was supplemented by firm economic control under the umbrella of the major international financial institutions, like the International Monetary Fund (IMF), World Bank and World Trade Organization (WTO). Diverse forms of cultural, diplomatic and media domination were also used in this endeavor. These global projections of capitalism are what we call imperialism. As a result of these strategies, formal decolonization in Africa masked persistent external economic exploitation that enriched a tiny local minority and international investors while the masses remained mired in misery. As Kwame Nkrumah put it, these neo-colonies had flag independence but not real freedom to determine their own future (Danaher 1994; Jalee 1968; Nkrumah 1966; Magdoff 2008; Toussaint 2007).

Kenya, Tanzania and Uganda, the three nations of East Africa that had attained independence from Britain in the early 1960s, remained in the neo-colonial mould. In the first decade after independence, their economies expanded in some ways. New industries were set up, agriculture output went up, major transport projects were completed, education and health services expanded, literacy rates rose, and so on. But this growth trajectory followed a common World Bank-led program for Africa, did not lay the foundation for a self-sustaining, strong economy, increased external debt, and reinforced external dependency. It was growth without development. On the social level, emergent business, bureaucratic and professional classes (the petty bourgeoisie) faced off the colonial era commercial bourgeoisie mainly of Indian origin and the European settlers. The former wanted to step into the shoes of the latter. As the masses saw the new *wabenzi* (those with luxury Mercedes Benz cars) reaping the fruits of independence for themselves, the sense of disquiet on the streets and villages grew (Leys 1975; Mamdani 1978; Rweyemamu 1973; Shivji 1976).

Action and Reaction

A system based on national and international exploitation inevitably generates internal and external conflict on a regular basis. The 1960s and 1970s were also times of global turbulence. To maintain and expand its imperialist hegemony, the US waged a brutal war on Vietnam and Laos, later extended to Cambodia, which took the lives of more than four million people. It installed, or overtly or covertly backed, dictatorships in Iran, Iraq, Turkey, Indonesia, the Philippines, South Korea, Congo, Ghana, Ethiopia, Libya, Saudi Arabia, Jordan, Brazil, Argentina, Chile, Nicaragua and other nations that oppressed their peoples with impunity. The other major Western powers mostly went along with such aggression, or engaged in their own acts of international perfidy. In one way or another, they stood behind the Apartheid regime of South Africa, the settler state in Rhodesia, vicious colonial rule over Angola, Mozambique and Guinea Bissau by Portugal and the oppression of the Palestinian people by Israel. France retained military bases and openly meddled in the internal affairs of its former colonies (Blum 2009; Chomsky and Herman 1979).

Violence inevitably provokes counter reaction. People all over the planet thereby rose up to confront injustice and exploitation. This occurred to such a wide extent that we can also characterize this period as one during which capitalism and imperialism were on the defensive. A general sketch is given here: In the still directly dominated regions of Africa, anti-colonial, anti-Apartheid movements gathered momentum. In the newly independent nations, awareness that indigenous rulers continued to serve the Western overlords and their own petty interests grew, leading to strikes, student unrest, and ethnic conflict. In Central and South America, popular guerrilla movements challenged the political and economic strangle hold of US companies and local land owning classes that kept the people impoverished and disenfranchised. Led by Nasser of Egypt, Nehru of India, Nkrumah of Ghana, and Sukarno of Indonesia, the nations of the global South established a community of non-aligned nations to counter the Western and Soviet power blocs (Hobsbawm 1994; Prashad 2008).

Imperialism attacked popular movements, directly or with the assistance of local stooges by unleashing violence at different levels. Leaders of popular movements, students, academics, trade unionists, peasant leaders and priests were assassinated by the thousands. Patrice Lumumba, Malcolm X, Martin Luther King, Che Guevara, Eduardo Mondlane, Pio Gama Pinto and Amilcar Cabral were among the notable leaders killed in this onslaught. Also, governments unfriendly to the West were destabilized, isolated or overthrown, as happened to those of Kwame Nkrumah, Milton Obote and Salvador Allende (Blum 2009; Chomsky and Herman 1979).

Of specific interest for us is that in those days students across the globe organized, in diverse ways, to challenge different aspects of the imperialist, capitalist system. University students marched to demand justice, peace and a better life for all humanity. In the US, they confronted racism, sexism and militarism. France, Germany, the United Kingdom, Pakistan, Iran, Chile, and Argentina, among others, were rocked by student revolts. In China, students waged a cultural revolution. The overthrow of the US backed dictator in Cuba and the defiance of the revolutionary state led by Fidel Castro and Che Guevara inspired and energized millions. American atrocities in Vietnam and the degenerate form of racism officially practiced in South Africa also sparked student demonstrations in African cities (Ali 2005).

The imperial onslaught and popular reactions to it occurred within a complex socio-historic process which had many local peculiarities and eventualities. Nevertheless, it was also a global process with common roots and similar manifestations.

An African Star

In the struggle against Western imperialism raging in Africa, Tanzania, under the leadership of Julius Kambarage Nyerere, came to occupy a prominent position. Mwalimu Nyerere, as he was known, was a fervent fighter for total decolonization of Africa and promotion of African unity. His diplomatic and material support to African liberation movements far surpassed that given by other African states. In the arenas like the UN and the British Commonwealth, Tanzania adopted a progressive foreign policy, generally siding with the anti-imperialist struggles and socialist nations in a consistent manner. The majority of African liberation movements were based in Tanzania; those that were not, established an office there. Civil rights activists from the US, anti-imperialist fighters like Che Guevara, Chedi Jagan and Amilcar Cabral, and progressive intellectuals like C.L.R. James and Eric Williams visited Tanzania (Othman 2005).

In 1967, to the intense displeasure of Britain and the US, Tanzania promulgated the Arusha Declaration making socialism and self-reliance (*Ujamaa na Kujitegemea*) the national policy (TANU 1967). Foreign banks and major firms were put under state ownership. A rural transformation strategy based on the cooperative mode of life was initiated, and a code to curtail wealth accumulation by the political leadership instituted. An education system formed in the colonial era that had promoted white collar skills and elitism was to be replaced by the policy of Education for Self-Reliance that stressed relevant practical education and service to the people (Nyerere 1967). A broad program of grassroots democracy to decentralize decision-making power for the rural areas, and to give industrial and other workers a say in the management of their firms was promulgated (TANU 1971).

These radical measures made Tanzania a beacon of hope, and inspired people struggling against injustice and exploitation everywhere.

Sparks at the Hill

From a modest start a year earlier, the University College, Dar es Salaam (UCD) became a constituent college of the newly set up University of East Africa in 1962. The campus moved to a lush, hilly, expansive terrain roughly five miles from the city center. From that time, the campus is commonly referred to as "the Hill." Established in the academic tradition of a British university, it boasted modern lecture theaters, a large, well-stocked library, tall towers serving as office blocks and halls of residence for students, swimming pool, and sports facilities. Most of the academic and senior administrative staff resided in elegantly built apartment blocks, or mini-bungalows spread across the hilly area that also had a decent network of connecting roads.

In all physical aspects and way of life, the university stood a world apart from the poor neighborhoods that surrounded it, and from the rest of the nation. No wonder the outlook of the academic staff and students at the Hill was similar to that found on other African campuses. The students -- children of peasants and workers -- were inflicted with an elitist (petty bourgeois) mentality. Their eyes and ears were set on a rapid elevation of their social status. Thus, when the government proposed a national service program for university graduates in 1966, they found it in conflict with such aspirations and staged a protest march to oppose it. As a result, many of them were expelled from the university, though most were re-admitted after a while (Kanywanyi 2006; Resnick 1968).

The expulsion, together with the radicalization of the national political atmosphere, had a strong impact on the attitudes prevalent at the Hill. A major conference on "The Role of the University College in Socialist Tanzania" was held in March 1967. Vice President Rashidi Kawawa and Health Minister A.M. Babu addressed the gathering. Babu, the only person in Mwalimu's Cabinet with solid socialist credentials, called for a fundamental transformation of the institution into a socialist university (The Nationalist 1967a; 1967b; 1967c; 1967d). Around the same time, prominent progressive scholars in the social sciences, law and natural sciences from the world over joined the university, or came on short visits. While most academic staff remained steeped in the traditional conservative scholarship, a growing number, especially after the Arusha Declaration, had a liberal, leftist, socialist, anti-imperialist, Pan-Africanist, or Marxist political orientation. The campus soon bubbled with progressive thought, generating sound scholarly material that challenged the Western domination in varied academic fields. Indeed, in that respect, it soon became a place without parity or parallel in the whole of Africa (Othman 2005).

At same time, Mwalimu Nyerere was urging the students to discard their selfish outlook and serve the people (Nyerere 1966b; Rodney 1968). A branch of the youth wing of the ruling party, TANU Youth League (TYL) opened at the Hill in March 1967. Inspired by Mwalimu, the Arusha Declaration, progressives like A.M. Babu and Walter Rodney, and the global climate of activism, a small number of students came to adopt a militantly leftist political orientation. First, they started a socialist club. Later, under the leadership of Yoweri Museveni, USARF was formed. The TYL branch was then was taken over by stridently socialist, anti-imperialist students, many of whom were also members of USARF. The activists worked with the growing bevy of progressive faculty members. As its first major action, in November 1967, USARF conducted a seminar on the African freedom struggle that secured good attendance from students, staff and people from the city. Walter Rodney, the principal speaker at this event, put a special emphasis on the need to integrate sound socialist theories within the academic curricula for all academic degree programs (The Nationalist 1967f; 1967g). The Hill TYL organized a seminar on socialism and rural development in January 1968 that was opened by Mwalimu Nyerere (Nyerere 1968b).

What was occurring at university campuses across the world in that era manifested itself in Tanzania, but with its own local features. Befitting a university, the Hill became a battle field of competing ideas. New pro-socialist and anti-imperialist visions of the world confronted the old business as usual, pro-Western, pro-capitalist ideology permeating the conceptualization and teaching of the social sciences and law (Arrighi 1968). Rightist students and academic staff battled, on the ideological plane, with leftist students and staff. Papers, proposals and memoranda were written and debated. Demonstrations, sit-ins and boycotts occurred. Old curricula were challenged and alternatives subjects and syllabi were proposed. USARF and TYL organized public lectures, conducted self-education classes, took part in adult literacy programs, held discussions on socialism and imperialism in schools, raised funds for African liberation movements, joined hands with villagers and workers in on-the-ground work, and even sent a delegation to the liberated areas of Mozambique. The ideological clashes on the campus thereby produced, in time, broad national manifestations.

A remarkable feature of these struggles was the extent to which the left-wing students educated themselves, and became a group independent of any political or other forms of patronage. While cooperating with progressive academic staff, they stood their ground on many issues. Time and again, they educated and led their lecturers, intellectually and politically. They were tenacious and committed to African liberation and socialism. They did not toe the party line, or blindly submit to authority. They often raised critical, fundamental issues without fear or favor. They examined deeds, not just words.

The magazine *Cheche* was an important, natural product of the ideological contentions. Started by the leftist students in 1969, it thereafter became the primary vehicle for pursuing them. A low-budget, time-demanding undertaking produced by purely volunteer effort under decidedly unfriendly conditions, it nonetheless attracted contributions from thinkers and activists like Walter Rodney, Tamas Szentes, Yoweri Museveni, Issa Shivji, John Saul, Dan Nabudere and Haroub Othman. Many articles in the magazine challenged the conventional wisdom on the history and contemporary situation in Africa, and fearlessly criticized the powers that be, both at home and abroad.

Because of the stand they took and their bold activities, USARF and *Cheche* were despised by the campus right wingers, state and party bureaucrats, and, of course, by representatives of Western imperialists. Russian, Korean and Chinese diplomats, for their part, were also displeased because these students did not follow the "correct political line."

The student radicals did not, it must be stressed, engage in any form of violence, illegal acts, or subversive activity. They promoted socialism, the national policy. But they were too independent; too outspoken; and too often stated the facts as they were. *Cheche* exposed the gap between the rhetoric and practice of socialism. This was why high ranking party and state bureaucrats abhorred it. USARF and *Cheche*, were thereby, and in a short time, proscribed by the government. The activists, for their part, did not take the blow lying down. They deftly reorganized, and returned to the ideological arena within a few months with another radical magazine.

This is the broad story underpinning this book, how *Cheche* came into being, how it functioned, what reactions it elicited, how it died, and how a radical successor emerged. It is told in detail by people who were at the scene. We also discuss how the banning of USARF and *Cheche* resonated within the broader political context. Was it an exception to the rule, or a reflection of the general state of affairs? And finally, after presenting what has and has not changed since those days, we discuss the relevance of the activism of the past to the present times.

The timeline for USARF and *Cheche* is sketched in Appendix B. It highlights the key milestones in the history contained in this book.

2

Activism at the Hill

Yoweri Museveni

"A country is not socialist simply because all or all the major,
means of production are controlled and owned by the
Government."
- The Arusha Declaration -

Editorial Note: This chapter is an edited version of an article that
appeared in *Cheche* No. 2 (Museveni 1970a).

Expectations and Reality

Tanzania stands out as one of the few African countries that are struggling against imperialism. I spent the past three years [July 1967 to March 1970] in Tanzania as a student at the University College, Dar es Salaam (UCD). For me and my fellow students, it was a period of intense activism. In this article, I will lay down a resume of some aspects of that struggle. I will use my personal experiences to illuminate the general struggle which we were engaged in at the College.

Before I came to Tanzania, I expected a lot, probably too much, of the Tanzanian revolution. At a distance, one gets an exaggerated image of the anti-imperialist stance of Tanzania. You get the image of clear-headedness regarding socialism, anti-imperialism and Pan-Africanism. You get the impression that the government leaders, ministers, top civil servants and party officials are devoted cadres with a high level of political consciousness. You get the impression that this and that type of situation would never arise in Tanzania where so much is supposed to happen. All such impressions, I have since discovered, are exaggerated.

But how does one get them in the first instance? Tanzania's foreign policy is what I think creates such impressions. The strong reaction towards German arrogance, the breaking of diplomatic ties with Britain, the resolute support that Tanzania accords to the liberation movements in the South are sources of pride and inspiration to African nationalists all over Africa. Remember this African nationalist is starved of any dignity; he is an heir of the oppressed, degraded, dehumanized ancestors. He is a relative of slaves both on the continent and abroad. Any act of defiance by an African state vis-à-vis the centuries old enemies of our people thus has high marginal utility. Sometimes it is overblown. It is against such background that we must understand the impressions of non-Tanzania African nationalists who almost invariably over evaluate Tanzania's militant anti-imperialist stand. That is, however, a dangerous attitude on our part because it can lead to disillusionment.

It was mainly because of my over-evaluation of Tanzania's achievements that while at home in Uganda, I was determined to come to Tanzania at any cost. I was so determined that I put UCD as my only choice on the university entrance forms. In fact, if, for any reason, I had failed to get admission to UCD, I would not have gone to university at all. This is because I was not so much interested in going to a college as in coming to Dar es Salaam -- to Tanzania. It is Dar es Salaam's atmosphere of freedom fighters, socialists, nationalizations, anti-imperialism that attracted me rather than the so-called "academicians" at the UCD. I considered my stay at the college as a means of staying in Dar es Salaam.

While in Uganda, I had looked at President Nyerere's leadership as a source of inspiration to the struggling people of Africa. Tanzania's staunch anti-colonialist policy and the President's commitment to the formation of an East African federation made his leadership exemplary. I regarded Tanzania as Africa's Prussia and President Nyerere as our Bismark. This was in the days when my political views had not coagulated into a (socialistic) ideological outlook. I did not know at that time that unity by itself could not mean much; and that what mattered was whether the purpose of the political unit was to serve the people or to serve imperialism.

Expecting all this from Tanzania, I arrived at the College in July 1967. I was, almost immediately, disappointed. I found the students lacking in militancy. Many were hostile to socialism, and some, even to the question of African liberation. There was no clear social commitment on the part of the broad sections of the student body. Most of our extra-curricular time was taken up by frivolous activities: drinking, dancing, and watching decadent Western films. I remember one occasion when I was really most unhappy. This was the time when Chief Albert Luthili died. A service in his honor was organized at the Arnatoglou Hall. Transport was provided to all the students who wished attend the service. Alas!! - only a handful of us turned up -- the majority being students from Southern Africa. Apathy towards, and ignorance of, many vital questions regarding the interests of the African people were the rule of the day. Teachers -- sorry! -- lecturers and professors were notably hopeless as far as the interests of our people went. I remember one eminent American "scholar" -- whose mannerisms were quite obnoxious -- once declared that the Arusha Declaration was "against national integration." To my surprise, I saw some students taking down notes!

USARF is Born

Against this background, a group of us decided to form a revolutionary student organization. We first formed the socialist club. But this tended to be just a study group rather than being an action front as well. TANU Youth League was at the time most ineffective, and very unpopular among students. Of course, unpopularity by itself does not mean much; in fact it is commendable if unpopularity is due to a correct revolutionary stance taken by any concerned organization to the detriment of the reactionary forces. But, in this instance, TYL's unpopularity was due, most likely, to a lack of commitment on the part of the leaders. Many students felt, I do not know with how much justification, that TYL was a vehicle for opportunism.

Around November 1967, we formed the University Students African Revolutionary Front (USARF). Our aim was to encourage revolutionary activities at the College, and to transform the college from being a center of reaction -- where Mazrui's "two concepts of nationalization" could be hailed as a mark of great scholarship -- to a hotbed of revolutionary cadres, cadres that would dedicate themselves, unto death, to the cause of the African revolution.

After USARF was formed, Stockley Carmichael paid a visit to Tanzania. He spoke several times under our auspices and made a great impression on the students. We organized teach-ins, film shows and demonstrations in connection with the international anti-imperialist struggle. People like Walter Rodney, Eric Williams, Chedi Jagan, and Eduardo Mondlane spoke to the students on our platform. The deep impact they made on a number of students swelled our ranks, and enhanced our reputation so much that the reactionary authorities at the College began to worry. I remember once when they tried to prevent us from showing films on the struggle of the Korean people. We resolutely frustrated their intentions and before long not only the Koreans, but the Cubans, Vietnamese, and Chinese comrades found their way into our forums. We waged such a resolute struggle against the interests of imperialism that the reactionaries thought we were mad. The imperialists were exasperated by our tenacity in frustrating their numerous designs on the College. For instance, on one occasion we foiled the plan of the American imperialists who had planned to bring to the college the arch-uncle Tom, Edward Brooke, whose intention was to dull our vigilance.

The formation of USARF was a major landmark in the anti-imperialist struggle on the campus, in Tanzania and indeed in the whole of East Africa. The campuses of East Africa had hitherto been strongholds of reaction. With USARF, they were now infected with germs of revolutionary thought. Sister revolutionary fronts were formed in Nairobi and Makerere. The reactionaries on the campus, especially the authorities, were particularly hostile to us. Notwithstanding, at UCD, we waged a resolute struggle. One example was the stand we took against the Rag Day when our militants engaged in physical confrontation with the reactionary students who supported the Rag Day.[1] We won victory after a police intervention. Rag Day was cancelled and it has never been revived. This victory and the visit by our militants to the liberated areas of Mozambique raised our morale and dampened that of the reactionaries.

---

1   The Rag Day is explained in Chapter 7, and poetically critiqued in Chapter 11.

We were generally on the offensive while the reactionaries were on the defensive as was, again, shown by our victory in the Law Faculty.[2]

Reactionary Backlash

Our rising influence and militancy in the latter part of 1969 and early in 1970 led the reactionaries to conceive a master-plan. I am one of those who believe in the wise leadership of President Nyerere. It had always been our view that he would go further than the Arusha Declaration if he felt that popular pressure demanded it. Indeed, he has, on many, occasions, said that "the youth should always be on his left" -- the youth, the army, etc. should drag him in a progressive direction rather than him dragging the country. The flourishing of youth groups like USARF and the possibility of further radicalization of the youth meant that the President may move further to the left. This possibility was a cause of deep concern and irritation for the reactionaries. They had felt comfortable with the 1966 situation whereby most of the undergraduate students appeared hostile to progressive measures. A situation where the youth, at least a group of them, were urging the President to move further to the left, to turn TANU into a vanguard party, to arm the peasants, etc. was not to the taste of the imperialists and their local allies. Their fears were further heightened when we started holding ideological classes every Sunday, publishing a paper and generally solidifying our revolutionary theory. To them, all this was fraught with danger. Hence they conceived a master plan: to create confusion and tension between us and the President and portray us as a danger to the government. Rumors of the communists who wanted to form a communist party to oppose TANU spread in town with snowballing effect. Wild distortions and unfounded amplifications of the rumors ensued. All sorts of slander was aimed at us.

It was in this context that the President's visit to the College occurred.[3] The ground had been prepared. In the session he held, the questions from us were arranged in such a way that he had no alternative but to regard us as spoilt children who did not understand elementary facts about life. He supported the Karadha scheme which we had opposed. The reactionaries were elated. We had been, according to them, crushed. Only one thing saved us. The President had not denounced us in specific terms, which was the main thing they wanted. During his second visit, they further pressed for this to happen. But to their bitter

---

2   Radical students occupied the Faculty of Law in March 1969 to protest the introduction of military law and other changes in the curriculum which they felt were inspired by American political influence (The Nationalist 1969a; 1969b; 1969c).

3   The details about and the aftermath of this visit are described in Chapter 4.

disappointment, the President began to realize that he was being used by the enemies of socialism to denounce the supporters of socialism.

Towards the end of my stay, USARF and the campus TYL were as determined as ever before to continue to play their part in the struggle for the materialization of socialism that the Tanzanians are waging. Socialism, I think, is the only hope for the world's oppressed masses.

3

The Spark Is Kindled

Karim F Hirji

"I am motivated, essentially, by the fact that every human being
ought to make a contribution towards human progress. We are
not just on this planet to eat, to sleep, and then we die. I think
we came because we have a contribution to make."
-Oronto Douglas-

Sparkling Spirits

It is a cool breezy Friday evening. Books and notes are cast aside; high
spirits permeate the air. Soothing tunes of Congolese and local bands
echo in the residence towers. Reggae or Calypso enlivens a few floors.
The cafeteria side bar is packed. Students with budgets on the low side
are glued to the gossip postings in the walkway tunnel nearby. Some
do their laundry; a few try to catch up on lost sleep. And more jostle in
Ubungo and Mwenge -- the neighborhoods nearby -- for food, fun and
dancing while others visit relatives and friends across the city.

A narrow bridge connects the residential and academic areas at
the Hill. The latter is dark, only a handful of staff offices are lit. Walter
Rodney types out page after page of *How Europe Underdeveloped
Africa*; Andrew Lyall and Haroub Othman leaf through a report on
restructuring the courses at the Faculty of Law, exchanging a word now
and then; Professor Ted Phythian, Ralph Masenge and Geoffrey Mmari
animatedly plan a meeting of the Mathematical Association of Tanzania;
Dr. Stephen Lucas has almost completed grading the pile of twenty five
essays on the sociology of education on his desk.

Apart from two postgraduate students and three sleepy staff, the library
-- a stellar repository of scholarly material rivaling any in East and Central
Africa -- is bereft of life. This is nowhere near the final examinations time
when, Friday or no Friday night, it is full of anxious, studious souls.

The lecture and seminar rooms are also mostly unlit. In one science
lecture hall, the Ismailia students have begun their Friday prayers. A
student and his girlfriend stand in a hushed argument in one seminar
room. However, something unusual is afoot in the larger of the two Arts
and Social Sciences lecture halls. A group of thirty or so students keenly
listen to one articulate comrade. Apart from an incognito state security
agent, those congregated are idealistic students. It is not a formal class,
but they are as attentive as if it was. Yoweri Museveni talks with a twinge
of a smile on his lips, but the topic of his oration is far from frivolous:
"What is the role of university students in confronting the major political
and economic challenges facing Africa?"

This gathering of the University Students African Revolutionary
Front (USARF), the first general meeting for the present academic year,
began at 6 p.m. Museveni has chaired the group for almost two years.
He proceeds earnestly.

Museveni reminds the assembled of the nations in Africa which
continue to suffer from brutal colonial, settler or Apartheid rule.
Nominal independence for the rest has meant little in terms of freedom

from economic and cultural bondage, or betterment of the lives of the people. Echoing an often noted theme, he says that students have a critical role in the fight for African liberation. To play it effectively they must, first and foremost, liberate themselves mentally. This process includes critiquing what their lecturers feed them. The pro-capitalist and pro-imperialist bias pervading the teaching of social sciences and other subjects has to be exposed. Alternative ways of approaching these disciplines have to be sought.

The words are familiar to me and many in the audience. We had occupied the Faculty of Law in March 1969, and challenged the content and orientation of law courses. The episode had culminated in the formation of a student vigilance committee with USARF activists Charles Kileo and Issa Shivji assuming the lead role (The Nationalist 1969a; 1969b; 1969c).

Museveni is a charismatic and inspirational speaker. His remarks are directed for the most part to the dozen or so new students. A few have already joined USARF while the others are considering whether or not to throw in their lot with us.

Two weeks earlier, USARF had sponsored an evening public lecture by Rodney. The topic was the Cuban revolution and its relevance to Africa. The eloquent lecture by a superb historian also served as an introduction to USARF for the first year students. That about a third of those present today are new faces is a testament to the success of that event.

Museveni's introduction leads to other items on the agenda. Kapote Mwakasungura, a comrade from Malawi, takes the floor. He reminds us that for the academy, it is a time of transition. Presently, UCD is a constituent college of the University of East Africa. But the next academic year, it will be a full-fledged university. There is a Presidential Visitation Committee to oversee the process. Kapote has headed a three-person team charged with drafting the USARF memorandum to this Committee. He now presents the initial draft in which the main weaknesses of the current system of university education are discussed.

We want to influence the reorganization of the academic structures and curricula. The memorandum is devoted to the teaching of social sciences. First, it notes the general failure of the university to produce well-rounded intellectuals able to reflect critically on important ideas of the day. Second, it points out that the social sciences basically serve as "an apology and a mechanism for defending capitalism." Thirdly, education is "not integrated into national life." Four remedies are then proposed. The artificial fragmentation social science disciplines needs to end.

Wider use of books and papers by socialist intellectuals, institution of relevant practical training, and recruitment of members of staff with a socialist world outlook are also needed (USARF 1969).

The draft of the report makes the essential points but needs further work in terms of style and discipline level details. There is a short discussion, after which he is given the responsibility to prepare the final draft. As there is no student from the Faculty of Science on his team, I am appointed to fill the gap.

Kapote is an easy going, mild mannered person. I find it a real pleasure to talk with this gentle soul. Underneath, he is far from happy, a deeply tormented refugee from his homeland. The relations between Tanzania and Malawi are, to put it mildly, strained. While Tanzania is at the leading edge of the confrontation with Apartheid South Africa, Malawi under Hastings Kamuzu Banda is an ally of that atrocious regime. This virtual potentate is lavishly funded by the US and Britain. His government spends more on maintaining his four large palaces than on health care for his people, and it brooks no political opposition. Kapote has told us about how his friends and family suffer behind bars under this cruel despot, and how, by a stroke of luck, he escaped that fate.

The agenda is too long. The meeting must end as the cafeteria will close soon. The next day we make our first trip to the Kongo *Ujamaa* village near Bagamoyo, forty miles from the Hill. This is not a tourist visit. Having left at dawn, we arrive just as the peasants begin work on the village farm. A brief, warm welcome is followed by several hours of toil. Some of us cut and clear the bush, some dig the soil with a *jembe*, and some plant previously prepared ground. Bernard Mbakileki and Andrew Shija sweat the most, inspiring the book worms like Henry Mapolu and me to put in our best. In the course of the day, the villagers tell us about the chronic water shortage and other problems they face. Mzee Selemani, the chairman, and the villagers are delighted at our presence, saying so in no uncertain terms. More than anyone, they are enamored with George Hajivayanis. His Afro-Greek complexion makes them think he is a *mzungu*. But as he smoothly blends with all, speaks exquisite Swahili spiced with the local dialect, jokes with the elders, and enthralls the kids, and when his words resonate what they feel in their hearts, the barriers melt away. It is as if they have known him for ages and *vice versa*.

We have brought along flour, oil and beans. An ample meal is prepared. Late in the afternoon, students, peasants and families sit on mats to consume it with gusto. Upon return to the Hill at 6:30 pm, our arms and feet ache from the grind of the day. Yet we are upbeat in spirits. I feel the trip was an essential expression of solidarity with fellow humans. It is not enough to talk and theorize about socialism. We have to physically participate in the struggles on the ground as well.

Ideological Sparks

As the academic year gathers momentum, I am somewhat laid back in my studies. The lectures in philosophy of education are insipid and shallow. The lecturer not only has a biased bourgeois perspective but also likes to spew out what he has memorized from one or two American textbooks. The absence of original or critical thought alienates me. There is little tolerance for dissenting views. So, I skip the class on a regular basis.

Two of the first books I read when I joined the university last year were *The Wretched of the Earth* and *Black Skin, White Masks* (Fanon 1965; 1967). Franz Fanon, the author of the books, was a radical psychiatrist from the Caribbean. Stemming from his practice in Algeria in the 1950s at the height of the struggle against French colonial rule, these books provide an astute analysis of the nature and dynamics of colonialism together with insightful ruminations on life after decolonization. His prose is majestic, his observations, stinging and erudite. He is a compulsory read if one is concerned about the liberation of Africa. For the esteemed establishment scholars of the West, however, these books are a big no-no.

The campus is about to get a first hand lesson on the extent to which the allegedly objective academics of the West are biased against Fanon. In a political science lecture this week, Dr. Francis Seth Singleton, a visiting American lecturer, blithely dismisses Fanon and his writings by pompously proclaiming that "Fanon is not relevant to Africa," and accuses him of promoting violence as an end in itself.

Unfortunately for him, Museveni and another USARF activist are present. They rise up to challenge him, and a heated exchange ensues. But the setting of a classroom prevents fuller discussion. So, in the spirit of open academic debate, he is asked to defend his stand in a public gathering. Dr. Singleton declines the invitation saying he is here not to engage in politics but to teach political science. That is a shallow excuse. Is not teaching political science and that from a particularly biased view point also a form of engagement in politics?

Undeterred, USARF goes ahead to organize a symposium on Fanon. The speakers are Rodney, John Saul (a progressive Canadian political scientist) and Grant Kamenju (a leftist lecturer in literature from Kenya). We have posted notices across the campus for the event. The lecture hall is overflowing. Students sit on the floor and in the aisle. Many more strain their ears near the windows and doors. Henry, George and I had come in early to secure a seat.

The place is hushed as the speakers poignantly narrate the life of Fanon, analyze his works, and describe the harsh reality of Algeria under French domination. In the process, we learn that it is as absurd to accuse Fanon of promoting violence or accuse Karl Marx of inventing class struggles as it is to accuse the doctor of spreading the case of malaria he has recognized. The doctor found what was there; Marx discovered that class divisions and conflict are inherent features of capitalism while Fanon observed that extreme violence in all walks of life is an essential feature colonial rule. Fanon, the psychiatrist, explained how unbearable oppression leads the dominated person to retaliate in a violent manner. His graphic description of colonialism does not glorify violence, but gives an honest account of what he encountered.

It was clear that Dr. Singleton has a double standard of morality. For him, his government is not violent, only those who oppose it are violent. Has he considered the bold statement by the assassinated Dr. Martin Luther King that the United States is "the greatest purveyor of violence in the world today"? Is he not aware of the many violent dictatorships in Africa that the US stridently supports? What of the vast tonnage of bombs raining down on Vietnam?

In the course of the symposium, we learn the US State Department is waging an all out global offensive to contain the spread of radical, especially Marxist ideas, among university students, trade unions and peasant movements. One way it does this is by dispatching a veritable army of pliant academics who articulate the US ideological line on world affairs. These scholars are ideological cold-warriors in disguise, and not simple academics.[1]

At the question and comment time, Ahmed Gora Ebrahim, a member of the Pan-Africanist Congress (PAC) of South Africa currently exiled in Tanzania, is among the first to rise up from the audience. He begins:

"Comrades, we must realize that Mr. Singleton is not a single entity."

All gathered roar and shake with laughter. Gora then derides the multitude of foreign and local "simpletons" who think US imperialism is an invention of the mind. He cites facts that reveal its hard reality. He ends by proposing that donations be collected to enable purchase of a one-way ticket for this "simpleton" to fly back to where he came from. He gets a loud cheer and wide support. In case the offer is not taken up,

---

1   To understand the relentless, comprehensive manner by which the US waged the Cold War on the ideological front, see Saunders (2001).

the funds are earmarked for the OAU African Liberation Committee. This is the highlight of the evening.

The next day, the campus is abuzz with the phrase "Mr. Singleton is not a single entity." Students call other students "simpletons."

In the aftermath, the campus TYL and USARF committees jointly write to urge the university and national authorities to expel Dr. Singleton. Their letter brands him as "a masquerading counter-revolutionary." Four days later, a local backlash ensues. A number of reactionary students and lecturers in the Department of Political Science issue a statement in support of "their man." USARF presents a counter analysis; and the ideological exchange rages on.

Sometime later, Sadru Champsi, a friend from my national service days, and now a second year political science student comes to my room. He sits on the fence, not in agreement with Singleton but not fully on our side either. He has a surprise in his hands: a book co-authored by the American lecturer (Singleton and Shingler 1968). A political science lecturer has loaned it to him for two days. As I earnestly beg him to let me have it for a day, he agrees. I immediately call upon A.S. Namana, the TYL secretary, and we pour over the tome. It confirms our worst fears; the man is a veritable cold war ideologue.

Within twenty four hours, we write a detailed review of the book that is cyclostyled, posted in the Tunnel of Love, and widely distributed on the campus.[2] Written under the name "Concerned," and entitled *Singleton: On the Rampage Again*, our review finds the book clothed in plain cold-war propaganda phraseology and reflecting the white man's superior attitude towards "the dark continent." Its basic aim, we write, is "to rationalize and perpetuate the U.S. strangulation of the peoples of Africa, Asia and Latin America."

Singleton is a sort of heavy weight in his own way, a 1970 PhD in Political Science from Yale University. His dissertation was on *The African States and the Congo Affair, 1960--65*. The recipient of the Helen Dwight Reid Award in 1970 for the best dissertation (from a US university) in the field of international relations, law and politics, he is a rising star in the US academic circles. (In the years to come, he will excel in the world of Cold War-oriented scholarship that champions US imperial interests.)

Despite the call to do so, Dr. Singleton is not expelled. In a sense, a number of comrades including me are glad. We should stridently confront people at the level of ideas but we also need to respect academic freedom. No matter how disagreeable the words, we should respect the

2   The Tunnel of Love is described in Chapter 10.

right of the person to say them. Some comrades seek short cuts. When you curtail the rights of others, you also curtail your own rights.[3]

Yet, this call is also a sign of the times. Globally, it is the right-wing that behaves in a nasty manner. Left-wing academics, writers and students all over Latin America and Asia are being pilloried, jailed arbitrarily, tortured and assassinated. In Tanzania, the Singleton affair typifies the era of ideological contention we are going through, though here it is a verbal -- as opposed to a physical -- struggle. It simmers below the surface in all sectors of society. But in this citadel of education, socialist- and capitalist-oriented ideas openly face-off. Because of the few newspaper debates we have initiated, the culture of open debate is beginning to spill over into the rest of the nation. But in the grander arena, ours is a tiny voice. For, make no mistake about it, it is the capitalist-oriented views that remain dominant. This is masked by the fact that an abundance of hypocrisy is in the air. Too many mouth socialist slogans to win favors from the big politicians, or to hide their true intentions and actions.

In class and personal encounters at the Hill, this confrontation rages. In my essays on sociology of education, I present a socialist point of view that is contrary to what the lecturer propounds. But I do sufficient research to back up my case. So he does not penalize me. The campus also has many narrow minded lecturers who cannot withstand any critique of the bourgeois oriented ideas they propound. My lecturer in philosophy of education is a typical case. So while I do well in other classes, I get failing grades in his class! Though, appearances can be highly deceptive: I was to find out thirty six years later that my American lecturer on sociology of education, whom had presented himself as a liberal open-minded academic, was actually a CIA agent.[4]

We are also busy on other fronts. On July 21, 1969, the day the first human landed on the moon, USARF held a demonstration. Comrades had painted banners and posters, and put up notices. But it was not a celebratory parade. Its aim was to expose and unreservedly condemn the tons of skin-scalding napalm, toxic defoliants and cluster bombs that were landing, with the blessings of Uncle Sam, on the people of Vietnam right at that moment. This combination of high technological prowess and utter lack of moral decency in the hands of an imperial power was frightening. Quite a number of first year students had participated in the demonstration.

---

3   Two reports of the Singleton saga are in The Nationalist (1969d; 1969f).

4   His name was Dr. Stephen Lucas. See chapter 14 for more information.

The Spark Is Conceived

This is the environment in which a landmark USARF meeting is convened. The day is Sunday, the 10th of August in the year 1969. Museveni and the other leaders of USARF are in their final year of studies. A new leadership has to be elected. Then there are the matters of ideological classes, a theoretical organ, and vigilance committee for the social sciences to be tackled.

After stating the agenda, Museveni invites Issa to introduce the key issues. Issa delves into the themes of intellectual clarity and rigorous social analysis. With eyes fast fluttering like the wings of a bee, his words pour out rapidly like water leaking from a barrel. Yet, they carry weight, as his comrades feel the depth of thought that underlies them. He ends by reiterating a keenly felt need: for a forum where presentations and debates on major issues of our times can take place openly, without hindrance from the political barriers and ideological prejudices that prevail in the academia.

Charles rises up next. With thick dark-rimmed glasses on a rectangular face, he typifies an erudite scholar. Even when addressing a large gathering, he speaks as if conversing with a close friend. You have to pay attention, for his tone is subdued, almost hushed. His flowery style notwithstanding, what he says also derives from careful forethought and analysis.

"My friends, we talk and talk endlessly; let us reflect and write and debate; this magazine will be a crucial tool in our drive for mental liberation. No revolution has gone far without being guided by a valid theory; the African revolution is not an exception. (Amilcar) Cabral asks us to wield the weapon of theory; this will be our weapon."

He also emphasizes the need to organize and start weekly ideological classes in which lectures and serious discussions of socialist theory and practice can take place on a regular basis.

As there is no dissent, a historically significant name for our magazine is chosen.[5] To be called *Cheche*, it will be a joint organ of USARF and the Hill branch of the TANU Youth League (TYL). During the past year, the two groups jointly organized many political activities. While the membership of TYL is restricted to Tanzanians, their core activists largely overlap.

The elections for the new USARF chair and committee proceed smoothly. Naijuka Kasihwaki, a first year law student with a flair

---

5 On the significance of the names of *Cheche* and *MajiMaji*, see Chapter 9, Chapter 14, and Appendix E.

for words and a diligent activist is the new chair. He will begin the ideological classes as soon as feasible. Other pressing matters need attention presently. Concrete steps to implement these resolutions are thus shelved. The appointment of the *Cheche* editorial board will take place after similar TYL elections are held.

For many of us, there is little time to rest these days. We are caught up in an unending hustle-bustle of progressive activities, from meetings, discussions, *shamba* work, demonstrations, to work on memoranda for the Visitation Committee, and so on and so forth. And it takes its toll. A month hence, I am down with fever. One friend says the cause is an excessive dose of politics. Another thinks it epitomizes the trauma of a break-up with a girlfriend. No matter what the cause, I undergo minor surgery in the Hill dispensary and take it easy. But not quite. Earlier, Naijuka had asked me to prepare a syllabus for the ideological classes. Recuperating in bed, I make a draft that includes a reading list for each topic. Issa and Charles give comments which are incorporated in the final version (see Appendix D).

That was during the first term break. At the start of the next term in early October 1969, our first priority is to organize FRELIMO Day to support the struggle of the Mozambican people against Portuguese colonial rule. We begin earnestly on the day we return to the campus to write and paint placards. An exhibition with material from FRELIMO, the African Liberation Committee, and TYL headquarters is arranged in the Nkrumah Hall. Open to students and the public the next day, it speaks to the time and energy expended by some comrades (Patrick Qorro, Ramadhan Meghji and George, in particular) to make it a success. Symonds Akivaga and I draft the joint TYL/USARF statement to be issued on FRELIMO Day, Tuesday, October 7, 1969.

The main event takes off at 4 pm with a campus wide march by a group of about fifty student activists, FRELIMO members, and representatives from the Dar es Salaam based African liberation fronts. Starting at the cafeteria, the procession goes around the residence halls, uphill to the administration block and onto the Nkrumah Hall. All the while, we boisterously chant *"FRELIMO oyee, Mreno zii, Kaburu zii."*
[6]Salim Msoma, with his shrill, penetrating voice rouses the bystanders. Speeches from the FRELIMO representative and Jonathan Kamala, the campus TYL chairman, climax the march. In the evening, a film show is staged. Among the films screened are *Vinceremos*, a film from Cuba

---

6   The chant means "Up with FRELIMO, Down with Portuguese Colonizers, Down with Apartheid."

with English subtitles, and a short documentary on the life and work of Karl Marx.

These events attract sizeable audiences. We hope that of the multitude of apathetic students, some have been inspired to explore broader issues. What have mostly been spontaneous and ad hoc type of actions on our part are now giving way to a planned set of activities. Two specific actions agreed upon during the last academic term are on the verge of emerging into the limelight.

That Saturday -- October 11, 1969 to be specific -- in a joint TYL/USARF committee meeting, *Cheche* is officially conceived. A three member editorial board (Karim Hirji, Henry Mapolu and Zakia Meghji) is elected and entrusted with bringing out the first issue as expeditiously as possible.

Another milestone is the start of the weekly ideological classes. Scheduled for Sunday from 9 am to 12:30 pm, the first one takes place the next day in the Law Faculty lecture room. About thirty USARF/TYL activists are present to learn about the Fundamentals of Marxism. Gora Ebrahim, a South African comrade and member of the PAC, and two third year students, Charles and Ally Mchumo, lead the session. Gora propounds his material in a jocular and rambling style; Charles and Ally are more systematic but their material lacks depth. We learn from each other and the ensuing discussion is thought-provoking.

These classes stir up a hornet's nest. On a Sunday morning, the Hill is in a state of slumber. Only the well-attired ladies and gentlemen heading to church service break the mould. On this day, many of them pass right by the expansive windows of the room where we hold our session. They seem to be gawking in derision at what "these atheists" are up to at this holy hour. At the evening meal in the cafeteria, devout Christian students complain why we are peddling a "foreign ideology" in Tanzania. Do they mean what they follow is indigenous to Africa? The fact is that while campus Christian denominations get lavish funding from foreign missionary groups, we never accept any foreign funds, be they from the East, West, or anywhere in between. No wonder we are usually broke!

We do not seek to memorize Marxism or embrace it as a matter of faith. Our opinion is that it is an ignored but key part of the intellectual heritage of human society. It has, moreover, deep relevance to the construction of a socialist society, a task our nation has set for itself. We want to study and understand it. But we will do it critically, with an open mind. Nobody cajoled or paid us, or has otherwise dictated that we pursue this course of inquiry. It is purely our own decision.

The Primary Spark

Will the resolution to publish *Cheche* bear fruit? It is a foray in a new direction. It is one thing to organize a protest march, or a series of lectures or classes. But a self-sustaining radical journal run by students with hardly any funds is another thing altogether. In the first place, no one in the editorial board has relevant training or experience. I am a second year student in mathematics. Henry is a first year sociology and economics student, and Zakia has but a year of political science and history courses under her cap.

But we have not been elected at random. Henry, having been an instructor at the TANU Kivukoni College[7], is conversant with the political issues of the day. He speaks and writes clearly and in measured terms. Zakia hails from a family of respected Zanzibari progressive political figures, and is one of the few female students seen at USARF events. In the past year, I had authored several public statements issued by USARF and TYL. My fiery style and reputation for strict discipline are what I think secured my place in the board. While the board does not have a formal hierarchy, effectively, I am the senior editor.

What we lack in expertise and experience is made up by a bucketful of energy and dreams. Like our comrades, we brim with the confidence, bordering on arrogance, one feels when promoting a just cause. We have the will to educate ourselves and learn from others. For example, to ameliorate my signal deficiencies in the study of social and political matters, I spent the past long vacation devouring twenty five books on African and world affairs. We also count on USARF members and progressive academics like Rodney and Joe Kanywanyi to guide us. Most importantly, we have the shining example of the millions of students across the globe who presently are challenging, in a diversity of ways, the existent bastions of injustice, exploitation and inequality, and formulating new visions and practices of human liberation.

And there is a room we can use. The campus TYL office lies in the annex to Hall I, on a steep slope overlooking the bookstore and cafeteria. This small, cramped space occasionally used by USARF naturally becomes the *Cheche* office. Being impatient as usual, I call the first meeting of the editorial board two days later. Midway during the lunch hours, I await my fellow editors. They come ten minutes later, complaining of the long lines at the cafeteria.

What will be the scope of *Cheche*? That is the first item. Will it mainly report events or be a theoretical journal? There is a general student

---

7   See Chapter 6.

body paper that does the former, though its substance and flavor is elitist and reactionary. Most publications in history, politics, economics and sociology at the university have tended to be right-wing, or of the pseudo-socialist variety. A few stalwart academics like Rodney, Archie Mafeje, Saul, and Tamas Szentes are breaking new ground. But a local medium for radical analyses does not exist. There is no venue to discuss and develop the activist students' outlook on human society, and none to debate, in an honest and open manner, the concerns facing Tanzania and Africa. What are the major obstacles facing the liberation of Africa? How does neo-colonialism function? Will the policy of *Ujamaa* pave the way to a genuinely socialist society? What is the relevance of Marx and Engels to Africa? How can the pro-Western and bourgeois bias in the academic courses be identified and challenged?

Cheche, it is agreed, will cover such matters and focus on theory. Yet, it is to deal with them in concrete, relevant terms. It is expected to complement and enrich other progressive efforts on the campus which include the work of the few academic staff who present a progressive perspective in their courses as well as the new compulsory interdisciplinary course called Development Studies.

Henry has come with a piece of good news, "I met Rodney this morning. He would like to contribute an article for the first issue."

"What will he write on?"

"He is not quite certain, perhaps on the working class in Africa."

I add, "Issa has been drafting a paper on the state of university education. He will now submit it to *Cheche*."

"Two in the bag already! We should also approach other final year comrades to contribute."

There are practical matters as well. Zakia wonders where the resources for typing and printing will come from. The coffers of USARF, which never amount to much, are almost empty. A large chunk of the funds raised last year was donated to the OAU Liberation Committee. The campus TYL office has a secretary. She will help with typing, and editorial correspondence. Henry, with his accurate touch-typing skill, is a great asset on the board. He will type some of the shorter pieces.

"I will approach Comrade Ngombale at TYL headquarters; I think we may get two or three boxes of stencils, printing paper and cyclostyling ink through him," are the usual practical words from Henry.

As we rush to our afternoon lectures, everyone gets the task of canvassing for articles and looking for resources. Little do we realize that this is the start of a truly eventful, hectic and often exhausting period in our lives.

Our extracurricular calendar is already bursting at the seams. Right that evening, there is a general TYL meeting to attend; on Tuesday, a public lecture on "Apartheid and Zionism;" on Wednesday afternoon, the 2nd Vice President of Tanzania, Rashidi Kawawa is scheduled to speak on "The Role of the Youth in Socialist Tanzania." He will be followed by a film show on Vietnam organized by the National Liberation Front of Vietnam; on Thursday, a film show and speeches will mark Che Guevara Day; and on Sunday, the second ideological class with papers on political economy to be read beforehand. Our plans include spending one Saturday of every month in an *Ujamaa* village. This type of schedule is the norm week after week during the current academic term.

* * * * *

The first tangible achievement is the cover design. Zakia tells us that Ramadhan Meghji, an activist she knows well, and a fine artist to boot, has volunteered for the job. In a week, he submits four sketches. The one showing a liberation fighter with a rifle, superimposed on the map of Africa, wins the day. He will put the sketch on a stencil at production time. He will also draw cartoons on typed stencils with blank spaces.

Continually canvassing potential contributors yields, in four weeks, three primary articles: Rodney submits a paper on African labor under capitalism and imperialism; Issa gives a critical piece entitled "The Educated Barbarians"; and Museveni pens a forceful thesis on why African people should take up rifles. A compilation piece on revolutionary thought and practice by Kwanza Kilewela is expected soon.

Detailed work (typing, arranging the lay out and pages, writing the editorial, etc.), begins on the 10th of November, 1969. The main articles are complemented by two page-long quotes, Fanon on tourism and Szentes on bourgeois economics. I compile a mixture of quotes with short commentaries about non-violence. George drafts three short poems to serve as page fillers. A strident message from the USARF and TYL chairmen introducing the magazine, and an editorial I write complete the issue.

The material is, as it comes in and after correction, given to Margareth, the TYL secretary, and a typist at the Law faculty, to put on stencil. Henry does so for the editorial and the smaller pieces. The issue is proofread by Henry and me with Issa doing that job for his long paper with its many footnotes. Such articles require keen fore-judgment to maintain adequate spacing on the stencil. A saving grace is that Rodney's article is already on stencil. And he has proofread and corrected it as well.

Throughout, the daunting demands of our studies do not cease. Each course keeps us fully occupied. Extensive reading, essays and tough assignments demand attention. We get less and less sleep, slog the weekends to put the issue in shape. Combined with the usual array of USARF and TYL activities, it is no wonder that our academic work suffers. Henry and Zakia miss crucial classes. I neglect my mathematics and education lectures to a degree that the head of the Mathematics Department expresses serious concerns. It seems as if his star first-year student is now going astray into the wilderness of radical politics.

I have two demanding subjects, differential equations and abstract algebra, this term. The former, taught by the head, Professor Phythian, has 8 a.m. lectures, three times a week. As the only student pursuing the pure mathematics and applied mathematics combination this year, I am also the only person in the class. The professor is always on time. Exhausted by political activities, I often wake up late, barely making it for the cafeteria breakfast. On a number of occasions, and even when Nizar Visram takes me on his scooter to the lecture area, I am half an hour late. The professor is gone. A note tells me to pick up the lecture notes from his secretary. Now that complex topic has to be read and understood on my own!

What rescues me is that Professor Phythian is a true English liberal, and a believer in academic freedom. When I run across him later, he confronts me with a serious expression on his face, "Karim, you say you want to change the world. How will you do that if you cannot even wake up by 8 a.m.?"

As I stand apologetically, not knowing how to respond, he bursts into his signature laughter heard miles away. It is a signal that he is not mad with me. He often tells me that what matters is whether I learn the material or not, and how I perform in the examination. That is the bottom line. As I had done well in the first year exams, he continues to display confidence in me. It is gratifying that he treats me as an adult whose opinions he takes seriously. At one point I express a critical view about another class he teaches, Programming in FORTRAN. I say that in Tanzania, we should focus on calculating machines, not computers. The former can satisfy our needs in schools, small business, agriculture and industry. And they can be made accessible throughout the nation. Nodding in agreement, he adds that we should also not neglect computers, and goes on to remind me, with a wink, to attend that class regularly during the next term.[8]

In time, our efforts pay off. The first issue is ready to roll off the press in November. The production is to be done on the Faculty of Law cyclostyling machine. Kanywanyi, a law lecturer, arranges the access. With help from a faculty worker, eight comrades sweat through two nights to print and sort the pages, and bind 293 copies of the first issue of *Cheche*.[9]

We emerge from the ordeal exhausted, nails and shirts stained by ink. Yet, we are in high spirits; the spark has lighted our torch. It has a majestic, stinging flame whose vibrations seem to follow the tune of the *Internationale*. We adore it, but it may look too reddish to others. How will the world at large receive it?

The Spark Sparkles

Cheche No. 1 is on sale on the 26th of November 1969. At seventy five Tanzanian cents a copy, it is within the budgetary reach of the students. That amount, though, does not cover the total production cost. Early that morning, George and Munene Njagi are at the cafeteria door, copies in hand. Most students are in a hurry to go off to the lectures, but a few stop for a look. Their comments vary:

"You people, what are you up to now?"

"Looks like an excellent job."

"You government puppets, don't you ever get tired?"

"More Marxist propaganda!"

"Rodney's article looks superb. I can use it for my history essay."

"Who are the educated barbarians?"

"You people, one of these days, you will be locked up."

About two dozen copies are sold. Henry and I later stand at the door of the university bookstore with fifty copies in our hands.

"I hope the manager opens this door soon."

"I am hungry. The breakfast service will end soon."

"I do not want to miss my sociology class."

Luck is on our side. In five minutes, we are inside. The manager expects us, and quickly counts the copies. After washing down two toasts and a boiled egg, we fulfill the normal demands of academic life.

---

8   Those were the days of main frame computers, punch cards and basic programming. User friendly personal computers and the Internet were not yet in existence. Yet, I think my viewpoint still has relevance (Hirji 2009b).

9   I recall this laborious exercise as vividly as if it occurred yesterday. But since chapters 6 and 7 describe the nighttime production work quite well, I do not dwell on it.

At lunch time, the editors sit together, but not by coincidence. Who will get the free copies? Who will deliver them? George, Ramadhan and the three of us are given five copies each to sell to students and academic staff. We are interrupted now and then.

"I just got my copy. Comrades, this is fantastic." Coming from James Wapakhabulo, a Ugandan member of USARF, the compliment is not unexpected.

Sebastian Kinyondo, the president of the University Students Union of Dar es Salaam (USUD), is less kind. Without hiding his contempt, he exclaims in his usual booming, verbose tone:

"What is the matter with you communists? You only know about guns and violence. This is the pinnacle of insanity."

Students at adjacent tables turn their heads. I am about to respond. But the fellow stomps off in his typical pompous style. He has a good reason to be angry. Two weeks earlier, in a general student meeting, he faced sharp censure from USARF members. Issa, Ramadhan and Eriya Kategaya charged him with mishandling the student body funds and lambasted his cabinet for indulging in trivial issues. USARF issued a public statement castigating the lack of direction and administrative confusion in USUD. We labeled USUD the Faculty of Corruption. Our statement was posted in the tunnel and discussed widely. Last week, in another general meeting, I had proposed he should be impeached. The motion, though, was not carried. Just after that meeting, he and I had come face to face.

"You wanted to impeach me! I will physically impeach you now." Given his bulk and my diminutive stature, it was not an eventuality I had wished to face. Fortunately, Kamala and Kasihwaki had been near by. Imposing themselves between us, they had challenged him: "First you will have to deal with us."

Kinyondo then had retreated, blazing with anger. He, Kamala and Kasihwaki hail from the same part of Tanzania, have passed through the same schools, but in the political arena, they stand miles apart. Years later, whenever I happened to meet Kamala, the pipe puffing ex-radical, he would invariably greet me thus: "Karim, I can physically impeach you!" and would shake with a howl.

Copies of *Cheche* are sent to the African liberation movements based in Dar es Salaam, a few libraries, schools, and sold to the public. The reactions we get, especially from the former, are supportive. Typical is the letter from the representative of the South West Africa Peoples Organization (SWAPO). Congratulating us, he also offers us the opportunity to interview Sam Nujoma, the head of SWAPO (and later the first president of liberated Namibia), who was expected to come to Dar es Salaam in a short while. We obtain a similar reception from the few progressives in the Tanzanian political establishment. Even embassies of socialist and capitalist nations, each for their own reasons we presume, seek out copies for themselves.

Cheche even flies beyond our borders to land in Kenya, Uganda, USA, Sweden, UK and Germany. After the second issue, requests from student movements, civil rights groups, universities and individuals across the world exceed both the number of copies produced, and the budget we have for postage.

The reactions from the State House and the bulk of the political establishment are, on the other hand, uniformly unflattering. Like the hard-core reactionary students and academic staff at the Hill, they accuse us of peddling a foreign ideology and adopting a foreign name. They say we promote violence. None of these accusations hold water. They derive from superficial impressions, and not the substance of *Cheche*, or what it stands for. Such charges sometimes reflect ignorance, but more often, a hidden anti-socialist agenda of the dominant party and state bureaucrats.

It is an auspicious and an ominous start. The spark has boldly taken off. It seeks to ascend into the stratosphere. Yet, powerful entities view its maiden flight with deep apprehension. Fiery political sparks are about to fly.

4

Tribulations of An Independent Magazine

Karim F Hirji

"It is only when we honestly describe the world that we can
begin to change it."
- Johann Hari -

Spreading the Word
During the second term of the academic year 1969/70, work on *Cheche* is one of many extracurricular engagements that keep us occupied. The Sunday three hour ideological class has a bulky reading load. The highlight is the class conducted jointly by Walter Rodney and Tamas Szentes, a Professor of Economics at the Hill. The latter, an erudite Hungarian Marxist, gives us the basic nuts and bolts of Marx's *Das Kapital*. Rodney expounds on the political economy of African labor under capitalism and imperialism. Even though Szentes has simplified his presentation considerably, it is difficult to grasp. Rodney, on the other hand, takes us through a gentle trip reflecting on how the classic Marxist theory bears upon African societies. One day, I tell myself, I must read the book, and understand it.

Regretfully, I miss one Sunday class. That weekend, Jonathan Kamala (TYL Chairman), Naijuka Kasihwaki (USARF Chairman), Zakia Meghji, Shiraz Ramji and I are bound for Morogoro. We are to visit the TYL Branch of the Faculty of Agriculture, have discussions on joint activities, and talk to Form V and VI students in two adjacent secondary schools.

Our first impression of the state of socio-political awareness at the Faculty is not encouraging. Their TYL chairman comes across like an establishment politician. His words lack substance but his style is pompous. The branch has a patron, a member of the academic staff. We are offended by this arrangement. Student organizations, especially at the university level, should be independent, without patrons or matrons. In the evening, Kamala, Naijuka and I make presentations to a small group on the history and challenges of socialism, and the role of the youth. TYL members take their time to stroll in. So we start half an hour late. As our talks end, members of the audience look at each other. None has a question or comment. Finally, a brave soul inquires: "Do you not think that socialism will destroy individual initiative and creativity in agriculture and business?"

Naijuka gives a terse response: "You can only destroy what is there. Look at the state of our nation, at the poverty of the masses. Where is this initiative and creativity you are talking about?"

I give examples from William Hinton's *Fanshen* and articles I have read from the Cuban magazine *Granma* to show how ordinary people's initiative and creativity mushroom when they are freed from economic and political bondage, and are empowered to make and implement decisions on matters affecting their lives.[1]

---

1   A new edition of this book is Hinton and Magdoff (2008).

The audience listens but does not appear convinced. They think we are on a propaganda errand. Do they realize that the view expressed in the question itself reflects the bourgeois propaganda they have imbibed? There are no further questions. The local TYL chairman gives a long tirade about party loyalty and *Ujamaa* drawn word for word from official documents. This is a disappointing encounter. The level of political apathy at this campus is far more pronounced than at the Hill.

The next day we are in a session organized by the Senior Discussion Society of Mzumbe Secondary School. With about thirty students in attendance, Kamala, Naijuka and Ramji talk on the same topics we covered yesterday. But today, we get searching questions followed by a lively discussion. There is keen interest! The younger students have fewer elitist hangovers compared to their university counterparts. Our hopes get a boost. A new generation of Tanzanian youth who will raise critical issues, question authority, and serve the common man, will surely arise.

On Monday, we are at the Marian (Girls) Secondary School for a similar purpose. Now Zakia, Kamala and Naijuka take the podium. But their words seem to fall flat. We mostly get a giggling type of response from the females, I am sorry to note. They are particularly attracted to the flamboyant Naijuka. I do not think we made any impact here. In the liberated areas of Mozambique and Vietnam, women comrades play an active role in all aspects of the struggle. Compared to them, our women have a long way to go. The socialization of women, combining outmoded traditions with petty bourgeois norms, inculcates a subservient mentality. Yet, one out of three is not a bad score, we tell ourselves.

That evening we hold a long meeting with the TYL committee. We urge them to embark upon a systematic program of developing ideological clarity and practical activities to support the move towards socialism in Tanzania. The TYL branch should not restrict itself to entertainment activities and officially celebrated events. Its function is not to toe the party line but raise that line to a sounder socialistic footing and hold the party bosses to account for the grandiose promises they make.

The next day, we are back at the Hill, and report to other comrades at dinner time. Issa Shivji says that the Sunday class we missed was conducted by Eriya Kategaya. The talk, about how human societies undergo major transformations, was based on W. Gordon Childe's *What Happened In History* (Childe 1960). It was a stellar presentation, according to Issa. I am quite sorry I was not present at this class, but am not that concerned about missing two days of my regular academic classes!

A Spark Fizzles

As the second term draws to a close, a grand event looms on the horizon. The Hill TYL in conjunction with the headquarters has organized the Second Seminar of the East and Central African Youth for the vacation month of December 1969. Charles Kileo and Ngombale Mwiru are the movers and shakers of the event. The theme revolves around the purpose, problems, prospects and strategies of the African Revolution. None other than Mwalimu Nyerere was to open the Seminar and give the keynote address. Unfortunately, he is unable to make it. The Second Vice President of Tanzania, Rashidi Kawawa, takes his place. Four days are set for the presentation of papers and small group discussions. A day in between is reserved for field visit to an *Ujamaa* village and the Ruvu National Service camp. Synthesizing the main lessons and formulating resolutions will take place on the final day. The Minister of Education will close the seminar.

The scheduled presenters are Rodney, Gora Ebrahim, Kileo and Ngombale Mwiru. Participants from all over the country and neighboring nations are expected. African liberation movements will be represented in full force. (The complete seminar program is shown in Appendix C).

I am eager to attend. But, to my chagrin, my pesky ailment has recurred. I have fever, feel weak, and am referred to a surgeon at the Agakhan Hospital in the city. For the entire duration of the Seminar, I languish in bed, and later undergo another surgery. It is a consolation that George keeps me informed. He also tells me about a grave misadventure that took place during this time (see Chapter 7).

I have a distinct reason for taking a keen interest. For, it has been agreed that the Seminar papers are to be published as the next issue of *Cheche*. The editors are excited about the prospect, ready to work as soon as the Seminar ends. Our target of two issues for this academic year will then be met. Further, we can finish the job in time to prepare for the end of the academic year examinations. The issue, moreover, will be a notable one.

Alas, that is not meant to be. A steep, unforeseen hurdle is encountered. In his typically incisive talk on the "Ideology of the African Revolution," Rodney proclaims that apart from a few nations like Tanzania, most so-called independent governments in Africa are stooges of Western Imperialists. It is a statement of plain fact, a rewording of the false decolonization described by Frantz Fanon. Nevertheless, it irks the state bureaucracy, and specifically President Nyerere. Since the Seminar has official blessing, Rodney's pronouncement transcends the norms of diplomacy. Officialdom feels compelled to distance itself from such heresy. The reaction is swift and sharp. Four days later, the party newspaper carries a strong editorial, written by Mwalimu or at his behest, entitled *"Revolutionary Hot Air,"* It roundly blasts Rodney's speech, and implies that the campus radicals are a bunch of irresponsible hotheads. We are surprised by the ferocity of the reaction. At the same time, it is a practical lesson that state diplomacy is but another name for hypocrisy.[2]

The *Cheche* editorial board faces a quandary -- should we proceed to publish the Seminar proceedings as the second issue of the magazine or not? The first issue had displeased the highest levels of the state authority. If the very next issue contains officially-condemned material, will that not be seen as a direct challenge to the President? The possibility that *Cheche* will be banned is not taken lightly. We discuss the matter with the USARF and TYL committees. There are two view points. One: Proceed as planned, stick to our principles and do not bend to the whims of the bureaucracy. Two: Take a long term view. Our magazine needs to thrive. It has the potential to exercise a substantial influence on the development and promotion of ideas that will further socialism and African liberation. The risk of being nipped in the bud is real. At this nascent a stage, taking such a risk is not worth it.

A number of comrades and I favor the latter course of action. In the end, it is the view that prevails. We decide to cool it for a while, the implication being that the second issue will not contain the Seminar proceedings and cannot come out before the next academic year starts, that is, six months later. This is, indeed, an exercise of self-censorship. Is it an appropriate act? Are we not being hypocritical? A month later, as the senior editor of *Cheche*, I am taken to task in a general TYL branch meeting for adopting that course of action. Several prominent TYL members -- Andrew Shija in particular -- disagree. My response is that working for social change and adventurism are not the same. At times, a short term compromise facilitates long term gain. (That our fear of being snuffed of existence is not an outlandish one will be known within a year.)

From the viewpoint of our studies, this is a blessing in disguise for Henry, Zakia and I. We now have room to attend to the long-neglected classwork. But only to an extent; for this term also brims with exciting activities. There are visits by and discussions with progressive students from Sweden and the USSR. With the latter, we raise the question of revisionism. Why does the USSR so often betray the ideals of

---

2 Hajivayanis (2010), Rodney (1969b; 1969c) and The Nationalist (1969i; 1969k). Other presentations to the seminar were reported in The Nationalist (1969j; 1969l).

internationalism? Why does it have oppressive internal institutions? Needless to say, we are hardly satisfied with the answers we get.

Comrade Betu, the local MPLA representative, comes to the Hill to give a lengthy talk to USARF members. He describes the conditions in the liberated areas of Angola, and the prospects for victory. He also invites us to visit these areas during the coming long vacation. I am pleased to be among the invitees.

On January 29, 1970, USARF and the Hill TYL organize the Lenin Centenary Celebration. A public forum and film show are scheduled. Salim Msoma is our liaison with the Embassy of the USSR for exhibits and films. We post notices across the campus; right-wing vandals tear them down; we put them up again. In the evening, the assembly hall overflows with students, staff, members of liberation movements, diplomats from socialist nations, and the general public. The three speakers are (i) Yoweri Museveni: Lenin, the Theoretician; (ii) Walter Rodney: Lenin and the Partition of Africa; and (iii) Gora Ebrahim: Lenin, the Internationalist. The gist of their talks is that Africa must pay attention to Lenin, and learn from both the achievements and failures of the Soviet revolution. In terms of general student participation, the event is a clear success.

The following week, the campus TYL branch produces a critical paper on the role of tourism in national development. It reflects the cumulative effect of several months of debate among the comrades. Issa led the effort in drafting it. Citing the history of the Caribbean and other Third World nations, it argues that tourism entrenches economic dependency and fosters skewed development. Interactions among peoples on the basis of equality and mutual respect is desirable. But the tourism under which travelers from rich nations seek cheap thrills and novelty in poor nations and exploit our workers is not. The latter is not compatible with socialism and will not improve the living conditions of ordinary people. Only big businessmen, bureaucrats and multinational firms benefit from such tourism. Further, it spreads the least desirable cultural attributes from the Western world to Africa, while sidelining those attributes from which Africa can benefit.

This paper is not well received by senior government officials. An evolving policy seeks to promote tourism as a key "national industry for development." An editorial in *The Nationalist*, the party organ, criticizes the paper. This is another sign of the growing discord between the Hill radicals and the state. In the light of other deficiencies in the national economic policies, we see the promotion of tourism as another leap backwards for socialism.

Around that time, *The Nationalist* proclaims that there are 600 *Ujamaa* villages in Tanzania. A number of scholarly studies and our experiences tell us that many villagers had welcomed *Ujamaa* at the outset. They favor cooperative work and sharing. However, the chaotic and authoritarian manner in which the policy is implemented makes them dislike it in no time. Now their lives are more dominated by party and district bosses. They still do not get fair prices for what they produce, and often, a part of that is snatched away by trickery. The unplanned and haphazard set-up of the villages has led to food shortage, water scarcity and spread of diseases. Theory and practice are a world apart. These contradictions signify that *Ujamaa* is akin to an utopian form of socialism.[3]

A Mighty Put Down

The political fireworks are just starting. A milestone in the rising tension between the state and campus radicals is the two-hour question-answer session with Mwalimu Nyerere at the University on February 4, 1970. The entire university community is present. On the one hand, it shows the unique sagacity and wisdom of Mwalimu. At this time, in neighboring nations and all over Africa, heads of state prefer to converse with students with a show of force.[4] Mwalimu, instead, has come down from his lofty pedestal to talk to us.

On the other hand, he is on a mission. He will answer questions that have been submitted before hand. Apart from other students, the TYL branch members have also set their questions, which were handed over together. Dr. Wilbert Chagula, the Vice Chancellor, selects the questions. The issues raised range from the challenges of constructing socialism in Tanzania to global affairs and student matters. Mwalimu responds in his typical erudite but populist and humorous style.

Yet, in many of his answers, he, directly or indirectly, takes the Hill radicals sternly to task. He openly ridicules the TYL for their "silly and immature" questions. He supports the Karadha loan scheme for state and party officials to purchase cars. We had opposed this as contrary to socialist tenets and instead urged the use of the resources to develop the public transport system. As the session proceeds, the university community directly witnesses us getting a sound political thrashing from the highest authority in the nation. Instantly we become the

---

3   See Chapter 12 for an evaluation of the policy of *Ujamaa*.

4   The harsh continent-wide suppression of students at that time is documented in Legum (1972).

laughing stock of the day. It is a dismal hour for radicalism at the Hill.
My comrades and I come out shaken and with our eyes directed to the
ground.

In a patently crestfallen mood, we discuss our fate in a USARF
meeting the next evening. Why did such a thing transpire? For one, Dr.
Chagula had selected trivial questions, leaving out the thoughtful ones.
He is no friend of ours. Two, questions posed by individuals were taken
as TYL branch questions. And, three, there was a lack of forethought on
our part. We should have planned better for such an important event.

These, though, are subsidiary factors. The key factor derives from
the inconsistent nature and incoherent implementation of the policy
of Socialism and Self-reliance in Tanzania. And we are vocal critics
of the policy, and especially of its implementation. Mwalimu was here
to defend the policy. No matter the questions, the outcome would not
have been that different. The tongue lashing we got was a culmination
of contradictions that have been brewing for over a year. Even if we had
refrained from asking any questions, our fate would have been the same.

The 1500 or so students at the Hill fall into four political groupings.
The leftist radicals are few in number, not more than 5% of the total.
Nationalistic students who are politically active in a way but follow the
ruling party are a larger group, about 10% of the total. The biggest group
by far comprises those who disdain "politics." They consider themselves
neutral, leaning to neither the left nor the right. Then there is a small
group of die hard reactionaries who hate socialism in any hue, form or
shape. While some say so openly, given the political realities of the day,
most work behind the scenes.

Student politics are dominated by these divisions. In many forums,
in class, and at the personal level, the left clashes with the right. We
oppose the war in Vietnam, they accuse us of promoting communism;
we oppose tourism, they call us dreamers; and so on. The debate at
times gets intense, as during the Singleton affair. The manner in which
Mwalimu has intervened into this debate is effectively a victory for the
far right. They are in a celebratory mood, elated by the official put down
we have received.

Yet, a paradox pervades this episode. While we criticize the manner
in which *Ujamaa* is implemented, we do not oppose socialism. To the
contrary, we declare that his policies are not socialistic enough. By
ridiculing us, Mwalimu weakens his natural allies, and plays into the
hands of the anti-socialist forces not just on the Hill, but more so, within
his own party and the state bureaucracy as well.

Two days later, in a radio address the nation, Mwalimu takes stock of the three years of the Arusha Declaration. He says that despite a few errors, the nation is headed in the right (no pun intended) direction. He announces that by the end of the year the government plans to assume full ownership and control of the import, export and wholesale trade. The campus rightists and the commercial bourgeoisie are dismayed by what looks like a further step towards socialism.

The next day, we discuss his speech. We are critical too, but for a different reason. Some comrades note that nationalization is not identical to socialism.[5] We wonder how socialism can be built without dedicated socialists. While he is a committed socialist, the ruling party is, from top to bottom, riddled with sell-outs and two-timers. They undermine his policy in one way or another, and use state institutions and firms to enrich themselves. TANU is a nationalist party. Sorely lacking dedicated and ideologically mature cadres, it is a socialist party in name only. This was the problem that had earlier plagued Kwame Nkrumah in Ghana, and contributed to his downfall.

Tanzania does not have an economic policy based on comprehensive socialist planning. An integrated plan to develop agriculture, industry and trade based on expanding the internal market is absent. Production of raw material for export and import of manufactured or semi-finished products drive the economy. That is not different from what Kenya or other African nations are doing. The nationalized institutions operate in the same mode they did before they were taken over. Why do our development plans always need the blessings of the World Bank, a pro-capitalist institution that does not lend a penny to stridently socialist nations like Vietnam or Cuba? The dilemmas associated with the nature and implementation of the policy of *Ujamaa na Kujitegemea* (Socialism and Self-Reliance) are grave and excessive.

Does Mwalimu see such contradictions? There are no easy answers to these enigmas. But that is all the more reason for open, critical debate among the people and those committed to socialism. The blind parroting of the Arusha Declaration by the big politicians only camouflages their anti-socialist practices. We are, on the other hand, not prepared or inclined to do that. On that day, I write in my diary:

> *Mwalimu Nyerere is a brilliant idealist dwelling in utter confusion and utopian expectations. Whether he is aware of it or not, effectively, he is entrenching neo-colonialism in Tanzania.*

---

5   See Chapter 12 for a discussion of state ownership and socialism.

These are times of dissent and discord in ways more than one. On the personal front, I have acrimonious exchanges with long time friends on politics and religion. Members of my ethnic community see me less frequently at the prayer house. They fear for my soul, and think I worship Julius Nyerere, not God. Old friendships fall apart; new ones flower. A poignant song in an Indian movie, composed during the deadly violence between Hindus and Muslims, puts it thus: "I will be neither a Hindu nor a Muslim, but a human being in the human family." That is what I declare to my relatives. They deduce a devilish spell has been cast onto me. Before I can protest, I am unceremoniously dragged before an exalted missionary to be put on the right path. When I stridently counter his arguments, he gives up. Other comrades in the same boat and I are then solemnly pronounced to be beyond local repair.

But we are not alone. Around the globe, from China to the USA, students pour into the streets. The present loci of the storm are in France and Pakistan. With them, we share a common goal -- a world devoid of injustice, hunger and misery. With so many compatriots, all cannot be gloomy. Despite our set-back, our spirits revive. Even on the local scene, a good omen or two are visible. In particular, in early February, the main daily English newspaper is taken over by the state. *The Standard* now has a new editor, Frene Ginwalla, a socialist and stalwart member of the ANC of South Africa.

Western media denounce this move as a curtailment of freedom of speech. That is most amusing. *The Standard* has hitherto posed as an objective paper. In truth, it was a pro-capitalist and pro-Western paper. What it covered, what it did not, and how the coverage was framed was tainted by that bias. The bias was disguised by professional terminology and style. But once you went beneath the surface, the lack of objectivity was in plain sight. The projection of socialist views was permitted in a marginal way only. Further, the paper had a particular gripe with the Hill radicals, and we were often misrepresented and derided in its pages.[6]

Now the pro-capitalist bias has been replaced by a bias in favor of *Ujamaa*. Yet, under Ginwalla, *The Standard* does not turn into a simple mouthpiece of the State. We pleasantly find out in a short while that she is an independent, knowledgeable, professional and visionary editor. Despite official disapproval, she is prepared to accommodate radical views. Her basic line is that socialism requires an informed citizenry and

---

6   The type of press freedom in 2010 is reminiscent of what prevailed in the 1960s. The mass media have become uniformly pro-West and pro-business, are saturated with the donor worship mentality, and in which socialist voices or views are almost totally absent.

wide ranging democratic debate. Hence, her main aim is to facilitate a public debate on official policy and practice.

An Unsparkly Hiatus

March is the month of annual examinations. Our extra-curricular activities grind to a virtual halt. But once free, we want to begin work on the preempted second issue of *Cheche*. But there is a quandary. My ailment has reappeared -- presumably due to the nights and days spent sitting on a library chair, and the intensive last minute toil. I am advised to consult a specialist surgeon in Nairobi. In a dejected mood, I depart for the distant city. The onus is on my fellow editors to prepare the ground for the next issue of our magazine.

I have so far lived a provincial life. This is my first time to fly, to leave Tanzania. Nairobi makes an instant impression. The splendid towers, the wide boulevards, expansive shops with eye-catching merchandise, well attired people, all a far cry from Dar es Salaam. Even the shoe-shine boy has a jacket and tie, though the fit is not anything to brag about.

This is one face of the system. Later I encounter Kabiru Kinyanjui, a Kenyan comrade from UCD. He shows me the other face, taking me on a long stroll through Mathare, the sprawling slum of Nairobi. Here a grotesque level of poverty non-existent in Dar es Salaam prevails. Thousands are crammed in tiny makeshift cardboard dwellings without sanitation or clean water. Crime and disease are rampant. One resident tells us that fourteen children recently died near his place, perhaps from cholera or dysentery. The city council now and then demolishes the squatter dwellings. Teenagers loiter about aimlessly. Nairobi boasts an abundance of beggars, pick-pockets and prostitutes. One boy tried to squeeze my pockets dry but I stopped him in the act. The well-to-do are insulated from this reality by high walls and armed guards. This is what capitalism offers -- the freedom to experience hunger and privation for many, and the right to a lavish life for a few. Fanon's divided city of settlers and natives comes alive here. I see that in Tanzania we have so far experienced quite a stunted form of capitalism.

At the guesthouse, I watch television for the first time. The glamour appeals to the senses but the substance is shallow. News toes the governmental line, and project the US and British spin on global affairs. Religious shows, drama and music programs from the West crowd the schedule. I find most shows not appealing, and deem it an escapist medium propagating the values of a bourgeois society. There are no locally rooted critical, entertaining or educational programs. The radio is not much better.

Not surprisingly, many Kenyans I meet have outlandish views of life in Tanzania. They think it is overrun by the evil communists from China. Many consider the USA a true defender of freedom, unaware of the millions murdered in Vietnam and Cambodia, and the extensive support it gives to dictators across the world. To assuage my loneliness, I read a variety of books on the history and philosophy of science, and world affairs. The first one I take up is A Schaff's *A Philosophy of Man* (Schaff 1968).

My surgery takes place within a week but I am in the hospital for two weeks. An elderly patient on the next bed writhes in a painful agony. Yet, his humor and spirit is our lifeline. The hospital ward is run efficiently by kind, competent and, I must say, quite pretty nurses. Time passes fast. After discharge, I have to have daily wound dressing for two months. My surgeon wants to make sure it heals completely. He says that the periodic recurrence I have had were due to deficient post-surgical care.

Several of my childhood friends, students at the University of Nairobi, are on the campus during the long vacation. So during these two months I put up in the student dormitories. A few days in this room, a few days in another -- a stratagem to impress the managers that I am a temporary visitor. Students here take to the streets on a regular basis, often clashing with the police. Earlier, the opposition leader Odinga Odinga had been barred from addressing the students. The students had protested loudly and the campus was closed down for a while. I recall USARF had issued a statement supporting them.

Every day begins with an unpleasant hospital visit. Good support from my friends lightens the ordeal. Soon I feel better. Yet, I feel uneasy. The government of Kenya is too subservient to the West. The atmosphere is too hostile towards socialism. I see that the main concern of students is with their own petty interests. They demand better living conditions and high allowances. They fight with cafeteria staff if a meal is not to their liking, or riot if some rule they dislike is proposed. I find it an elitist student body that shows little regard for the plight of the common man.

In a while, I resume daily physical exercise. Two months on, the wound has healed. Instead of spending my vacation in the liberated areas of Angola, I have languished in a citadel of capitalism. But it has not been in vain. I have seen a more mature version of capitalism, met interesting people and devoured twenty books. Among them were Franz Mehring's vibrant biography of Karl Marx, Norbert Weiner's reflection on *The Human Use of Human Beings*, Oscar Lange's methodological treatise *Wholes and Parts*, Sigmund Freud's discourse on *The Future of an Illusion*, and Arthur C Clarke's futuristic rumination, *Voices from the Sky*.

Now I am repaired and re-energized, anxious to head for home. A letter from Issa a week ago had conveyed disappointing news: no work has been done for the next issue of *Cheche*. I reply:

> *It was extremely disappointing to read that no articles for Cheche have been received; not even Museveni's. I hope you are in the process of writing one, and I would like you to tell Mapolu to assign one to all comrades who are in Dar. I too shall write one, probably on the sociological aspects of cybernetics. I met Kanywanyi here when he came for the law conference, and he too has promised to write something. Has Meghji kept the stenciled cover designs in the TYL office? Cheche No. 2 must and will be produced, this I am determined to accomplish.*[7]

The Second Spark

Back in Dar es Salaam by early June, I start work on the second issue. A lot has to be done. As the long vacation is not over, my fellow editors are not around. So I take up residence on the campus. The issue needs to come out soon after the new academic year begins, which is just a month away.

Persistent harassing and cajoling for articles pays off. Dick Urban Vestbro and Gunnar Persson, lecturers at the University of Lund in Sweden, contribute a paper entitled *"How Socialist is Sweden?"* Yoweri Museveni writes on *"My Three Years in Tanzania."* Two pieces on the Portuguese colony of Guinea Bissau are included: One briefly describes the liberation struggle, and the second is a reprint of Amilcar Cabral's *"The Weapon of Theory."* Haroub Othman reviews Cabral's latest work, *Revolution in Guinea* (Cabral had visited Tanzania last year.) The paper *"The Role of Youth in the African Revolution"* by Dan Wadada Nabudere arrives in the mail. A Ugandan lawyer, Nabudere is a progressive activist who has been detained by Obote's government without good cause or due process. We plan to publicize this fact and campaign for his release. Shiraz Ramji writes a note on *"Mathematics and Ideology."* I pen a satire on my stay in Nairobi. Once on the campus, Henry drafts the editorial, and I finalize it. These articles and various filler pieces that include an informative article on the CIA, and cartoons drawn by Meghji complete the issue.

The "Nightshift Comrades" get into action (see Chapter 7) with the results that *Cheche* No. 2 is on sale in the second week of July 1970. A day

---

7   Letter from Karim Hirji in Nairobi to Issa Shivji in Dar es Salaam, dated 7 May 1970.

earlier it had been reviewed in *The Standard*. The reaction from students and academic staff is heartening. We soon get requests for copies from all over the country and abroad. I write in my diary.

> *Editing a magazine is quite a job, though it provides rich and challenging experiences. Though we have only made a small beginning, Cheche should develop into an established and scholarly organ for scientific socialist thought.*

A New University?

The second issue of *Cheche* has come out in changed circumstances. The Presidential Visitation Committee had handed in its report in November 1969.[8] The Committee's mandate was to propose the changes needed to transform our university into an institution serving national social and developmental goals As of July 1, 1970, we are students in an independent national university, the University of Dar es Salaam (UDSM). Mr. Pius Msekwa, the former National Executive Secretary of TANU, is the new Vice Chancellor overseeing a modified administrative setup (The Nationalist 1970b; 1970c).

In Africa, higher education has to meet the manpower needs of a developing society. University education converts the child of a poor peasant or worker into a teacher, doctor, lawyer, engineer, or government official. He or she also ascends the social ladder. This raises many questions. Has the education alienated him or her from the masses? Will the graduate simply aspire to have a car, house and comforts, or also effectively serve those who paid for his education? Has the training equipped him or her with the skills, knowledge and aptitude required to face the challenges encountered in building an integrated, internally oriented economy? Or has he or she simply mastered traditional, business-as-usual skills? Does he or she have the foundation to foster self-reliance by developing relevant technology, or adapt the existing ones to new tasks? He is not asked to live in poverty, but simply to restrain himself and seriously attend to raising the living standards of the society as a whole. Fanon has observed that the post-colonial petty bourgeoisie succumb to the temptations of the neo-colonial environment to such an extent that even a minor personal sacrifice is unthinkable. How can the education system be reoriented to counter that tendency? (Saul 1968).

Those are the fundamental questions the Visitation Committee is to have addressed. In that regard, USARF, the campus TYL and the TANU study group (comprised of the few socialist cadres in TANU) had

---

8   See Chapter 3. Also The Nationalist (1969e; 1969h).

jointly presented "a voluminous memorandum dealing with nearly all aspects university affairs including curriculum reorganization, students organization, staff recruitment, etc." (Hirji 1971a). This document advocated transforming a university graduate to be "red and expert. " In other words, he or she should be a dedicated socialists armed with adequate intellectual and practical skills who can contribute to a genuine national development program. As the inauguration day for the national university had approached, we had reliable word that this memorandum had been accepted in full by the Visitation Committee.

Indeed, Mwalimu Nyerere, the Chancellor, had inaugurated the new university with a stellar, inspiring address in which he had not only stressed the traditional functions of an academy, namely, teaching, research, intellectual discourse in an atmosphere of academic freedom but also the need for bold, innovative, critical thought relevant to the serve the needs of society. He had urged the academicians to challenge established orthodoxy and chart new vistas.

> In its teaching activities, and its search for new knowledge, therefore, the aim of the University of Dar es Salaam must be to service the needs of a developing socialist Tanzania. Nyerere (1970)

Three weeks into the new year, there are hopeful signs that his words have substance. The progressive forces anticipate a fundamental shift in what is done and how it is done at the Hill. For one thing, the previous administration was openly and categorically hostile to progressive ideas and the radical students. Mr. Msekwa, on the other hand, says the right words, and meets with the Hill TYL committee once he takes up his post. And he seems understanding and cooperative. The students are now well-represented on faculty boards.

Yet, not all is well. The reactionaries among the academic staff and bureaucracy mount fierce resistance to prevent any change from the *status quo*. They campaign under the misleading banner of preserving academic standards. As weeks go by, it is apparent that the reactionaries have secured the upper hand. The signs suggest only some cosmetic changes. No overall or detailed plan of how Mwalimu's words will be put into action exists, and there is no official push along that direction. Much is left to the initiative of concerned individuals who have to swim against the tide of entrenched orthodoxy.

As time passes, the trends indicate that even under the new set up, and despite the fine inaugural address by Mwalimu, UDSM is likely to remain a neo-colonial institution that will churn out elitist graduates with stunted intellectual horizons and circumscribed technical skills.

We fear that half-hearted measures together with the installation of pseudo-socialist political yes-men in critical areas of the academy may eventually get us a university that is neither a stellar socialist university, nor a functional bourgeois academy. Instead, we may end up with a run-down intellectual dwarf from which it will takes decades to recover.[9]

Why?

As days pass, our fears mount, and quite rapidly. Signs of a decisive leftward shift are not in sight. The pseudo-socialists at the helm do all they can to side line intellectual independence, free inquiry and scientific socialism. They display more authoritarian tendencies than the previous administration. Despite earlier promises, the students are not being consulted in terms of the setting up of a new general student organization, new administrative rules for the halls of residences, and other matters. Soon the entire student body is alienated. Students decry "political interference" in the academy, and blame "socialism" for the problems they face.

Our reaction to these trends is to heighten our activism. Our critical commentaries and sharp statements continue. This takes the general student body by surprise. Since many of us also belong to the Hill TYL, they naively consider us as loyal ruling party followers. Now that senior party men administer the campus, they had expected us to quieten down. Instead, we shout louder. Why, they ask?

Indeed, we ask that of ourselves. Why undertake the literal avalanche of extracurricular activities, including producing *Cheche*? Financially, we do not get a cent; academically, our standing suffers; socially, we are isolated; psychologically, we have to endure vitriolic insults; and politically, there is no dearth of hostility from university, state and party officials. Mwalimu's visit to the campus, when we became objects of pity and ridicule, was the climax of this onslaught.

Yet, we persist, even more energized! Are we mad, as some opine? Or, are we political fanatics, as others declare? Or, are we agents of the USSR or China? Those who one day say we are agents of the USSR, the next day call us agents of China, oblivious of the contradiction involved. Or, are we opportunists or government stooges, as we are now and then branded? If so, we seek favors from the authority in a decidedly unconventional manner!

Our activism derives from our convictions about the crucial role of a university in a society striving to build socialism, from the fact that

---

9   And sadly, that is exactly what transpired. See Hirji (1990).

we take Mwalimu's words quite seriously. University students, whatever their field of study, need an integrated perspective on human history and social change, require broad knowledge about the challenges of building a socialist economy, and need to be critical thinkers as well. Their training must be technically and scientifically rigorous. It must inculcate an innovative spirit. Further, they need practical training of the sort that brings them closer to the masses of people, and their day-to-day issues and problems.

Our activism strives to push the academy in that direction. Our work is educational in nature; we seek to learn, question what we are taught, and conduct educational work for other students at the Hill and beyond. We want to recruit the broad masses of politically apathetic or lukewarm students to the cause of socialism. Thus far, the university has not played the role it should be playing in the construction of a socialist society. So we struggle to make that happen.

That is why we do what we do. We are not saints, but inexperienced students with faults, failings and personal inclinations. But our dreams and strivings are for the total liberation of Africa, and for a humane, just and egalitarian society where no one will go hungry or lack the basic necessities of life.

5

Not So Silent A Spark

Karim F Hirji

"If I give food to the poor, they call me a saint. If I ask why the
poor have no food, they call me a communist."
- Don Hector Camara -

Campus Activism

The academic year 1970/71 begins with a huge gap in our ranks. About fifteen senior comrades had graduated three months earlier. Yoweri Museveni and Eriya Kategaya are in Uganda. Charles Kileo is a teacher in Tabora. Andrew Shija is a TANU cadre. They had inspired and guided us. I miss the infectious spirit, cheerful demeanor and unblemished dedication of Comrade Shija. Many regular faces at USARF/TYL activities are absent. It is a relief that Issa Shivji remains at the Hill as a tutorial assistant in the Faculty of Law. Though, he will soon depart for further studies.

Nonetheless, USARF and TYL have a full calendar of events on the campus. Abdulrahman Babu, the rare erudite and committed socialist in Mwalimu Nyerere's cabinet, speaks on capitalism and imperialism to a capacity crowd. According to him, an economic policy based on multi-sectoral planning, state control (not just formal ownership) of major enterprises, and focus on the internal market points the way forward for Africa. Gora Ebrahim lectures on the Middle East. His signature style entwines humor and sarcasm with a load of informative material and critical analysis. USARF holds a campus wide march to protest the impending sale of British weapons to Apartheid South Africa. Representatives of African liberation movements give speeches and the USARF statement is read out. We collect funds for these movements. The general student body holds a demonstration in town on the same issue.

Ideological classes go on. In one Gora speaks on historical materialism and I, on the application of the scientific method to social analysis. After the class, we have a contentious exchange. I feel his approach is narrow and dogmatic. He thinks I am a Trotskyist in disguise!

We have a cordial meeting with Frene Ginwalla in her office. She stresses open debate on social and economic development, and socialism in particular. African and foreign news in *The Standard* are no longer framed in the typical Cold War terminology and perspective of the Western media. Debates initiated by USARF and TYL take place. Henry Mapolu's long analytic letters appear occasionally in this newspaper, generating a lively exchange. Henry, Nizar Visram and I get a joint book review column. Every other week, we take turns to write a review. I submit the first one that explores G William Domhoff's exceptional work, *Who Rules America?*, a meticulous study of the class structure of the American society. The facts he amasses demolish the myth, trumpeted by the right-wing staff and students at the Hill, that the USA is a meritorious, equal opportunity society. With detailed data, he shows that the main sectors of the society including education, media, and the service and manufacturing sectors are controlled and dominated by a tiny elite that also owns a large portion of the wealth of that society.[1]

In time, and to our dismay, we gather that the official reaction to *Cheche* No. 2 has not been a favorable one. Initially, there was a positive review of this issue in the party paper, *The Nationalist*. This is followed six days later by a highly critical "letter to the editor" that is no ordinary letter but has official blessing, and may have been written by the editor, Benjamin Mkapa, himself. It takes our magazine to task for not examining the concrete aspects of the socialist endeavors in Tanzania. *Cheche* is criticized for dealing with events and abstruse theories relating to far away places and distant times without showing their relevance to the local conditions and problems. It is castigated for unfairly dismissing the products of the current education system as "reactionary bureaucrats and technocrats." The message seems to be to avoid foreign ideologies and adhere to the Tanzanian version of socialism. There is a germ of truth in what the critical letter says, but then it concedes that it is too soon to judge a journal after just two issues.[2]

We are paid a visit by Mwalimu's personal assistant, Annar Cassam. The message is to tone down our rhetoric. Henry and I earnestly argue with her, and do not relent. She leaves plainly frustrated. We learn later that her report had indicated that there are "some hard nuts to crack on the campus!"

There is a backdrop to this encounter. After the sound public reprimand he gave us, Mwalimu had called the radical students to a private meeting. The first one was in early March. He had again called us to his private residence in Msasani on June 16, 1970. I was not present at the first meeting but took part in the second one. What an encounter it was. Here were we, virtual nobodies, sitting down face to face with not just the Head of a State but also one of the most distinguished leaders in the world.

About ten of us sat in the living room, some on the soft couches, and others on the carpet. Mwalimu emerged smiling, casually attired. Two assistants were present; I do not recall anyone else. We were not searched; and I did not see any guards around. It was as perfectly informal and friendly a get together as one could visualize.

---

1   This excellent book has been updated several times. The latest edition presenting an up to date class analysis of the USA is Domhoff (2009).

2   See GK (1970) and Mwana wa Matonya (1970).

Mwalimu began by saying, with a wry smile on his face, that he sought continued dialogue with the "true socialists." Then he dwelt on the difficult task of building socialism in a very poor nation. He told us he had tried to read the works of Karl Marx, but only after the Arusha Declaration was promulgated. It was not easy to comprehend Marx, he noted. But he had found Lenin more understandable.

Then he asked us to raise what we deemed the main issues of the day. We first drew attention to the class character of the struggle for socialism in Tanzania. Not every one in the country supported socialism. The lower social classes did so but the upper class was bitterly opposed. The ideological struggle at the Hill was a reflection of this contradiction. We said that Tanzania would find it extremely difficult to build socialism if it kept one foot in the capitalist camp and one in the socialist camp. We had to form strong alliances with the socialist nations. We also talked about participatory forms of government. In particular, we requested a greater representation for students in the affairs of the university.

Mwalimu listened keenly to us. Now and then, he expressed his views. On alliances with socialist nations, he was skeptical. Otherwise, he seemed to concur. Two days later the proposed amendment to the University Bill that had been tabled before the Parliament was modified. The Minister for Education raised the number of student representatives on the faculty boards from one to five. This was in line with what we had requested.

In social gatherings, I am normally reserved. But in a political or general meeting, I am invariably boisterous and outspoken. Yet, on that day, I was tongue tied. I recall that Charles Kileo, Andrew Shija, Issa Shivji and Jonathan Kamala doing most of the talking on our side.

In the face of the public put down we had got from Mwalimu in February, all of us were apprehensive about this meeting. But it went well, leaving us encouraged and in jolly spirits. Given this background, the official reaction to *Cheche* No. 2 is somewhat perplexing.

A Stupendous Spark
During the time I was in Nairobi, Issa had undertaken extensive research relating to the nationalized companies in Tanzania. His effort revealed little known facts about the arrangements under which these firms operated after being taken over. The things he uncovered, and the broad conclusions he drew were crucial to both the character of the socialist transformation in Tanzania, and the need for open discussion about this process.

It was proposed, and the editorial board concurred, that his report would come out as a special issue of *Cheche*. After the usual nightly printing exercise, it came out on September 3, 1970 bearing the title *Tanzania: The Silent Class Struggle*. The main thesis in this path-breaking work was that nationalization had done little to foster the disengagement of the Tanzanian economy from the global capitalist system. Formal state ownership had not translated into actual state or popular control. Thus, the nationalized British banks now functioned under management contracts with multinational banks from other capitalist nations. Issa revealed a complex web of neo-colonial type arrangements under which most of the nationalized firms operated.

In an accompanying editorial, Henry and I state that socialism in Tanzania cannot be constructed under a disguised and enhanced form of dependency on the international capital. To build a self-reliant, integrated and prosperous economy, we need to disengage from the system. A vigorous debate on this question is required in order that a "rigorous exploration of the forces of both progress and reaction in the Tanzanian revolution" can be undertaken.

With this special issue, *Cheche* has come of age. The appearance is more professional. Locally and abroad, its reputation as a medium of socialist scholarship is rising. Many commend the analysis presented. We thereby expect that a serious debate on the construction of socialism in Tanzania will unfold.

Our plan is to start the debate with the third regular issue of *Cheche*. But we are overly ambitious. Many students talk about the special issue, but they are not inclined to put their views to paper. And because it offers a solid critique of Mwalimu Nyerere's version of socialism, the seasoned and progressive academics need more time to formulate their response. One of the first commentaries, written by John Saul, appears in *The Standard*.

Cheche No. 3 comes out about six weeks after the special issue with a mixture of articles. Among them are three commentaries on *The Silent Class Struggle* by A. S. Namama, Yoweri Museveni and myself. Each of us basically concurs with Issa's thesis, gives supportive evidence, and takes note of the wide gap between the theory and practice of socialism in Tanzania. The last point is succinctly formulated by Museveni.

> *Peasants and workers, not being philosophers but men of water and ugali, are not very much impressed by what Mazrui called "documentary radicalism" -- i.e. documents of a revolutionary character. They tend to be impressed by revolutionary practice.*
> *Museveni (1970b).*

In addition, this issue has a review of the book *Nyerere on Socialism* (Nyerere 1969). The reviewer, John Saul, notes that the book is directed at students and the common man with the view to stimulate socialist debate in Tanzania. While he makes some critical points, it is generally a laudatory review that commends Mwalimu for his desire to promote discussions on socialism. He calls this desire as "one of the more promising portends for socialism in Tanzania." But Saul does not note that earlier Kwame Nkrumah had been more serious about stimulating such a debate in Ghana by founding a journal specifically devoted to such a purpose.[3]

Cheche No. 3 also contains a revealing commentary on how economics is taught in Africa written by Glyn Hughes, a school teacher. There are, in addition, a satire on vacations by Gora Ebrahim, a short piece on CIA and Black Power, an expose of individuals and companies from the West acting against African interests, two poems, and letters from readers. Our editorial announces that *Cheche* No. 4 is expected to have further "informed comments/discussions" of *The Silent Class Struggle*. The earlier accusations that *Cheche* was preoccupied with abstruse theories devoid of contemporary local and practical relevance no longer hold water.

Both issues sell well, on the campus and in town, and are sent across Tanzania, East Africa and abroad. Our mood is upbeat as we look forward to continued open and critical debate among the university community and others about the construction of socialism in Tanzania.

Ideological Sparks

Progressive students and academic staff are also active on other fronts. One fight is to consolidate Development Studies, a new compulsory interdisciplinary course that took off last academic year under the stewardship of Lionel Cliff. The change did not come about without a struggle. The very idea of such a course is an anathema to academics -- the majority of our social science lecturers –who have been trained and immersed in the traditional specialized bourgeois approach to the study of human society.

The roots of the new course lie in a cogent report prepared in 1967 by nine progressive academics, including Giovanni Arrighi, Grant Kamenju, Sol Picciotto, Walter Rodney and John Saul arguing for an conceptually integrated course of study at the university. The fragmentation of perspective in the current system of education generates

---

3   That journal was called *The Spark*. See Chapter 9.

conformist individuals. What Tanzania (and Africa) needs are rounded intellectuals able to think critically and facilitate social transformation.[4] The extracurricular lecture series -- the Common Course -- offered initially was not adequate to overcome the deficiency. The USARF and TYL memorandum to the Presidential Visitation Committee had also called for such a course. The Department of Development Studies was established in 1969 with Development Studies, or an equivalent course, required for all students. It does not replace traditional disciplines like sociology, history or political science but complements them with a cohesive perspective on society and human development, and elucidate the ideological underpinnings of the conventional content, methodology and teaching of these disciplines.

The top echelon of the university administration, and many lecturers remain opposed. The former dislike the robustly progressive orientation and lack of fealty to official TANU ideology. Their vision does not transcend political education that regurgitates the tenets of *Ujamaa*. The latter, on the other hand, consider the present course as political education that breaches the norms of academic freedom. The narrow-minded academics fear that their claim to objectivity is being shown as hollow in the thorough socio-economic analysis presented by Development Studies. They neither study nor analyze the holistic, dynamic perspectives on human society and social change. What they do not comprehend, and are slothful to delve into, they thus brand as politics or propaganda.

Due to the political climate after the Arusha Declaration, and the tenacity of the progressive forces at the Hill, the reactionary forces are unable to prevail on this front. But they do not give up. The administration allocates inadequate funds and support staff for the Department and fails to hire even a minimal number of lecturers. Lionel Cliff has faced major hurdles in teaching the entire first year student group with limited resources. Yet, he puts up a remarkable effort, and with assistance from like minded academics and senior students in terms of giving lectures and conducting seminars, the course takes off better than anticipated. Development Studies, it must be said, constitutes a major pedagogical innovation not only for the universities in Africa but elsewhere as well. It is a pioneering effort that needs to be lauded, supported and further refined.

Nevertheless, rearguard actions continue. A group of seven "respected" dons, with a strong contingent from the Department of Political Science,

---

4   The Nationalist (1967g), Saul (1968) and Saul (2009), Chapter 1.

issues a memorandum to urge a re-evaluation of the purpose, content and organization of the new Department and what it offers. It says that students and academic staff are dissatisfied with what has been done. The aim, clearly, is to turn the clock back.

We discuss this matter in a TYL meeting, and prepare a counter-statement. Issued with the title "Students Unite to Support Socialism," it notes that the course has already begun to enlarge the mental horizons of our students. We point out what the reactionary academics fail to do, namely that a serious and thorough examination of the purpose, content and organization of all the departments at the University, and the courses they offer are needed. Our university still produces graduates who are divorced from reality and are not intellectually well-equipped to serve the interests of the people in a poverty stricken nation.

Our strongly worded statement calls for a cultural revolution in education. The combined efforts of progressive students and staff make it not possible, at least in terms of formal structures, for the reactionaries to win this fight. They do not get support from the political establishment, and Development Studies continues its existence.

Our Wednesday afternoon *shamba* work goes on. USARF leads the students in picking cashew nuts on nearby farms. The money raised goes to the African liberation movements and other causes. Ideological classes continue.

The new main student body is in a state of transition as well. We attend its meetings to push for a more progressive orientation. But the leadership is hostile. Harsh statements and counter-statements ensue. Many student leaders are corrupt, and misuse of student funds is an ongoing scandal. Several of them are forced to resign this term when one more case of financial impropriety is exposed.

One day, Mr. Lee Kwan Yu, the flamboyant, learned Prime Minister of Singapore, lectures at the Hill. He is accompanied by his host, Mwalimu Nyerere. The assembly hall is filled to capacity as he lauds the capitalist path to economic development. The right-wingers applaud him, posing questions that make him disparage socialism even more. Mwalimu has an ambivalent expression on his face, but respecting his guest, he does not say a word. Henry and I raise our hands to challenge the man. The Prime Minister, beaming confidently on the podium, points to me. Fireworks begin as we exchange views. Without mincing my words, I say he has presented selective evidence, and go on to compare India and China. He calls me a dreamer. Mwalimu smiles in amusement. I stand to respond but am shouted down by the man from Singapore. However, our message has been given.

An American group called Moral Rearmament visits the Hill. USARF clashes with them. I write the USARF statement on the hypocrisy of burning millions with napalm and supporting dictators like Mobutu and Suharto on the one hand, and talking about morality on the other. Rodney gives another one of his popular public lectures. This time he talks on "Kidnappings and Hijackings: Two New Revolutionary Weapons." He refers to the plight of the forgotten people of Palestine, more than a million of whom have been ejected from their land and languish in squalid camps. He talks about the death squads of the US-backed dictatorships in Central and South America that murder students, trade union leaders and priests with impunity. When some oppressed peoples resist with tactics like hijackings and taking hostages, the world media react as if they are the root and source of all the violence on the planet. The daily, official and massive violence practiced by the capitalists and imperialists is, for them, non-existent. Walter shatters the double standards, calling a spade a spade.

That plain truth, stated in a melodic style reminiscent of the tunes of Bob Marley, does not sit well with the authorities. Many leftists on the campus are also at odds with his words. Prof. Szentes call him an adventurist. But Frene Ginwalla publishes the text of his speech. Three years ago, Rodney had been expelled from Jamaica for standing up for the interests of the poor and disenfranchised. Now some bureaucrats in Tanzania urge Mwalimu, as they had done earlier during the Second Seminar on East African Youth, to do likewise. The British Ambassador issues a strongly worded condemnation of Rodney. However, several university students including me write letters to the editor of *The Standard* to support him.

Rodney is almost done with his magnum opus, *How Europe Underdeveloped Africa*. For several weeks, he has given draft copies of the chapters, one at a time, to Henry and me. We read the drafts, and meet with him. Imagine a stalwart historian giving his manuscript to two upstart students, and sitting down for hours to listen to their comments. The final version shows us that he did take what we said into account. A humble man, a brilliant scholar, but one whose plain words make oppressors of the world tremble with rage.

The Spark is Extinguished

By early November 1970, USARF and the Hill TYL have held their annual elections. A new editorial board for *Cheche* is elected. Zakia and I, being final year students, step down. Henry is now the senior editor. Others on the board are George Hajivayanis, Naijuka Kasihwaki, Wilbert Kavishe and Munene Njagi. George is also the new USARF treasurer, and a member of the TYL committee. The new board is working on production of *Cheche* No. 4, which is to carry in depth analyses of the *The Silent Class Struggle*.

While other ideological struggles continue, I have at least relinquished some responsibilities. Now my formal studies cry out for attention. The final examinations are four months away. On a Monday evening, November 9, 1970, to be precise, I am at my desk. Having had an early dinner, I plan to review and do exercises from two books. Should I start with Ruel V Churchill's *Complex Variables and Applications*, or with Richard A Dean's *Elements of Abstract Algebra*?

Nazir Virji, my roommate, is absorbed in Thomas Hardy's *Far From the Madding Crowd*. A literature major, he adores Brecht, Ngugi, Dickens and Hardy. Get him started, and he spends hours dissecting their fine points. He looks forward to the day, five months from now, when he can teach literature to Form V and Form VI. He has diabetes, a childhood affliction. Daily, he injects himself with insulin. I wince at the sight and worry. He laughs and tells me "that is life."

Our room is above the ground level in the Hall I tower block. At around 8 p.m., a pebble strikes our window. It is his typical knock -- George is outside. He will soon barge into the room with the invariable question, usually expressed in broken Gujarati, "Karim, what has Mr. Fatehali brought this time?"

He refers to my father. My parents live in Upanga, five miles from the Hill. When I go home, which is not often, my mother feeds me as if I have been starving for days. She always complains how thin I look. If I open my mouth to say a word, an hour long lecture follows. Every Sunday, she makes my father drive his small truck to the Hill to deliver an assortment of Indian sweets and spicy food. My protestations that that is not necessary are to no avail.

George is a dedicated comrade whose light hearted manner and boundless energy enliven our activities. With an unkempt beard, he is a Fidel Castro look alike. He smokes like a chimney, eats like a pig, and is often hungry. On Sundays and Mondays, he knows there is food in my room. Whenever the pebble strikes, I know who is there, and for what purpose. But this time, he does not march in. Instead, another pebble strikes, and another one. As I open the window, he signals to me to come down. I think he looks pretty mad.

"What's your problem?"

"Karim, we have been banned. USARF and *Cheche* are dead."

"What?" I exclaim in utter disbelief.

Earlier, George with other members of the TYL committee had a meeting with Mr. Msekwa, the Vice Chancellor. I had assumed that a presidential visit or another major event was to occur. Instead, our progressive edifice is engulfed in flames. The boss has conveyed a specific order from President Nyerere. USARF and *Cheche* should cease their activities immediately. They no longer exist. The reason given is that USARF is redundant and unneeded because since TYL is a "revolutionary organization" that has the monopoly of political activities in all educational institutions in Tanzania. Further, the name *Cheche* is Russian in origin. A magazine that promotes a foreign ideology is not needed in Tanzania. That is the forthright message, plain and simple.[5]

I am speechless, devastated. I write in my diary that night: "My soul has been torn apart from me." George goes on: "Other comrades are finishing their dinner. We have agreed to meet later at Joe Kanywanyi's house."

"Let us go to Walter's place to inform him."

We have a long meeting that fateful night. Rodney, Kanywanyi and about ten student activists are present. Nothing can undo the death sentence handed down -- that is clear. But we decide not to take it lying down. At the least, The university community and world at large should know about the ban and our reaction to it. Kasihwaki and I have the task of drafting our death-bed statement. We work till late to produce *Our Last Stand* (Appendix E). Other comrades produce copies and distribute them over the campus, the city and abroad. Both *The Standard* and *The Nationalist* give front page reports of the ban and a summary of our statement.[6]

The reactionaries have secured their desired prize. The sole strident voice of the left, the staunchest proponent of socialism in Tanzania, has been extinguished. Yet, *Our Last Stand* proclaims that:

> *Organizations can be banned,*
> *individuals can be liquidated,*
> *but ideas live on.*

---

5   See Chapter 8, Chapter 9, Chapter 10 and Appendix E for further elaboration.

6   The Standard (1970) and The Nationalist (1970d). This issue is further discussed in Chapter 10.

6

On Producing A Student Magazine

Henry Mapolu

"A socialist must be concerned with the lot of the poor not as
a philanthropist but as an active fighter against the causes of
poverty and misery among the people."
- Chenge wa Chenge -

In July 1969, I joined the University College at Dar es Salaam to pursue a BA degree. It was the era of the Arusha Declaration. Not only had a new ideological orientation towards socialism been pronounced, but it had then been followed by nationalization of "the commanding heights of the economy," namely, banks, industries, farms, and other enterprises. A move on this scale was unprecedented in sub-Saharan Africa. To the imperialists, especially the British, and the big domestic capitalists, this takeover was egregiously earth-shattering but to the ordinary person in Tanzania, it was positively inspiring.

The spirit of socialism was in the air all over the land, including at the country's only institution of higher learning. I too had been captivated by socialistic ideals; I was a mature-age entrant at the College, having previously been a junior member of the academic staff of Kivukoni College -- then considered the country's fountain of political ideas (Harris 1968).

At the university, I encountered a group of students with similar inclinations, who, moreover, seriously explored and debated the social, economic, political and philosophical dimensions of socialism and were engaged in activities designed to promote it. I joined them immediately and enthusiastically. Soon I was attending public lectures, visiting *Ujamaa* villages, doing *shamba* work, raising funds for African liberation movements, demonstrating against the sale of arms by Britain to the Apartheid regime of South Africa, and against the American war on the people of Vietnam, and so on. As it was, the workload for my studies was heavy. With this demanding, extensive, and purely voluntary extra-curricular work, life became doubly hectic. Yet, it was a fun-filled and emotionally fulfilling time as well.

Producing the Spark

My consistent participation in these activities resulted, in September 1969, in my election to represent the campus TANU Youth League (TYL) at the national TYL level. The following month, I was elected onto the first editorial board of *Cheche*, a new student magazine being launched by USARF and the campus TYL. The board had three students. Little did I realize what a tumultuous period in my life this was to herald. Despite the requirements of our studies and practical hurdles of those times, we were able to produce four issues of *Cheche* within a year. However, after the fourth issue, it was banned by the authorities. Not to be deterred, we re-launched it in 1971 under another name, *MajiMaji*, and I continued as a member (in fact, the senior editor) of the new editorial board. Two issues of *MajiMaji* came out that year, before a new editorial team was elected. More than two of my undergraduate study years were spent editing this magazine. Further, I also wrote articles for the earlier issues of *MajiMaji*.

Subsequently, under some twenty editorial teams, *MajiMaji* continued to appear for more than 15 years, at times frequently, and at other times, only once in a while. Inevitably, it changed over the years -- both in form and content -- reflecting the changing circumstances at the University, the country, and the world, and also reflecting the altered visions of the new teams. As my involvement was during the initial phase, my reflections bear upon the first days of *Cheche* and *MajiMaji*. My experiences may diverge substantially from those of the editors during the latter half of the Seventies and during the Eighties. In any case, I hope my reflections will enrich the diversity of editorial experiences, and the joint lessons gleaned from them will, I trust, be of some relevance particularly to the African youth of today.

I focus on two aspects: first, on the physical work involved in producing a student magazine in those days and the impact of it had on those who performed it; and second, on the kind of issues the magazine raised, and the responses that the different sectors of society gave to it. I will also reflect on the general underlying factors that led to the total proscription of *Cheche*.

Stencils and Cyclostyling

Looking back at the actual manner in which copies of *Cheche* -- and later *MajiMaji* -- were produced, one cannot avoid noticing the momentous ways in which the world has changed. Producing a student magazine in Dar es Salaam at that time was a truly laborious process. After the editorial deliberations on acceptability, each contribution (article, poem, book review, story, etc.) was typed on a stencil using a manual typewriter. Electric typewriters, which made the job somewhat easier, were not available to us. Some students of today may have seen a typewriter, but do they know what a stencil is?

In those days, photocopying was done rarely since it was very expensive and the machines were not as versatile as those of today. For many offices and educational institutions, typing stencils was the first step for producing, at low cost, multiple copies of a written document. About 15 inches long and 9 inches wide, a stencil consisted of three sheets joined about two inches from the top of the last sheet. The upper sheet was waxed plastic-type paper, the middle one was carbon copy paper, and the last was a thicker paper sheet. (Some stencils did not have the middle sheet). The top segment of the stencil had intricate perforations used to fit it onto the production machine. Typing a stencil (technically called cutting a stencil) produced tiny perforations through which ink would flow. It also gave a readable copy on the last sheet.

This work required expert level typing skills. The waxed top was delicate; a spoiled stencil wasted money. Correcting a typing error was a complex maneuver: first you had to apply a special fluid exactly on the mistake, wait a minute for it to dry, and precisely re-type the correct letter over the erroneous one. After typing an entire page, the mistakes made and corrected appeared as red dots decorating the top page. Imagine correcting not just a letter but a whole sentence -- not to speak of an entire paragraph! For good copies of the final document, even a single error was to be avoided as it could blemish all the magazine copies.

Once the stencils were cut, they were put, one at a time, on a cyclostyling machine. Again, I wonder which student of today has ever heard of the word "cyclostyling." Another name for it is mimeographing. Varying in capacity, these machines either ran on electricity or were manually operated. Most of those in Tanzania then were manually operated and were about the size of a modern desk-top photocopier. With a paper tray at the bottom, their main external parts consisted of a roller drum on which the stencil was loaded, a side compartment for the ink bottle, a handle and a metallic cover.

To load a stencil, first the last two sheets were carefully torn off. The waxed sheet was then aligned so that the perforated top fitted exactly onto the corresponding metallic projections above the drum. This held it in place. To ensure even print margins, the sheet was gently but firmly placed on the drum so as to be free of the tiniest of a wrinkle. This required skill and patience. Otherwise one could damage, tear, or misalign the stencil. The drum had a thin layer of ink on it. During printing, ink had to flow evenly and at the precisely required rate; a slight smudge on an initial copy could be a big blot after a few more copies. This might necessitate reloading the stencil or, heaven forbid, production of a new stencil.

With the stencil loaded, paper tray filled and ink bottle in place, the handle of the cyclostyling machine was turned at a regular pace, not too slow or not too fast, so as to bring out copies that were neither too light nor too dark. One turn bought out one printed page; five hundred turns gave five hundred. With the required number of copies of that page produced, the stencil was carefully removed, and stored in a neatly unfolded manner in the original box for re-use. For the next page, the next stencil was loaded, and so on. The ink flow was continually monitored, and the paper tray was periodically replenished as well.

As one page after another was printed, the task of collating started. A wide work area, with at least five or six persons for the job, was needed. Each collated copy was combined with a stencil-produced or otherwise printed covers, and stapled with a heavy duty stapler. Finally, one person went through each copy to look for the badly produced copies. Only copies of acceptable quality were distributed. To produce four hundred copies of a fifty page issue usually took seven to eight student volunteers the better parts of two nights. I say nights, because we did not own a cyclostyling machine, and depended on faculty or departmental machines which were normally in use during the day. Further, working on weekend nights at times allowed us to use the machines to which we only had a semi-official access. All in all, the physical production of an issue of *Cheche* or *MajiMaji* was a long, laborious and tiring process.

In this era of the personal computer with attached printers and much cheaper and flexible photocopiers, the extent of this effort is difficult to visualize. As students, our resources were extremely limited. We had no access to external "donor" funds; and even if any were offered, as they at times were, we would have and did, in a spirit of self-reliance and self-determination, rejected them outright. It was our magazine, and we did most of the work ourselves. Our unlimited enthusiasm is what kept us going right from the stage of soliciting articles, editing, taking care of the administrative tasks, writing editorials and the like to the typing stage and the extremely tedious final production process. At the end, with several volunteers and the better portions of one or two weekend nights, the issue was brought to life. The late hours over which we did this work will always remain in my memory. To this day, I can visualize my comrades taking turns to operate the cyclostyling machine, one watching over the ink tank, adding more ink as needed, another collecting the emerging sheets and arranging them, and so on.

Even now, the memories of those days invariably return to me whenever I pass by the spot along what is now Samora Avenue (then Independence Avenue) where the company that was at the heart of the cyclostyling technology, Gestetner, was located. I used to look at this company with envy. They had a virtual monopoly on the supply of cyclostyling machines, stencils, the ink needed for them and even the fluid used for correcting the typing errors on stencils! I used to think they had secured an immortal business line! As reproduction of documents would always be needed, I harbored the impression that this company's abundant profits were guaranteed eternally! But I was woefully wrong: who knows about Gestetner today? Today's key words when it comes to document production are Xerox, HP, Microsoft, Intel and the like. As in the past, globalization ensures that even the most rudimentary transaction carried out in the remotest part of the world is mediated through the auspices of big capital.

The rigorous march of technology and the inevitable periodic crises of capitalism produce such upheavals. In Africa, to this day, we blow with the winds that prevail from outside. That brings a superficial appearance of progress but has little benefit for the majority, and does not give us the ability to stand on our own feet. We need to grasp and apply the idea of appropriate technology. The latest is not necessarily the best. When the latest gadget breaks down, we do not have the means to repair it. When the electricity supply dies, an electrical water pump comes to a standstill, but the hand driven pump still does the job. In rural areas and schools, use of appropriate technology can make a real difference between education and no education, good health and poor health, and even between life and death.

Sparkling Comradeship
Despite the drudgery and loss of sleep involved in producing the magazine, at the end, we never felt tired! We were enthusiastic and devoted to the work. It was our own choice; nobody forced us to do anything. As we worked, we chatted, joked and without fail, had a fabulous time.

These factors made the night toil appear absolutely light. The camaraderie that evolved amongst us, and the once-in-a-lifetime opportunity to be acquainted with people from diverse backgrounds and staying in different halls of residence made it a time to savor and enjoy. With substantial numbers of students from Kenya and Uganda, the University in those days had a truly East African student composition. Also, a sprinkling of students from places like Malawi, Sudan, Zimbabwe, and Ethiopia added a rich diversity to the student body. The spirit of Pan Africanism held forth in the minds and lives of the students. Working for this magazine strengthened that spirit. The nocturnal work brought together like-minded people from practically all the academic faculties on the campus. An aspiring lawyer, a budding economist, a student of languages, a sociologist in the making, a chemist and a mathematician in training -- all worked in unison to bring it to life, and in the process, enriched each other's lives. The process of physically producing the magazine thereby became an experience in itself -- even without looking at the intellectual benefits relating to the contents of the magazine.

In our endeavors to promote socialistic ideals, we shared a lot, and helped each other. People contributed according to their talents and skills. Apart from the editorial and nocturnal teamwork, I gave extra input in the sphere of typing. As one of the few students at the campus with blind-typing ability (i.e. typing without looking at the keyboard), my skills came in quite handy. As I have noted above, typing fast and without errors was a very valuable skill to have in that era, and I put it to good use for both *Cheche* and *MajiMaji*. Many comrades contributed immensely in various other ways. I cannot forget Ntalyaga (Ramadhan) Meghji, a fellow student and artist for our magazine. He designed the cover, and drew the cartoons. For the initial issues, he did this directly on a stencil using a special pen, a task needing patience and concentration. It was through this difficult process that the face of our magazine was sculpted.

Because of our lack of experience and skills, the print quality of the first issue was poor. The cyclostyled covers, made of ordinary pink colored paper, had a faded appearance and were not attractive to behold. Similarly, the cover of the second issue lacked visual appeal. Starting with the (third) special issue, we managed to acquire funds to pay the University Printing Unit to produce the cover on firmer and better quality paper. From then on, *Cheche* and later *MajiMaji*, had the appearance of a semi-professionally produced magazine!

I am able to report the budgetary details, thanks to Karim Hirji who has somehow managed to keep the records pertaining to our work. The budget of *Cheche* No 1 reveals both the paucity of our resources as well as the ability to get by with the little we had. The editorial committee secured a loan of shillings 160/= from TYL and USARF, and a lecturer in the Law Faculty, Joe Kanywanyi, contributed the princely sum of shillings 3/=. Ten reams of cyclostyling paper were donated by the national Youth League office; 45 stencils came from the College TYL branch supplies; and half a ream of pink cover paper and cyclostyling ink were donated by the Faculty of Law. Further, from the TYL/USARF funds, we purchased one ream of the cover paper (Tshs 23/50); one box of large staples (Tshs 2/=) and 5 reams of white paper (Tshs 72/50). For typing two articles, we paid the total of Tshs 33/= to a typist in the Faculty of Law. We incurred a postage charge of Tshs 13/10 for mailing the printed copies. The rest of the work was done by volunteers free of charge.

For the first issue, a total of 293 copies were printed of which 230 were sold at the price of 75 cents each, making our sales revenue amount to shillings Tshs 192/90. After returning the sum borrowed from USARF, we had the grand sum of Tshs 171/80 left over in the account at the end! For the second issue, a similar story prevailed. About 500 copies were produced. The sales revenue amounted to Tshs 815/=, and we had a balance of Tshs 272/85 in the magazine account at the end.

How the economy has changed! Today, with this sum, you can just get a large-sized banana or two oranges. Even for those days, it was a modest sum. The minimum wage was about Tshs 200/= per month, and a secondary school teacher earned Tshs 1,100/= or so per month. In terms of the US dollar, at the exchange rate of Tshs 10/= per US dollar, our account balance after the second issue stood at US $27.29.

Impact and Reactions

What distinctly mattered was not so much the appearance but the substance of the magazine. In that respect, it was a unique and exemplary undertaking. Soon after the first issue came out, the reputation of *Cheche* literally spread world-wide. The contents of each issue were path breaking in political terms and refreshingly rigorous along intellectual lines. The form did not compromise the substance. I cannot help contrasting that with many magazines I see today that are glossy and immaculate in appearance but quite shallow in content.

Cheche was banned after only four issues -- actually only three plus a special issue -- were produced. Other contributors in this book examine this question in greater detail. The question on which I would like to reflect on is this: why were so many people, other than the students of the College, interested in it? After all, it was just a student undertaking, and those involved in it represented an extremely tiny proportion of the student population at the College -- only the radical left.

All sorts of people and institutions from beyond the campus went to great pains to get hold of a copy whenever an issue was out. I recall noticing diplomatic cars showing up at the Hill to pick up copies! Messages came from libraries, people and organizations across Africa and in Europe and North America, asking to be put on the mailing list. Once an issue was out, the *The Standard* (later to be called *Daily News*) -- at that time, the only English-language daily newspaper -- tended to take notice of it. On at least one occasion we had the honor to have an editorial dedicated to the contents of an issue! Senior members of the academic staff wrote articles for this student magazine. Looking at the table of contents of the three issues of *Cheche*, I find amongst the contributors well known scholars then (or later) teaching at the College: Walter Rodney (History), Tamas Szentes (Economics), Dan Nabudere (Law), Haroub Othman (Law), and John Saul (Political Science) (see Appendix A). Why this interest in a student magazine? And, when sentenced to death, the order came from the State House itself!

A major reason for this widespread interest lay in the fact that the period from 1967 to roughly 1975 was a period of rigorous serious soul-searching in Tanzania. A lot of questions were being asked: Where are we? Where are we headed? Where should we be going? How should we move forward? Many views competed to occupy the center stage. The official media mostly gave the official line. There were few platforms in which such matters could be explicitly posed and seriously discussed without political interference. External platforms gave their own biased perspectives on what was going on in Tanzania.

Cheche -- and *MajiMaji* later on -- were home-based ventures that addressed these issues in a politically consistent, intellectually challenging and generally coherent manner. Although a student magazine, it did not concern itself with student matters. Indeed, day to day, facile student politics were never at the heart of the magazine. Rather, it delved deeply into national and international social, political, cultural and economic affairs. That was another reason behind its broad appeal. As I look back, I do not see any other institution or organ that put forward and deliberated upon such critical issues and pointed to some avenues for their resolution with the same diligence as this student magazine did.

A number of important and open debates did occur in the main newspapers of the time. At times, it became a vibrant national debate. For a while, *The Standard*, though owned by the government, served as a platform for expressing diverse ideological strands. Indeed, it has been said that there has never been as much press freedom in East Africa as the time when this paper was under the editorship of the South African, Frene Ginwala! But even in this context, several of these debates were initiated or led by the same group of university students who stood behind USARF and *Cheche*.

Cheche, for its part, ventured too far for the authorities to countenance, and was too independent. They wanted to control political debate, to steer it in a particular direction and away from other directions. They did not want too deep, too probing questions to be raised. *Cheche* did all that. It critiqued the official policy and suggested alternatives unpalatable to the elite. So, it had to be banned.

Freedom of Speech

It is usual to blame the demise of USARF and *Cheche* on the existence of the one party rule prevailing in Tanzania at that point in time. Under this line of reasoning, socialism is synonymous with one party rule and censorship. What happened therefore was bound to happen, and needs no further comment. In my view, this way of reasoning is simplistic, unenlightening and factually misleading.

The fundamental flaw in this form of reasoning emerges from noting that one party rule (or one man rule), in name or in fact, was common in Africa at that time. It was found in the avowedly pro-capitalist, pro-Western nations like Malawi and Zaire as well as in the declared socialist nations like Tanzania and Congo (Brazzaville). The repression of political dissidents and silencing of opposition voices was, if anything, more common and took harsher forms in the US supported regimes like those in Malawi and Zaire as compared to Tanzania. University students there faced arbitrary detention, torture and death if they spoke out. In contrast, USARF and *Cheche*, and the radical students associated with them, were not dealt with in a manner anywhere approaching such brutalities. In Africa, and even in Asia and Latin America, there was no direct correlation between dictatorial and militaristic rule on the one hand and declared socialist or other forms of government. Whether the government was diplomatically or politically aligned to the East or the West, suppression of the opposition and blanket censorship were common. The knee-jerk tendency to blame it all on socialistic one-party rule ignores this crucial historic fact.

Yet, the fact remains that USARF and *Cheche* were silenced, and that needs an explanation. This matter is explored in a broader theoretical context by invoking Marx's sound observation that the dominant ideas of any era are those that serve the interests of the ruling class. Whether you examine the prevalent ideas about life in general, important information, ways of conceptualizing issues, the common sense notions, or opinions on major in issues and events in society and history, what dominates social discourse is that which is aligned with the basic interests and visions of those who control the economy and political power. It is only during periods of major societal transitions that exceptions to this basic rule tend to emerge.

Further, it is incorrect to attribute such ideological dominance solely to a direct mechanism, state-run or otherwise, of curtailment of thought and opinions, or restriction of expression. Ideas and views can be more effectively censored when there is no central censor, when there are a multitude of indirect ways undertaken by varied parties not acting in unison but which serve to promote some ideas and ways of thought and downplay or sideline other views and ways of thinking. It then becomes a matter of common tradition and folklore, to say this and that and not to say this or that. Yet, the "this" or "that" which comes to the fore is invariably in line with the world outlook of the rich and powerful, and the "that" which usually lies unnoticed on the ground is precisely that which challenges their hegemony or perspectives.

This is how things actually are even in the industrialized capitalist nations. The supposed freedom of speech is a freedom to express yourself but not the real freedom to be heard, no matter what your views. You can shout and shout. The dominant views on the television and other major media, in schools, universities and political discourse will, however, be those that favor corporate interests, and the military industrial complex. And because there is no overt censorship in most matters, people come to think that they are making up their own minds, free from external influences. Yet, these influences drench their lives, day in and day out, from childhood to death, to curtail even the way they think about things, let alone the facts about different issues (Borjesson 2004; Herman and Chomsky 1988; McChesney 1997).

In the US, for instance, you can, as a leftwing party candidate, run for president. But unless you have major corporate backing and hundreds of millions of dollars to advertise on TV and for other campaign expenses, you will go nowhere. Your face will never appear on TV. No major newspaper will devote more than a few words to you. You will not be invited to any television debates. On election day, nobody but a tiny, tiny minority will know about you, and among them even fewer will vote for you. The soundness or otherwise of your program is never an issue. It might as well be that you had been banned. In fact, if you are banned, probably more people will pay attention to you (Bleifuss and Freeman 2006).

Take another illustrative case: During the lead up to the war in Iraq a vast majority of the American people believed that Sadaam Hussein possessed weapons of mass destruction, was about to attack the US, and was involved in the 9/11 attacks in New York. All these ideas were known to be utter falsehoods even at that time, and now we know that they were outright lies. People outside the US were much more skeptical about these outlandish claims. How can it be that in a nation with a free press and media, with an advanced system of education, the vast majority of people were duped so readily? This only becomes a puzzle if you think of it as an exception. It is indeed the way things usually are, be that in the US, UK, Norway or Africa. The dominant world view is that which serves the (economic) ruling class.

In a society in transition, when the ruling class is not yet entrenched economically and culturally, there may be greater diversity of views or there may be an overt clamp down on dissent and ideas. It is a matter of the political balance of forces and other factors. When the ruling class or elite lacks confidence in its ability to rule, it resorts to outright suppression. And that is how the issue of censorship in Africa in the post-Independence era needs to be approached.

I cannot do justice to this fundamental issue in a short article. But I note some of its ramifications for the present. Africa is firmly integrated into the global capitalist system, basically as a land to be exploited for the benefit of major multinational corporations. Thereby, it has both external and internal mechanisms that restrict the freedom of speech and expression. These mechanisms are strongly biased against anti-imperialist and anti-capitalist ways of looking at issues. They do not give the ordinary person an honest and full account of what is happening in Africa and the planet at large.

Both in the international media that saturate Africa's air waves and local media of all forms, voices that champion the interests of the poor and powerless in an uncompromising way are silenced, or marginalized. Attention is given to scandals, squabbles and personalities but the prevailing socio-economic system as such is not questioned. "Donors" are praised and corruption is condemned. But there is little talk of economic exploitation. If the powerful collide, it is usually the "donors" who are seen as the good guys. Socialist and consistently anti-imperialist voices are effectively banned from these media (Bello 2010).

For Africa to move ahead and stand on its own, the media and students need to pose fundamental questions: Why are things they way they are? Who bears the responsibility? Who benefits and who suffers? Can that state of affairs be changed? How can that be done? What can we learn from history, that of our own and of the world in general? Is capitalism good for Africa, or is socialism the better strategy?

These are the burning questions *Cheche* posed, without fear or favor, during its time. The youth of today, in particular, the university students must, I say must, explore such matters, in an as bold, in-depth and incisive a manner as that radical voice of the past did. The fate of Africa depends on whether they will take up this challenge or not.

7

Sisterly Activism

Zakia Hamdani Meghji

"The incorporation of the great masses of...women in the liberation struggle...is one of the prerequisites for the victory of the Socialist idea and for the construction of a Socialist society. Only [in] a Socialist society will ... the family as an economic unit...vanish and its place will be taken by the family as a moral unit, [and] the woman will become an equally entitled, equally creative, equally goal-oriented, forward-stepping companion of her husband; her individuality will flourish while at the same time, she will fulfill her task as wife and mother to the highest degree possible."
- Clara Zetkin -

Radicals and Rags

Growing up in *Unguja* town during the colonial and post-colonial times exposed me to many persons with a progressive, anti-imperialist outlook. Abdulrahaman Babu, who led the *Umma* party, and Abdulrahaman Hamdani, my brother and a party activist, influenced my vision of the world. By the time I joined the University College at Dar es Salaam in 1968, I was acquainted with and supported the ideals espoused in the Arusha Declaration, and had firm confidence in the admirable leadership of Mwalimu Nyerere.

Not surprisingly, I found myself immersed in radical political activities from my first day on the campus. At that time, I did not harbor any political ambitions. Like my fellow activists, I was appalled by the misery of our peoples, and enthusiastically wanted to play my part in changing the world into a more just and humane place. My participation into the effort to terminate the Rag Day was a clear expression of that spirit. Following a tradition carried over from British universities, our college had reserved a day in the academic year when students would wear rags to express their solidarity with the poor and raise funds for them. We discussed this during a USARF meeting and concluded that this sort of activity was simply a mockery of the poor. It was a band-aid, not a genuine solution to the problem of mass poverty. So it had to be opposed.

On that fateful Saturday, the 9th of November 1968, USARF members including I woke up early. Before anyone had a clue as to what was happening, we simply deflated the tires of the vehicles that would carry students to town for the Rag Day. We also stood and blocked their exit. In no time, the few of us confronted more than a hundred ragged hypocrites. The campus police intervened to prevent an escalation of hostilities. When we explained our stand, even the ordinary policeman agreed with us.

USARF was roundly criticized in *The Standard*, a mouthpiece of reaction in those days. We were called enemies of poor children. But we defended our action saying that it was the capitalist system which perpetuated poverty. Charity was a way to cover up an unjust system, a device by which the rich soothed their conscience. We wanted to change the system, and make poverty history.

By this act, USARF made history. Never again was the Rag Day held. The area near the bookstore was renamed the *Revolutionary Square*. USARF and the Hill TYL then organized *shamba* work and visits to *Ujamaa* villages on a regular basis. In these activities, students labored with the masses almost every week.

The ending of the Rag Day carries a particular personal significance for me. That was around the time that I bonded with my husband to be, Ramadhan Ntalyaga Meghji. He was radical student whose views strongly impacted me. He was an artist and a poet. I was immensely moved by the poem he wrote on this occasion, which I have kept to this day. I am glad this unpublished poem has now found an appropriate venue (see Chapter 11). In 1977, when I was pursuing my masters degree at the University, I often passed through the Revolutionary Square. The memories of that eventful day in 1968 were then fresh in my mind, and to this day, they still are.

Ramadhan's poem has an indirect reference to a classic novel by Robert Tressel with the title, *The Ragged Trousered Philanthropists*. This is a hilarious but profound expose of the capitalist system. It shows us that the ragged and impoverished workers are the true philanthropists of our time. Their labor creates the wealth. The rich expropriate it, and then give a few crumbs back now and then. In reality, it is they who receive charity on a daily basis from the working class. This book was taught in the literature classes in those days and was also a popular reading for the comrades. I read it with much delight and learned a lot in the process as well. Today, it is as, if not more, relevant. Now that a new edition has been issued by the Oxford University Press, I recommend the university students of today to acquire and read it (Tressel 2009).[1]

Amongst the individuals at the University who made an impact on my world outlook was the revolutionary historian from Guyana -- Walter Rodney. As an undergraduate student, I took a course in African History in which he was the lecturer. He impressed me with his scientific and thoroughly-researched interpretation of history that challenged the colonial Euro-centric interpretation. I realized how erroneous my previous vision of African history had been. Whereas at high school, it was like how Europe developed Africa, here it was the contrary perspective: how Europe underdeveloped Africa. Rodney was at the time writing his major book, *How Europe Underdeveloped Africa*. In the lectures, he presented the main points from it, giving us an opportunity to discuss them and give our own points of view. His lectures were extremely thought-provoking. In time, I became close to Rodney and his family -- his wife Patricia, son Shaka, daughters Kanini and Asha. They would invite me and other students to their house on a regular basis. He loved to do this. After the meal, the comrades would continue to discuss and brainstorm about world and local affairs

---

1 Talking of charity, the hypocrisy of international "aid" to Africa is well exposed in Hancock (1989).

until late at night. When later we walked back to our halls of residence that were about five minutes away from his house, we were well-fed and ideologically contented as well, looking forward to another day of struggle.

Radical Sisters

In the wide variety of radical activities on the campus I participated in, one thing often bothered me -- too few female students were present. Then, I was the only female committee member of *Mlimani* branch of TYL. When I went to USARF/TYL meetings, demonstrations or *shamba* work, I saw only two or three female students. Often, I was alone. When *Cheche* was launched, I stridently supported the initiative as I had become more politically conscious by then. I wanted the radical ideas to be known to all students. I was elected into the editorial board, and was the sole female member. I was prepared to put all my efforts to work for its success. The dearth of female students in these activities was both a reflection of the subordinated position of women in our land, and the petty-bourgeois aspirations of the few who had a chance to rise above the ranks of the common woman.

I gained a real practical lesson into the actual position of women in Africa during one of the short vacations. In September 1970, the Hill TYL organized a trip to Mpunguzi *Ujamaa* Village in Dodoma in which I took part. Having come from Zanzibar's Stone Town, I never had any meaningful exposure to the rural life. Our group had two members of the academic staff (Walter Rodney and Grant Kamenju) and the Dean of Students, Ms. Muthiga Muthoni (a Kenyan). A few non-university people including Ndugu Moronda from the TYL Headquarters and members of the liberation movements based in Dare es Salaam joined us as well. Of my fellow students, I particularly remember George Hajivayanis and Ndugu Mdundo.

Our aim was to experience life in the villages and understand social differentiation in direct terms. The situation of women in the rural areas was also of specific interest. I was touched by the atmosphere in the village and soon became engulfed in their day to day activities. I was really touched by young children waking up before sunrise, carrying buckets of water on their heads, and walking long distances to and from their homes. The water was muddy. We also drank it. Overall, we tried to share the daily lives of the villagers in every respect. Contrary to my expectations, I discovered that Dodoma was a semi-arid area, full of shrubs. It had few trees and became extremely hot and dry. We had come under the impression that in terms of agriculture, it had no potential except in livestock. Yet, here we were, in a village with vineyards grown as a cash crop, and sorghum as a food crop.

One thing I immediately saw was the subordinate position of women. Women and young girls did most of the work both in the farms and at home. Women cultivated and prepared food while men stayed under the baobab tree chewing tobacco and talking of trivial things. Even in our group, the women went along with the village women and our male colleagues joined the male villagers. When the women put a bucket of water on my head, I could not balance it. All of them burst into laughter. Every woman was expected to able to do this. I came from an urban society where water is obtained from the tap. Nevertheless, the village women found it very amusing that I could not balance the bucket on my head. I grounded with my sisters, explaining to them the question of oppression of women in male dominated society. We discussed about differentiation in the society, question of development, poverty and how to overcome it, the importance of education for girls. They seemed to understand the practical issues better than I. They were living it, experiencing the hardships, but somehow accepted the status quo as they were not empowered to change it. I realized that we women have a long way to go. In the course of staying in the village, a baby girl was born and they named her Zakia. I was overjoyed and felt that they had really accepted me.

Our meals comprised *ugali* and vegetables cooked by village women. Each day, we sat together and gave a summary of what had occurred. Each one of us shared his/her experience. The villagers raised a number of questions but I recollect that it was mostly the men who participated. This experience opened my eyes, showing me that are two different worlds in Tanzania. At the University, we had a comfortable life with imported beef, eggs, chicken and milk. But our brothers and sisters on the other side hardly made ends meet and lacked all basic amenities. I returned to the Hill a new person, understanding much more the suffering of the people. In the academic classes on underdevelopment in Africa, I was more aware of the real situation and appreciated the arguments in relation to our concrete situation.

During my stay, my skin was really burned with the scorching sun. When I went back to Zanzibar, everybody was astonished at what I had done. Some fellow students mocked me for being "revolutionary" and a follower of Walter Rodney. After our trip, we wrote a report on the situation in the *ujamaa* villages in Tanzania. It was a factual but critical report which pointed to many deficiencies in the practical implementation of the policy of Socialism and Self-Reliance in Tanzania. It was published in the *The Standard* and generated a lively debate in its pages. Many bureaucrats, however, were not pleased by our report.

After completing the University in 1971, I first lived in Moshi. My husband and I taught at the Moshi Cooperative College. In those times, we invited Rodney and Gora Ebrahim to lecture our students. Rodney came with his family and stayed at our place, and gave a talk on his book, *How Europe Underdeveloped Africa*. Gora talked about the liberation struggle in Southern Africa. Their talks generated lively discussions that aroused students. For quite some time, the students related the challenges facing the cooperatives in the nation in the context of underdevelopment.

In retrospect, I would say that my University life was the most productive stage of my intellectual development. As a member of USARF and the *Cheche* editorial board, and by participating in the elimination of the Rag day, celebrating Che Guevara Day, working in villages, and taking part in frequent discussions and arguments with comrades and friends molded my outlook profoundly. I was privileged to be included in a couple of meetings with Mwalimu Julius Nyerere held at his Msasani Residence with the University TYL branch committee members. These experiences formed the basis of my future interests, and made me what I am. Those times remain the most memorable days of my life.

8

Night-Shift Comrades

George G Hajivayanis

"Above all, always be capable of feeling most deeply any injustice
committed against anyone, anywhere in the world."
- Ernesto Che Guevara -

I joined the University of Dar es Salaam in July 1969. By then, USARF had been militantly active for two years. *Cheche* was born some five months later. USARF and its organ, *Cheche*, reflected a sharp break from the student movements so far prevalent at all the East African university campuses. Now there was a growing class-oriented subgroup of students. They identified with the plight of the poor, the oppressed and the disenfranchised. It was a trend that was bound to challenge the post colonial regimes in Africa that had betrayed, in a depraved manner, the hopes and aspirations of the masses.

As I reflect on my student days, I remember in particular my work as a "night shift comrade" to produce four issues of *Cheche*, and later, two issues of *MajiMaji*. Many weekend nights were spent in hard work, cyclostyling and binding copies of the magazine. They were, at the same time, nights full of jokes and talk, the joyful hours of grounding with my comrades. I also took part in many other activities that challenged the existing state of affairs, and called for a better organization of human society.

Life As A Poem

But before going into all that, let me backtrack somewhat. From what I have seen from my earliest days, I have come to believe that life is a poem, a long winding poem filled with mystery and wonder. One stanza makes you smile or laugh, the next makes you brood or cry; one expands your mental horizon, the other breeds prejudice and ignorance; one brims with pain, loss and fear, another showers love, comfort and bounty; that is how the poetry of life runs its course.

We all are poets. Sometimes we write our own verses. Often, external forces and the conditions in which we get caught up modify or dictate what we put down.

The first line of my poem was penned by a man and a woman in Dodoma in the colonial times. The man, my father, was a Greek named Galinos from the Island of Lesvos, and the woman was my mother, Ida. She was of German and African descent from the then Tanganyika. My maternal grandfather had migrated from Stuttgart to German East Africa to work on the construction of the central railway line running from Dar es Salaam all the way to Kigoma. As a child of mixed race, neither here nor there, I was exposed to some of the best and some of the worst aspects of life. I was at times called *mzungu* but I never had any of the privileges of the white man in the colonial era. I always felt one and at ease with my fellow Tanzanians, spoke Swahili as fluently as anyone else, and experienced the many difficulties of life that the common man in those days did. I speak Kigogo, some Gujarati and Greek as well. From secondary school onwards, my education was in English. Later in life, I learnt French and some Italian. In me and for me, humanity was evolving towards a single indivisible family. When Martin Luther King said no man is free until everyone is free, I could not have agreed more.

Childhood Sparkles

In the colonial period, Dodoma was a racially divided town. The British officials lived South of the railway line while the Asian (Indian) and other communities lived to the North. The Asians were mostly shopkeepers. They lived in seclusion from the Africans. The remnants of the caravan traders, the Swahilis of Dodoma, also stayed in the Northern zone. My father ran a small butchery. So this area was also our home, and this is how I ended up enrolled in an Indian school. In this school I experienced the crudest of colonial racism and was fondly called "*golo*" by my classmates. This was a derogatory terms Asians used for Africans. My school fee was double that of the children from the "purer race." That is why when President Nyerere converted all schools to public schools in 1964, I was ecstatic.

We lived very close to the Catholic Church. My mother's extreme spirituality meant that my siblings and I had to attend mass everyday. We resented this so much that during thunderstorms, we wished, in vain, that the church would be destroyed. We were, nevertheless, a lucky family. Not everyone had their own patron saint. We had one, St. Martin de Pores of Lima, who was our spiritual guardian. All colored people prayed to him since, just like us, he grew up in the in-between world. This was the logic of colonial Christianity. As we lived in perpetual misery, I doubt if he ever paid heed to our requests. Perhaps he did answer our prayers, but that answer always was No!

My childhood was joyous and full of adventures. We played *tapo* and hunted birds with *manati*. And there were many battles. Poor Hindus were pitted against the wealthy Ismailis. Being neither Hindu nor Ismaili, I found myself aligning with my poorer Hindu neighbors. The rich kids monopolized the play grounds. So we confronted them, which often escalated into hostile feuds followed by a physical settling of scores. The most exciting event was the annual kite competition at the end of the rainy season. There was one cinema in town, Cinema Paradiso. Occasionally we managed to get in and watch Charlie Chaplin and Raj Kapoor.

As a child, I witnessed the harsh poverty of the peasantry. They lived miserable lives; few had access to clean water or health services; the eyes of their children oozed with pus; their families often went hungry; they were cheated when they sold their produce; the colonial administrators and big traders cared not a bit about their plight. These people hardly ever wrote their own verses; all was dictated to them, whether they liked it or not. Their hopes and dreams rarely saw the light of the day. Their children often went into permanent sleep after only a few lines had been written in their odes. This made the poet in me blaze with fury and ready to rise up.

It is from this Apartheid-like society that I acquired the culture of peasant solidarity, the jocular, easy going, chatty demeanor of the Waswahilis, a tinge of Western individualism combined with a modicum of oriental sentimentalism. I grew up with a longing for justice, showing rebellious tendencies from my school days. My heart always beat for the poor and the wretched of the earth.

Groundings at the Hill

As I reflect on this grand poem written by and for me, one portion stands tall. It has the exciting stanzas of my time as a student at UDSM. In the three years from July 1969 to March 1972 lie a host of enjoyable and fulfilling moments of my life. In that respect, I was a part of the many people the world over engaged in struggles for justice and equality. Liberation movements of all shades, in Africa, Asia and Latin America, were on the rise. In Vietnam, the USA -- a mighty imperial power -- faced imminent defeat at the hands of a tiny, underdeveloped former French colony. It faced strong resistance in Laos and Cambodia. Wars of liberation were afoot in the Portuguese colonies in Africa. The Apartheid regime in South Africa faced strong internal and external challenges. Ethiopians and Eritreans rose up against a noxious feudal regime. Revolutionary forces bloomed in Central and South America. Socialist Cuba was an inspiring example of the way forward. A cultural revolution led by the Red Guards was underway in China. Even in Europe and the USA, students and workers challenged the system. In Tanzania, the Arusha Declaration had just been issued. Mwalimu Nyerere aspired to build a society based on African Socialism. Forces of reaction were mostly on the defensive in general, while progressive forces were in the ascendance. This was the general global and local socio-political scenario when I joined UDSM and became one of the group of night shift comrades.

A week into my university life, I attended an evening public lecture by the radical historian Walter Rodney entitled "The Cuban Revolution and Its Relevance to Africa." It was organized by USARF. Both the floors of the large assembly hall were filled to capacity. Rodney was a brilliant, inspirational speaker whose profound analysis combined with a solid commitment to justice and human liberation. I had heard about Fidel Castro and Che Guevara but he widened my vision. What did the Cuban revolutionaries do? And why and how? He explained the role of the United States in backing, for decades, the brutal dictator Batista who converted the island into a touristic brothel and a gambling casino for rich Americans. He ended by telling us about its major achievements and the difficulties it continued to face.

Inspired by Rodney and the student activists, I soon joined USARF. I took part in demonstrations against the war in Vietnam and in support of African liberation movements. I did weekend work in *Ujamaa* villages. I distributed USARF fliers and statements. I discussed African and world affairs. It was in these activities that I came to know many of my subsequent night shift comrades. For many activities, a lot of preparatory work was needed. A demonstration had to have placards and banners. Notices had to be posted, and statements, cyclostyled and distributed. Many comrades showed up for the main event only. I made sure that I would also contribute my share of the preparatory work. My close friend Ramadhan Meghji, a second year student, was good at drawing and painting. He and I had a good time thinking up the slogans and phrases for the banners and drawing the posters. In the protest against the US aggression on Vietnam, the common slogans included "Yankee! Go Home!" and Che Guevara's elicitation, "Create One, Two, More ... Vietnams!"

We also took part in a number of self-help projects that existed near the university campus. They included construction projects, and *korosho* picking activities. The people were motivated to use their co-operative spirit to uplift their lives. During the harvest season, the picking was done every Wednesday afternoon when there were no classes. On Saturdays, literacy and adult education classes were held near the campus. University students volunteered as teachers, and many USARF members took part.

The radical students and the night shift comrades in particular came from diverse social backgrounds. Some had relatively well-off families and some had modest origins. The variety of races, regions and religions of Tanzania were represented. Students from Uganda,

Kenya, Malawi and other African countries were there. Yet, despite the differences, ideologically, we were united, committed to the liberation of Africa, and the improvement of the conditions of the peasants and workers everywhere.

Though materially better off than the working classes, we were intellectually drawn to the ideology of the working class. This meant that eventually, we had to "commit class suicide," that is, give up our petty-bourgeois pretensions and firmly dedicate ourselves to a life time of struggle for the cause of the toiling, poor peoples of our nation, Africa and indeed, the whole planet. That is what I strongly believed in at that time, and that is what underlay my participation in these activities. In addition, unlike some comrades, I had had a first hand experience of the naked poverty of the masses. So I did not, in any way, feel aloof from them.

At that time, several construction projects were underway around the campus. Ramadhan and I were in the habit of having our lunch at one of the several the *mama nitilie* makeshift kitchens that served the workers engaged at the construction sites. We sat on the ground and had our lunch with them. The laborers were puzzled why we ate there and not at the university cafeteria. Nevertheless, they were happy that we talked and shared a meal with them. While our intent was to disengage from our social backgrounds and identify with them, there was a sense of incompleteness and artificiality to the exercise. We wanted to be with them but were not of them. At the end, while they returned to hard labor, and a night in the slums, with at best a modest meal, we returned to our books, a cafeteria dinner and a good night's sleep in a tall tower. Yet, I think it was a worthy effort on our part. Of course, the issue is not simply to be like the common man, but to live a life that truly serves the common man. Yet, if you become too distant from the vast suffering humanity, most likely you will one day betray your original goals and just become a pretentious talker at best, and even an exploiter or oppressor, at the worst.

Despite our desire to identify with the man in the street, our way of looking at life did not always fall in line with his outlook. I remember an incident when we worked in a brick-making project at Ubungo. From morning to late afternoon, we sweated profusely, almost breaking our backs. In the course of our work, we talked about a self-help housing project at Mwenge. One among us suggested that the bricks we were making could be used for those houses. Upon hearing this, an elderly man interrupted angrily, "No, no! Never! We are building a mosque with these bricks." Then one of us responded that as people in the slums of Mwenge were living like sardines, the mosque did not have the same urgency as the house. That did not go down well, especially with the elders. In an instant, we were surrounded by angry believers wielding machetes with fire coming out of their ears. Luckily for us, as we sought to scamper in different directions, a wise elder intervened to explain our ignorant naiveté. All in all, that day we did learn one thing -- religion is indeed the opium of the poor, and never would we tamper with it again.

Yes, an element of romanticism flowed in our veins, and some comrades poked fun at us. But, I must admit, there was also another side to this story. Ramadhan and I were the more frequent comrade-visitors to Hall 3, the female students' hall of residence. We solemnly said we were grounding with our sisters so as to recruit them for progressive activities. Our dual romanticism drew sarcastic but friendly taunts from the comrades. We would be asked in a mischievous tone, "How was the lunch?" or "What is the progress of the ideological class in Hall 3?" Everyone would then burst into laughter, as heavy as the sound of *masika* rains. Through sarcasm, we educated ourselves and bonded firmly to each other and our cause.

Mapinduzi by Night

This was the global background, and the campus atmosphere in which *Cheche* was born. Its first issue came out in November 1969. I was not on the editorial board at that time but had written three short poems for the first issue. The scenes around the time it was born are still vivid in my memory. A week before, just after supper, I heard the sounds of typing in the TANU Youth League campus office located directly below my room in Hall I. I crept by to peep through the window and saw Karim Hirji and Henry Mapolu proofreading and correcting the stencils. I knew then that our first *Cheche* was in the offing.

About ten of us gathered for the first ever night shift to produce the copies of the first issue. It was a weekend. The convenient time for the cyclostyling and binding work was at night. It was incognito work done so as not to attract undue attention from the authorities. We used university facilities but on a semi-official basis. A supportive member of the academic staff opened the door of the Law Faculty cyclostyling room for us, and left us to work there. We worked mostly in silence for two consecutive nights. On Monday morning, just before the sun shone from the Dar es Salaam harbor, the last copy was bound. Two hours later, as students gathered for breakfast in the cafeteria, we were at the door, selling *Cheche* Number 1 at price of seventy five cents a copy. That day,

I missed all my classes. I took a short nap in the morning but at lunch time, I was back at the cafeteria door. Exhausted to the bone, later I must have slept for many hours to relieve my fatigue. This was but one the many weekend night shifts I participated in during those days. I did not miss the work for a single issue. In my second year, I became a member of the editorial board of the newly renamed magazine. Thus was born the family of the night shift comrades, who, three, four or more times in an academic year, labored to bring out issues of this magazine.

What made the night toil bearable were the litany of jokes and light-hearted talk we engaged in from start to finish. Many of the jokes we told were drawn from Gora Ebrahim, a South African comrade who often visited the campus. He had a thousand and one jokes, all very political in substance. With his creative mind and a good command of English pun together with his strong South African accent that emphasized the consonants, it was always a pleasure to listen to Gora. Among the comrades, his jokes were told over and over, often acquiring different narrations. We wondered if he had acquired this creative and humorous bent while serving as a political detainee in South Africa.

One version of one of Gora's tall tales I remember was about a large group of new inmates in the notorious prisons of Apartheid South Africa. An older inmate asked one of them, "How is it that so many of you have come in together today?"

The reply, "We were arrested at a bus stop, and accused of loitering. In court, the magistrate asked each of us for name and address. I was the first. I gave my name but had no address to give. He asked me if I was a man of "No fixed abode." I said yes. The next person gave his name and said that he was my neighbor. And the next and every other accused said the same. This infuriated the magistrate. So he sent all of us to prison. Now we really are neighbors."

I can still picture Gora cracking a joke but with a serious composure. That in itself makes me laugh. That he always had a joke for the day was also a joke. One time, a comrade (was it Karim?) asked, "Have you heard Gora's latest joke?"

"Which one?"

"You know, the one he heard a month before being released from jail."

We all burst into laughter, knowing well that that was more than a decade ago. But then Ramadhan softly said, "For heaven's sake, why don't you give Karim a chance to tell us the joke."

Seizing the opportunity, Karim went on, "Gora swears that this is a historic fact which proves that South Africa is a land of miracles. A child was born headless. The doctors, though, managed to transplant a pumpkin onto him. His mother was very happy, now that her child had a chance to make it in life. But alas and behold, it turns out that the current Prime Minister of Apartheid South Africa was this very child."

Henry burst out with his sharp and short laugh and all followed suit. The night shift also gave us a chance to make fun of each other. Recalling the brick-making saga, we described with added spice how we had tried to escape the impending beating from the angry crowd. We recreated each other's furtive glances as the machetes were brought out, and exaggerated that so and so had raised his hands in surrender. We would roar with laughter.

But then we quietened down, realizing that we had to work in silence. Yet, soon another joke or tale was on its way. Munene Njagi, a dedicated Kenyan comrade, had a peculiar way of saying things; we poked fun at that, and he too laughed at himself.

One other activity which we joked about was teaching the adult literacy classes. They were organized by the ten-cell leaders. It so happened that the attendees were mostly women. Men would find the most inconceivable excuse not to attend. I remarked once, "Comrades, you know the attendance in literacy classes in not good?"

Henry quickly responded, "You mean only the women attend!"

And Ramadhan quipped, "In my class, the men have a good excuse. Once, all had to attend a wedding. One man said he had to take his sick daughter to a clinic since his wife was at the literacy class ..."

Karim, the serious guru, opined that women were probably happy to get a venue to escape from domestic serfdom but Issa Shivji slyly remarked to Ramadhan, "It does not seem that you are that unhappy to have a 100% female class!"

We all burst out with laughter, only to be hushed down by Karim and told to not make mistakes in collating the issues of the magazine. While Ramadhan and I were the light-hearted ones, Karim and Henry were the serious types. Karim especially was a disciplinarian with a perpetual serious expression on his face, always at work. He would order people around and say things very bluntly. This tended to annoy me, so I often pulled his leg. He would then just look at me, not knowing whether I meant what I said or not. That was how, with zest, jest and hard work, the night shifters developed a strong bond that is alive to this day.

What we found most difficult was to clear up the waste -- the paper and the black ink -- when we had finished cyclostyling and binding. We mopped not only the floor but also the cupboards. It was an effort to remove the black ink smeared randomly in different corners. The room had to be left immaculately clean so that no one should have inkling about the incognito working shift.

Bonfire and Cuba

During December 1969, I attended the Second Seminar of the East and Central African Youth. It was held at our campus. Many students from East and Central Africa were present. The conference gave me hope that one day we would have a Pan Africanist government, an Africa living up to its heritage as the birth place of human civilization. The papers read at this conference would be published as the second issue of *Cheche*. (Appendix C shows the program of the Seminar).

I was one of the student activists responsible for cyclostyling and distributing the conference papers. In the course of this week, and for the first time, I came to value the importance of different forms of struggles, the legal and the clandestine, and the need to think deeply before one acts. The conference was a legal venue. Unfortunately, it got stuck in a quagmire of the sort we could not have imagined. Comrade Rodney had presented a paper on the ideology of the African revolution. In this, he had blasted the neo-colonial regimes in Africa that served the Western masters and not the people. He had also implied that they should be overthrown by the people. By saying this up front, comrade Rodney had crossed the red line. The conference had the official backing of the TYL, the youth wing of the ruling party. And, the state authorities could not condone such subversive ideas.

That evening, we were tipped that by midnight, some of us would be arrested. We felt we had to destroy the conference papers that were said to promote dangerous ideas. There was very little time to dispose of them. The task fell on Ramadhan and me. Just before dusk, the two of us rushed to Hall 4 to burn the papers. Unfortunately it became a bonfire engulfing the grassy surroundings of the residence hall. The fire brigade from the city was called. A truck arrived a few hours later, but with an empty tank. The fire we had not been able to put off with pails continued to burn, only to later subside by itself. Happily there was no damage to the buildings. No one was injured. As the cause of the fire remained a mystery to others, we were not arrested. (See Hajivayanis [2010] for further elaboration of this incident).

It was a well-intentioned but hasty and careless move. The idea of going to prison scared us. We had not discussed the matter with the comrades and spontaneously brought about an inferno that could have created an unforgivable loss. We did not realize, as Mao Tse Tung said, a revolution is not a dinner party. During the night shifts, the incident became a cause for derisive laughter. A cheeky comrade would say, "So you burnt a house to roast a pig!"

With such radicalization on the campus, I fell in love with the Cuban revolution and its heroes, especially Che Guevara and Camillo Cienfuegos. I admired the grand achievements of the revolution, the alphabetisation of the masses -- education and health care for all! I was inspired by Che's ideas of the creation of a new man, who carries a socialist spirit and abandons individualism and materialistic lust. I even had a home library named Sierra Maestra, to link myself with my heroes.

Some comrades found this out and my fantasies became a source of amusement during the night shift. Fortunately Omowale, a Caribbean comrade, always came to my rescue. He would say, "Yo cantryy izz endowed with sieerraas, and one day you will have to learn to climb 'em." This did not really help as it evoked further friendly mocking which led to bursts of laughter. I would feel ridiculed but nevertheless stuck to my guns.

Shifting Winds

Our motivation in producing *Cheche* was to serve the working people of the world, disseminate ideas that promoted a class-based understanding of society and social change, speak the truth to the powers that be, and educate our fellow students. The process helped us clarify our own ideas, debate the different interpretations of history, society and development, and intellectually engage the broader group of apathetic students. Our zeal and enthusiasm derived from a deep sense of commitment to a worthy and worthwhile cause. We put at risk our studies and careers, and expected no rewards. All we did was purely voluntary.

The day the first issue of *Cheche* came out, the campus was caught by surprise. No one had imagined what we were up to, or capable of producing such a thing. It represented bold statement of defiance. The student body was, to put it starkly, electrified. In the days that followed, the university community stood polarized in its stand towards *Cheche*. Many liked it, but many opposed it, and what it stood for. It was the same with the academic staff. We were congratulated by some but others derided us as a wild bunch of radicals or political stooges.

The university administration and the state establishment were deeply annoyed at us, though they dare not directly come out against us. Socialism was supposed to be the official ideology. And here was a magazine that fervently championed not only socialism but African liberation as well. This contradiction sharpened as more issues were produced. Our magazine not only had a campus wide impact but also spread to secondary schools in the nation. School students led a difficult life and were at that time under the policy of socialism and self-reliance. They did *shamba* work, raised poultry and other tasks as their contribution to a socialist society. The policy was good and could have at the least improved the nutritional standards of the school meals. But the school authorities often misappropriated the harvest and the funds, and the students hardly got anything. This bred anger, forming a basis for radicalizing the students. The militant spirit of *Cheche* appealed to some students. Our magazine, which stood for building a socialist society not just based on words but also in deeds circulated in several schools. But at the same time, it created enemies among the authorities.

Soon afterwards, a special issue of *Cheche* was published. This was a critical, concrete analysis of the nature of the socialist experiment in Tanzania by Issa Shivji. He documented that nationalization was not the same as socialization. The nationalized companies, through management contracts and other devices, continued under external capitalist control. The state bureaucracy stood apart from and did not have the same class interests as the masses. Despite the socialist rhetoric, the reality was one of neo-colonial domination, even in Tanzania. On the campus, its analysis was controversial and polarizing. Yet, this had already been done by Frantz Fanon for post colonial Africa. I guess many found it hard to believe for Tanzania. But facts were facts, and the hidden reality Shivji had unearthed could not be denied.

With such trenchant, fact-filled analysis, *Cheche* and its parent USARF were turning into a nuisance or worse in the eyes of those in power. There had been previous face-downs between them over several matters. To the big guys, what we said and that we were allowed to get away with it represented an abuse of academic freedom. These tendencies were an anathema to them, especially as we had found an audience among students, the future of the nation. To say the least, they were unhappy.

At that time, there was a sizeable quantity of radical literature circulating in the country. Works of Marx, Engels, Lenin, Mao Tse Tung, Ho Chin Min, Che, Fanon, Cabral and modern Marxist authors from the West were readily available. Many were distributed gratis from the cultural centers. But *Cheche* was not in the ball park in that it was indigenous, and gave a concrete, radical analysis of the local situation. To those in the upper echelons of the state, indigenous ideas that challenged the official way of thinking were something to fear. The special issue of *Cheche* was the last straw.

The end was swift and decisive. Prior to this step, I or my comrades did not have an inkling about the severity of the oncoming reaction. One evening, the campus TYL committee was summoned by the Vice Chancellor, Mr. Pius Msekwa, to report to the council chamber. A few weeks earlier, I had been elected the campus TYL Secretary. So I went too. I recollect our wait for the boss of the campus, a patient wait that lasted a few hours. We were not given an agenda for the meeting. So as we waited, we stole inquisitive, curious glances at each other. Finally, he sneaked in, as if from nowhere. We became aware of his presence when he was already seated amongst us. This was extremely unusual for a man of pomp and glory. At his appointment as the VC of the newly established UDSM, I vividly remember his triumphant entrance into the campus. Escorted by the cadres of the ruling party, the retinue resembled the entrance of Julius Caesar into Forro Romano after the conquest of Pompeii. The VC was from the top hierarchy of the party and seemed to have the aspirations of running the University as a party college. Needless to say, we stood in the way of that vision.

Our eyes were fixated on him. He opened his mouth, looking for words, but no sound came forth. After a while, he managed to utter a few words that evade my memory. Then he took a deep breath and came to the point. The essence of his speech was that he had just come from Mwalimu Nyerere's residence at Msasani where he had been summoned for an extraordinary meeting. This is why he was late. He had a "message" from Mwalimu, a simple message: During its historical struggle, TANU never had any foreign assistance! Although Mwalimu recollected one incident in the history of the party whereby the nation of Burma had donated a cyclostyling machine for printing party documents. Mwalimu was demanding the same of the campus TYL -- that it should not have any links with what is foreign. The name *Cheche* was derived from Lenin's *Iskra*. USARF was promoting a foreign ideology. All that was unacceptable. The message, in fact an order, from the Chancellor of the University and the country's President, was that USARF and *Cheche* had to close down. They were no longer in existence.

That was it! We walked out of the meeting extremely deflated. We were upset at the misleading rhetoric coached in the language of party chauvinism. The charges put on us were not credible; the real reason was different. The news of our demise spread like wild fire on the campus.

The die-hard conservatives were celebrating. They could not stand against our arguments, and despite their alleged misgivings about state interference, had relied on the state to suppress us. The next evening, we released the statement *Our Last Stand* that firmly defended our ideas and ideals. We had no option but to comply with Mwalimu's "request." Yet, we did not give up. *Cheche* was soon reborn under an indigenous name, *MajiMaji*, the name of the valiant movement that had united a multitude of ethnic groups to fight German colonial rule. A rose by any name is as fragrant. The fundamental thing was to disseminate progressive ideas. But as USARF could not be revived, the campus TYL took up the banner.

In the next academic year, I participated, now as an editor, in preparations for the first two publications of *MajiMaji*. It was a demanding task, but I have to say, I felt that the comradely spirit that existed in the early night-shift sessions had weakened. Some comrades had completed their studies and moved out, some felt disenchanted with orders dressed as requests. The close camaraderie in the cyclostyling room, abounding with humor and banter, had lost its luster.

The Cheche Spirit

I left the university a different person, inclined towards a scientific world outlook. I began to understand the origins of wealth and the wealthy, to grasp the motive of history and history itself. I had set aside childhood superstitions and its moribund myths. My stay at the university flourished in comradely solidarity which I cherish and store in my memories to this day.

The banning and resurrection of *Cheche* reflected the spirit of that era, a spirit of defiance towards imperialism and desire for true human development in Africa and all over the world. Unlike today, the imperialists and capitalists were on the defensive. Ordinary people and our intellectuals had high hopes and dreams. It was a time of rapid change, in outlook and reality. For the night shift comrades, it was a wonderful time to be alive and take an active part in those transformations.

One thing that many comrades retained for long was the romanticism for names associated with progressive leaders and places. For our children, we had names such as Rosa (Luxembourg), Yenan, Amilcar (Cabral), etc. My first daughter was named Ida, after my mother, a woman of great tolerance and strength. Like other comrades I could not resist naming my second daughter after what I considered a very militant woman -- Inessa Armand, Lenin's comrade in arms. When Issa

Shivji came to see the baby and learned that I had named her Inessa, he looked at me in disbelief and burst out with his unique laughter, "Inessa Armand! George, what will happen if Krupskaya comes out from her grave right now?" Krupskaya was Lenin's wife.

Following the bonfire incident I had become quite close to Walter Rodney. Four months later, a group of USARF and TYL comrades stayed and worked at several *Ujamaa* villages in Dodoma. They included Grant Kamenju, Muthiga Muthoni, Zakia Meghji and Rodney. Rodney had also brought along his little son, Shaka. He was well-loved by all of us. I still remember our work with the peasants in their plots and at their homes. We had nocturnal discussions with the peasants about the policy of socialism and their future. They really appreciated him. They still lived in the same conditions of poverty and deprivation as in the colonial era.

After my graduation, I taught in Morogoro. Soon afterwards, Rodney, Pat (his wife) and children were traveling to the south of the country. He was taken ill on the way and they came to stay with me and my wife Salha. As he recuperated, we spent much time talking about everything under the sun. My students and colleagues were also able to dialogue with him. We learned a lot. It was during this time that we planned to do a paper on Greek settlers in Tanzania. He was fascinated with the phrase *Tajiri kama Griki* (rich as a Greek); his interest as a historian lay in discovering the sources of wealth accumulation. Unfortunately, I went for further studies and never had the opportunity to do this research with him.

My house in Morogoro acted as a magnet for my erstwhile night shift comrades. On the way from or to Dar es Salaam, they would drop by, sometimes as a group. We would have a feast, talk about the good old days, and discuss how to spread the message of socialism in schools. The jokes and stories of the night shifts were recycled. We talked about the latest issue of *MajiMaji*. Often, I would get extra copies to distribute to the schools and colleges in the area.

But over time, the zeal waned. Instead of committing class suicide, as we had dreamt about during student days, my comrades and I became more petty-bourgeoisified. We were absorbed in the hum-drum of work and family life, earning a decent living, and away from the lives and conditions of the masses. In one way or another, we failed to live up to the ideals. Our ways of thinking and looking at the world reverted to the bourgeois mould. Only a few comrades, here and there, kept the cause alive. It was not a pretty sight.

Yet, it has not been in vain. Human progress does not follow a straight line. We are not angles. In a sense, life is a relay race. One generation takes the baton up to a distance. In our time, the night shift comrades sacrificed and contributed to the ongoing struggle. The youth of today have to pick up, not drop, that baton. But not in a mechanical way. They need to examine our efforts, weigh the good and the bad, and work out their own analysis, directions and strategies. That is how it is, as I reflected a long time ago in *Cheche* No. 1:

For Humanity

Hills of fire rose in ....battlefields,
Made thousands of us ....betray,
A handful stood to ....challenge,
For the cause was for ....Humanity.

9

Revisiting Cheche

Christopher C Liundi

"To those who see in it a theoretical character we should recall that every practice has a theory, and that if it is true that a revolution can fail even though it be based on perfectly conceived theories, nobody has yet made a successful revolution without a revolutionary theory."
- Amilcar Cabral -

As the year 1970 was drawing to a close, dark clouds hovered ominously over the University Hill. When they finally descended, they brought forth a decisive bolt of lightening whose socio-political reverberations went far in time and space. That was the day of November 9th, 1970 when the chief bureaucrat of the University pronounced, on behalf of the State, the verdict on the fate of USARF and *Cheche*.

It was a final verdict with no room for appeal. USARF and *Cheche* had to forthwith cease all their activities. It was a strange but not an unexpected decision. In this paper, I examine the background and ramifications of this fateful move.

From my school days, I had been concerned about the liberation of Africa. As was the case for many people in Tanzania, the promulgation of the Arusha Declaration had a profound impact on my political perceptions. Organizing our nation along socialist lines would, I believed, bring economic development for the masses and promote social harmony.

At this point in time, I was an official at the TYL headquarters. I was responsible for liasing with TYL branches in educational institutions, including the University of Dar es Salaam. During this process, I became quite close to USARF and *Cheche*. Henry Mapolu, one of the *Cheche* editors, represented the University TYL at the TYL headquarters. As a result, we were in regular contact.

The following year, I joined the University through the Mature Age Entry Scheme to pursue a BA degree. My fields of study were political science and education. Naturally, I became a TYL activist at the Hill, as a result of which I was later elected as the TYL branch chairman, and was also a member of the editorial board of *MajiMaji*. What I write thereby derives from first hand and intimate knowledge of the activities and the political climate of that era.

The Spark Arises

The Arusha Declaration opened up new political horizons in Tanzania. People marched across the country to support the Declaration. The birth and growth of USARF was a part of this trend. USARF was a home-grown, open organization of and for the students with no hidden agenda. It secured support from a number of progressive lecturers at the university which helped to sharpen its intellectual and ideological visions. Its express purpose was to galvanize political awareness to make way for establishing a robust socialist political environment and develop a student network in support of this cause. To me it seemed as if the founders and activists of this group were influenced by the wise declaration of Mahatma Gandhi that, "You must be the change you wish to see in the World."

Students are a dynamic social group. Inquisitive and energetic, they often venture beyond the status quo, with their heads, or arms and legs. At critical junctures in history, their dynamism has had profound social consequences. Though they come from specific economic classes, as students their social status is a fluid one. As such, they are potential class choosers. Often, they act as if they have nothing to lose. They have the capacity to politically align with any social class whose cause or vision they find persuasive. It has been remarked that the "youth are more vulnerable to suggestion and persuasion, because they are the least likely to hold rigid beliefs or attitudes." (Holsti 1967, page 254). The dynamism of the youth has been seen and felt across time the world over.

In the late 1960s and early 1970s, the Dar es Salaam University campus was an arena for lively, heated contentions among competing ideas. Capitalism, socialism, liberalism, Marxism, nationalism, Pan Africanism, fascism, imperialism, neocolonialism, idealism, materialism, utopianism, adventurism, do-nothingism, opportunism, fanaticism -- all the "Isms" were vigorously debated in the classroom and outside. USARF and the University TYL were at the center of this maelstrom. And unlike other student groups, they were organized and dedicated. They staged public lectures, giving the community a chance to meet and share the views of prominent thinkers, personalities and academicians. They held free Sunday ideological classes which offered a rare but worthwhile opportunity to students to enlighten themselves about what was going on in the country, the continent and the world at large, without forgetting their home base, the University campus. These well-attended classes proved to be significantly constructive and instructive. They also held demonstrations in support of varied progressive causes.

In addition to the educational activities on the campus, USARF and TYL organized work visits to nearby and rural villages, discussions with factory workers, and practical *shamba* work for the students in farms near the Hill.

During this period, Apartheid South Africa heightened the repression of black Africans. Portuguese colonialism ran wild. Liberation movements like FRELIMO, ANC, PAC, MPLA, ZANU and ZAPU were getting stronger with the assistance from of the African Liberation Committee. Tanzania consistently stood as the robust rear base of this continent-wide struggle. Activist students, in fact, many in the

University community, were afflicted by liberation fever. In December 1968, USARF led a visit to the war zone in Mozambique, a move that enhanced its zeal and provided it with first hand experience it could use to counter the anti-liberation propaganda emanating from Western quarters. The activists were aware that they were not living in a vacuum. Their actions gave them on-the-spot experience and enabled them to combine theory with practice.

It was against this background that USARF and TYL launched their revolutionary magazine *Cheche*. It was an organ to discuss their ideas in black and white, and soon it became a springboard of communication between them and the public at large. One major objective was to strengthen the process of building socialism in Tanzania and accelerate its pace. They were heeding the call by Amilcar Cabral to develop a sound revolutionary theory as an integral part of the process of social transformation.

Contradictions Ripen

Such were the concrete conditions that led USARF and TYL to become catalysts of ideological change at the Hill and beyond. But they faced obstacles. Misunderstanding and trouble between the Hill activists and the powers that were soon emerged. The desire for change burning in the minds of activist students was not well understood by the state and party bureaucracy. Moreover, inside the lecture halls and seminar rooms at the campus, reactionary professors were facing a hard time. They were heavily criticized by activist students for their unfounded pro-imperialist and anti-socialist positions. That gave further discomfort to the authorities. The frequent posting of critical statements on university, national and international matters on the notice boards across the campus by USARF and TYL created a radical and contentious atmosphere that also became a subject of close scrutiny by organs of the state. As the reputation of USARF and *Cheche* grew, the authorities became more suspicious and nervous.

It did not take long before the State descended on them and literally nipped them in their revolutionary bud. On the ill-fated day, the University Vice Chancellor (VC) summoned the TYL Executive Committee to his office to convey an important message. The message was in the form of an order stating that USARF should cease to exist, and should stop publishing *Cheche*.

To legitimize the order, the VC revealed that it came from the State House. It was being conveyed to the leadership of TYL because TYL was supposed to have the monopolistic privilege of conducting political activities on the Hill. USARF had no recognized role in that regard. There was no public ban, no written, legal order. But the authoritative nature of the message was clear. Close your shop, or face the consequences.

This move was a typical manifestation of political intolerance in newly independent Africa. The level of freedom of expression at the Hill was consequently reduced. Genuine enthusiastic radicalism among the youth was muzzled. *Cheche* was completely owned and published by students, registered only at the University. It was purely a student affair. Why did the state have to take such a drastic step and intervene in their affairs? What reasons were given? And what were the real reasons?

Strange Reasons

One declared reason behind the ban was that *Cheche* had a foreign name. The double standard in placing this charge against one magazine and not against other publications was described in the final USARF statement, *Our Last Stand* (see Appendix E). We can also explore this issue.

In 1900, a group of Russian exiles in Europe launched a Russian language Marxist journal called *Iskra*, meaning The Spark. Printed in Germany, it was smuggled into Tzarist Russia to foment a revolutionary uprising. Among the socialist luminaries who at some point served on the editorial board were Vladimir Lenin, Georgi Plekhanov, Vera Zasulich and Leon Trotsky. An English equivalent of the motto of this journal reads "From a spark, a fire will ignite."[1] This phrase was also echoed in a famous quotation by Mao Tse Tung: "A spark can start a prairie fire."

Cheche is the Swahili equivalent of the word spark. Because of this political background, just that word became a source of apprehension to the bureaucrats. They viewed *Cheche* with suspicion from the day of its birth. They assumed that *Cheche* had a hidden agenda to spread Russian communism in Tanzania.

There was, however, an African side to the story. Kwame Nkrumah, the first president of Ghana, wanted to build socialism in his nation. The two essential requirements for this exercise, he emphasized, were "ideological clarity" and "devoted socialists." Accordingly, he had encouraged the formation of student socialist study groups and discussion of scientific socialism in the media. Because the mass media in Ghana were still dominated by the colonial bourgeois mentality, in 1962, he started the weekly journal *The Spark* that was explicitly modeled after

---

1   This information was obtained from www.wikipedia.com under the entry "Iskra."

Iskra. Nkrumah, however, did not want to imitate what had happened in Russia but strove to formulate an ideology of the African revolution that was "socialist in content and continental in outlook." (Panaf 1974; Arhin 1993, pages 93--94).

Yes, the activist students at UDSM were inspired by the ideas of Marx and Lenin. But this was a part of their internationalist outlook. Like Kwame Nkrumah and with awareness of his theoretical magazine, they wanted to learn from the struggles for liberation and socialism conducted by people everywhere, be it China, Guinea Bissau, Russia or Cuba. To call their magazine *Cheche* was a well-thought out decision. But the issue of the name was a secondary one. The basic imperative was to assist our nation and Africa in spreading the ideology of socialism. The clarion call of *Cheche*, on the first page of each issue, was an internationalist one:

> *Oppressed world unite*
> *You have nothing to lose*
> *But your chains,*
> *You have a world to win*

Cheche, in its successive issues, linked activist students with other students and the public at large. It stimulated debate on economic, social, political and educational matters. It invited students, progressives and the critics as well to come to the fore and speak their mind. During its life, it proved to be a formidable tool of progressive education that critiqued biased pro-imperialist ideas prevalent in our education system at that time. Students, members of the educated elite and even some bureaucrats learned from it. It brought forth a fresh perspective on life, society and history.

Perhaps for these reasons, it was a menace to the bureaucratic bourgeoisie. They deemed it a political provocateur. As it gained ground in readership and became richer in content, the TYL at the Hill and USARF further cemented their alliance in the march towards the socialist D Day. According to some quarters, USARF had committed the crime of firing unguided verbal missiles on various political issues concerning the State and its functions, even though it did not represent any local or national body, inside or outside Tanzania.

The accusation against it was that it gave the impression that Tanzania was pursuing a Russian model of socialism rather than *Ujamaa na Kujitegemea* (Socialism and Self-reliance). The latter was a home-grown "Ism" while the former said to be was foreign. *Cheche* was branded by some big shots as a "fanatic, arm-chair, theoretical, extremist and infantile" entity. Its articles were regarded by them as inflammatory. It could not be tolerated. Hence, its demise.

At the time of the ban, practically the entire student body and other members of the University community complained bitterly that students were being deprived of their chance to air their views on political and other matters. USARF, for its part, wound up its affairs with a final statement entitled *Our Last Stand* (See Appendix E). Dated the 12th of November 1970, it carried a telling conclusion:

> *We do not doubt the wisdom prompting our ban. But one thing must be remembered. Organizations can be banned, individuals can be liquidated, but ideas live on. USARF (1970)*

A Million Flowers

Looking back, it is apparent that the clamp down on *Cheche* and USARF was detrimental to the political and mental development of the students at the Hill and youth in Tanzania as a whole. Blocking their political growth could be counterproductive even from the viewpoint of the authorities; muzzling such a voice can backfire and create a breeding ground for clandestine activities. When a situation reaches that point, it becomes politically unhealthy.

Fortunately, after this death sentence was enacted, progressive student activism at the Hill did not cease. It went on, but in other forms. Another student organ called *MajiMaji* was published under the auspices of the TYL branch of the University. This branch now enjoyed an elevated status, higher than the other youth league branches in the nation. For many years, the fiery political stance of *Cheche* continued to be reflected in the pages of *MajiMaji*. And now, more students rallied behind it.

Yet, the ban on USARF and *Cheche* had a number of deleterious long-term effects for the development of socialism and freedom of expression in Tanzania.

USARF was a Pan African student group, with members from several African countries. TYL membership was open to Tanzanians only. The ban on USARF deprived progressive students from other African nations from playing a significant role in the campus political activities. They could attend political events but could not be leaders. This was a blow to the growth of a genuine, progressive Pan-Africanist vision that had begun to take hold among University students. That restriction could only foster narrow minded nationalism. Divisions of this sort only benefit imperialism in its quest to continue to divide and dominate Africa.

Further, the ban also gave a strong message to students across the nation. There was a limit to political tolerance. If you cross the red line, you will be silenced. The construction of socialism in Tanzania faced many challenges in terms of strategy and tactics of implementation. These challenges could be faced and queries tackled only by means of an open, frank and even critical discussions among the broad sections of the public, including students. The ban placed a big psychological if not real hurdle that hindered the process and prospect of starting such nationwide discussions. Many politicians then just hypocritically parroted the Arusha Declaration which was not to our nation's long-term benefit.

I have wondered what would have happened if the Minister of Education had at that time gone on the radio with the following announcement.

> *My fellow Tanzanians: We want to build a society based on equality and freedom from exploitation. This is not an easy task. No text book gives all the steps by which you can do this. There is no formula. No single person has the answer to every problem. We can learn from the experiences of others but we also have to work out our own specific solutions.*

> *In the past, our University students had elitist attitudes. They often did not have the interest of the common man in their hearts. Now it seems that things have begun to change. Some students at the Hill are saying that we are not socialist enough! They want more radical and faster change. They have even started a magazine in which they criticize, in a pro-socialist way, the policies and work of our government.*

> *Mwalimu Nyerere has talked to me about this. He agrees with some of what they say and he disagrees with other things they talk about. A number of things they call for are not practical or are misguided under our conditions. Yet, Mwalimu admires their spirit. They are friends of socialism, not its detractors or enemies.*

> *Mwalimu Nyerere has asked me to urge all students in our nation to emulate their spirit and become friends of socialism. Students across the country and all our people need to conduct honest and open discussions of the problems we as a nation face. What are the problems? What are their causes? How can we resolve them?*

We need to discuss such issues at regional and national levels.
We need to write, have public meetings, and conduct other forms
of exchange. No one should feel restricted. Every one is free to voice
his or her opinion, provided it is done in a law-abiding manner.
Let us follow the example of the University students. And at the
same time, let us not give them the monopoly of engaging in this
important debate. All of us should participate. It is our inalienable
right and sacred duty.

Instead of the clamp-down on USARF and *Cheche*, had such a step been taken, the history of socialist development in Tanzania could have been a different one. A million flowers may have bloomed. The creativity and energy of the youth would have been sparked and channeled in a positive way into the difficult struggle for socialism in Tanzania. The youth would have been empowered.

But what I dream of did not occur. Instead, the youth became more dormant and socially apathetic. As years went by, they withdrew into personal affairs. When the nation's doors were opened, they lacked a firm cultural foundation or nationalist pride. Globalization cast a tantalizing hypnotic spell on this apolitical youth. And now it is almost unknown for student groups in the country to organize and fight for the rights and interests of the common man. If they fight, it is for their own narrow interests.

In conclusion: Instead of gathering support or praise, the gallant Revolutionary Front and its organ, *Cheche* met an unceremonious and painful demise. The ink with which the verdict was written has, however, not dried. The struggles of the people of Africa for justice, dignity, equality and development continue. With them, the spirit of USARF and *Cheche* continues to march on.

10

From Cheche to MajiMaji

Karim F Hirji

"Activism comes with a lot of pain, a lot of frustration, a lot
of discomfort. But I think that at the end of the day, you will
realize that progress has been made."
-.Oronto Douglas -

USARF is dead; *Cheche* is history; we are sad and sullen. My diary reads that our will remains firm. We will not fade silently away into oblivion. Naijuka Kasihwaki and I spent last night composing *Our Last Stand* (see Appendix E). Henry Mapolu looked at our draft before we finalized it. Of the seventy copies cyclostyled, a dozen go to town and *The Standard*. Early this morning, it was pasted around the campus. So there it stands, casting a brooding shadow, in the Tunnel of Love, calling forth men and women to bear witness to a tragedy.

Sparks in the Tunnel

The roadway underpass from Hall I to the cafeteria is called the Tunnel of Love, or Tunnel of Scandal. Nearly ten meters long, it is well-lit, though now and then, a few light bulbs are missing or broken. The wood-framed large notice board at one side, strewn with notices and statements, is hard to miss. One portion is reserved for university announcements, and the other portion is for the student union (DUSO) and other student organizations.

By tradition, individual students also post their ruminations here, making it the campus free speech board. Saucy, witty write-ups highlight nightly escapades of a male student in Hall III, allusion of an affair between a lecturer and his student, or an exposé of misuse of DUSO funds -- such are the perennial topics of free expression. A naughty report quickly attracts a buzzing crowd. The more vulgar or roguish the post, the more the vacuous cerebella congregated around it.

This practice dates from the early days of the university. USARF has added a novel twist. Our group issues, on generally a weekly basis, commentaries or statements on varied university, national or international events and affairs. Of recent, the Hill TYL branch has followed suit. At times, the two groups issue joint statements.

When USSR invaded Czechoslovakia in October 1968, USARF issued a statement unreservedly condemning the act. When seven academic staff issued a memorandum recently to rescind Development Studies, a Hill TYL statement resolutely defended the course. When the government proposed the KARADHA scheme to give favorable car purchase loans to civil servants, USARF and TYL branded it an anti-socialist move. Several joint statements pertained to overall and specific problems within DUSO. When the Kenyan government harshly dealt with the opposition politician Mr. Odinga Odinga, and the police brutalized the students at the University College in Nairobi, USARF and TYL issued a strong condemnation. Some USARF members now and then pen individual statements on academic, national and global matters. When Professor Ali Mazrui gave a series of pompous pro-Western presentations on at the Hill, Munene Njagi and I composed separate critical evaluations of his ideas and analysis.[1]

These statements are distributed and posted around the campus. One copy always lands on the free speech board. What was once primarily a medium for petty gossip is now, in part, a venue for airing views on vital societal issues. Being militantly and uncompromisingly worded, a USARF statement invariably attracts a crowd, though not as large as one which unveils a sexual scandal. Nevertheless, students do gather, and converse about what we have put up. The university and national authorities are often displeased about what we say in these statements and how we say it, but thus far, they have not been able to dampen or silence our voice.

After posting a statement, some USARF comrades usually stick around the tunnel. For two reasons: One, to guard against rightist vandalism. The pro-Western lackeys that are around always claim they favor freedom of speech. But when it comes to what we post, they make an exception, and are inclined to tear it down. Two, this gives us a golden opportunity to discuss and debate. We do not hesitate to pick an argument with anybody who loudly opposes our point of view. Sometimes they approach and harangue us. The exchange always follows a pattern. From the topic at hand, it migrates towards broader matters; then we debate capitalism, socialism, imperialism, dictatorship, democracy and the like. Unfounded and facile arguments against socialism are regularly encountered. A learned student holds up his hand to say all the fingers are not equal. Human nature, he wisely declares, abhors equality. But we are the better read, the better prepared. We counter puerile simplicity with a nuanced social analysis, piling on a barrage of facts and figures from history and the present era to back up our case.

The temperature in the tunnel rises as we argue and argue. Other students mill around. The vitriol goes on for an hour or two, until all are at the point of exhaustion. We stand our ground; they stand theirs. The words become loud and cantankerous, and yet it does not ever degenerate into a physical confrontation.

---

1   Fortunately, from the 1980s onwards, Professor Ali Mazrui changed his tune and became a prominent Pan-Africanist scholar critical of the Western domination of Africa.

Jonathan Kamala, Munene Njagi, Ramadhan Meghji, Naijuka Kasihwaki and I are the vociferous leftists at this venue. It is fun to watch Kamala confront a bunch of right-wingers, usually well-attired political science or law students. As his opponent speaks, he stuffs his pipe and lights it. Barely giving the fellow time to speak, he launches his counter tirade. By the time he is done, the pipe needs re-stuffing. So the ritual is repeated, and repeated. It looks as if Kamala cannot decide whether to overwhelm his antagonist with politically potent prose or massive puffs of cancerous smoke.

At last, our ideological opponents make an exit, muttering caustic words about the "dogmatic communists." Kamala gives me a cheerful thump on the back and exclaims, "Karim, we clobbered the reactionaries. Let's go and have a soda."

And now, it is we who have been clobbered by the power of the state. This morning, two days after the ban on USARF was issued, comrades hang around the tunnel. We have had our breakfast. But the desire to rush to class is absent. A sizeable crowd forms, attempting to decipher *Our Last Stand*. Those at the back strain their necks to read what it says. A few with their own copies read out to those who surround them. Rumors about the demise of USARF have been afloat for a day; this is a material confirmation in black and white.

On this occasion, no one argues with us. The mood is somber. Silence prevails, as in a funeral. As we stand crestfallen, some pat our backs. The reactionaries also say *pole*. For the first time in my memory, the bulk of the student body sides with USARF. They are going to miss the loudmouths with little regard for authority. Even while they disagree with what we champion, they acknowledge that we do take a principled, independent stand, and cannot be bought off by anyone. Many lament the death of *Cheche*. Are we going to let them down?

The Revival
Just two weeks prior to the ban, a new editorial board for *Cheche* had been elected in a joint meeting of the USARF and TYL committees. Its five members were: Henry Mapolu, Munene Njagi, George Hajivayanis, Naijuka Kasihwaki and Wilbert Kavishe. Henry is the only carryover from the original board. Over this time, I have been working closely with them to put this issue into shape.

The ban has preempted all that. We hold a second meeting that weekend to draw up concrete plans. Members of the former USARF Committee, the TYL branch Committee, Walter Rodney and Joe

Kanywanyi are present. The general outline is, in a sense, obvious. Now the comrades have to work within the confines of the TYL. After all, *Cheche* had been a joint organ, and no restrictions have been placed on the TYL campus branch. Henry suggests we publish under the auspices of TYL but with a new name. Of the several names proposed, we settle for *MajiMaji*, the name of the historic uprising against imposition of the German colonial rule in Tanzania. Now, for sure, no one can fault the magazine for having a foreign inspired name.[2]

Henry systematically outlines the steps we need to pursue. And, I am impressed. When we began our work on *Cheche*, I had had a few tussles with him about the pace and style of his work. After a year on the editorial board, and intense activism, he has matured into a clear-headed leader. He speaks sparingly but when he does, it is in a sharp tone, and in short and to-the-point sentences that follow precise rules of logic. A implies B; B implies C; so A implies C. It is hard to misunderstand or not understand what Henry says. I cannot say that for too many comrades.

> *There is a political vacuum in the current situation. Nature abhors a vacuum but we can seize on it. If we are tactically circumspect, we can make strategic gains. True, working under the umbrella of the party youth league will entail some loss of ideological and practical freedom. But if we tread with care, we can go far even in this challenging terrain.*

With the case carefully outlined, it is agreed that *MajiMaji* No.1 is to be produced soon, with essentially the same material that was to be in *Cheche* No.4. The editorial board will remain unchanged despite one potential complication. Munene hails from Kenya, and thus is not and cannot be a member of TYL. In theory, he is not eligible to be on the board. As Pan-Africanists and internationalists, we disregard that petty distinction and forge ahead.

As we devise the comeback, a major regional Social Science Conference is held at the Hill. In this December 1970 conference, one session is devoted to *Tanzania: The Silent Class Struggle*. Issa Shivji is for now at the London School of Economics. So I have the task of presenting the paper. Walter Rodney and John Saul give commentaries. The turn out is large; in fact, it is the highlight of the conference. A spirited, contentious discussion ensues. Overall, the reception towards the basic thesis, that the character of the nationalizations in Tanzania has compromised the progress towards socialism, is positive. Even those who disagree with

---

2   The history of the *MajiMaji* uprising is found in Iliffe (1979) and Kaniki (1980).

the verdict of the paper admit the issue is a vital one, and needs broader discussion at the national level.

The commentaries by Rodney and Saul are to form the backbone of *MajiMaji* No.1 (as had been planned for *Cheche* No.4). I am confident that Henry and his team will pull it off. I would like to work with them but now I am in dire straits. Academically, it is make or break time. For two solid years I have dreadfully neglected my studies. The final degree examinations for pure mathematics, applied mathematics and education are only three months away. I will have little time even to sleep if I am to do a decent job in that domain.

Yet, when Henry asks me to write the editorial, I oblige. I am also present in the nightly production shift. The new editors come through magnificently, and at a fast pace. *MajiMaji* No.1 is on sale in early January 1971, just as the new academic term begins.

Substance
The editorial of *MajiMaji* No.1 condemns the ban on USARF and *Cheche*, and castigates the hypocrisy underlying the reasons given for that act. It also declares that "genuine dedication to socialism cannot go hand-in-hand with pernicious double talk."

Two commentaries on *The Silent Class Struggle* follow. Walter Rodney, in *Some Implications of the Question of Disengagement from Imperialism* complements Shivji for bringing attention to crucial questions. But he critiques Shivji for "rather loose" generalizations about the petty bourgeoisie. According to him, the absence of entrenched bourgeois class interests in Tanzania make the victory in the struggle for socialism virtually certain. John Saul, in *Who is the Immediate Enemy?*, also praises Shivji for raising basic issues. Nevertheless, he says that Shivji is preoccupied with imperialism and does not reflect on how a revolutionary state confronting imperialism will be formed. For both Saul and Rodney, the leadership of Mwalimu Nyerere appears to be the principal factor that will almost inevitably propel the nation towards socialism.

They are followed by an astounding article by Paul Semonin, an economist. Entitled *Nationalization & Management in Zambia*, it is a detailed account of the nationalization of copper mines and other companies in Zambia. We learn that for varied political and economic reasons influential multinational companies and banks operating in Africa prefer that the state have minor or even major holdings in the companies they invest in. Contrary to what is blindly dished out by bourgeois economists, the real bourgeoisie are not blindly wedded to the free market, or automatically decry state involvement. They welcome it when and as long as it serves their interests. Nationalization is not necessarily socialism; it can also be the very opposite of socialism. (My article in *Cheche* No.3 had shown that nationalizations of foreign companies and setting up of state-owned firms had indeed occurred in many, if not most, African countries after independence.)

A long article exposing the real nature and function of the World Bank in the global economy from another source is reprinted. Karrim Essack has a long review of Kwame Nkrumah's *Class Struggles in Africa*. These are complemented by a social commentary, letters from the readers, and a list of progressively oriented books on varied topics. In sum: The first issue of *MajiMaji* sparkles with the spirit of *Cheche*.

Distribution

While about 300 copies were produced for *Cheche* No.1, slightly more than 500 copies of *MajiMaji* No.1 have been printed. The latter goes to more places and people as well. About two hundred sell on the campus, and a hundred go to the office of *The Standard*, for sale to city residents. About ten go to Kenya and Uganda. Each African liberation movement gets free copies. A letter from Joachim Chissano, the local representative of FRELIMO acknowledges the receipt of one copy, and requests three copies for each future issue.[3]

Some libraries and colleges in Tanzania are sent a copy or two. School teachers request personal copies. Watiku A Nyerere, from Korogwe Secondary School needs a copy and back issues of *Cheche*. Harko Baghat, also a teacher in Korogwe, obtains three copies, and donates Tshs 10/=. Adhu Awiti, a scholar from Kenya, carrying out research on rural stratification in Iringa, sends a supportive note enclosing Tshs. 60/= and requesting that copies be mailed to three people in Kenya whose names and addresses he supplies.

The demand from overseas rises. The Africa Research Group in Cambridge, Massachusetts and the American Committee on Africa in New York exchange materials with us. A similar arrangement holds with PANAF Books in London and the Africa Group of Stockholm. Available funds do not permit posting many copies overseas. Henry writes to the overseas customers that " [t]here are no conditions whatsoever for people reprinting our material." Anyone can reproduce more copies for

---

3   FRELIMO letter dated Jan 13, 1971 with Reference No D/B1/J2 in the TYL Office File for *MajiMaji* No 1. Joachim Chissano was later elected as President of Mozambique.

distribution. *Zenith*, a Scandinavian socialist journal, will accordingly reprint *The Silent Class Struggle* and its commentaries.

The sales revenues do not cover even a third of the production cost of nearly Tshs. 1,000/=. Donations from academic staff come in once in a while. John Saul recently contributed Tshs. 50/=. Purchasing printing paper through the Department of Development Studies enabled us to secure the wholesale price. Lionel Cliffe facilitated this arrangement. A few student activists give what they can, their contributions ranging from Tshs 5/= to 70/=. Other than that, *MajiMaji*, like its predecessor, is self-reliant. In particular, it has no internal or external donor backing. This is a crucial factor that has to be maintained if the magazine is to retain its vitality and ideological independence. It does not get any funds or material from the TYL main office as well.

Reactions

MajiMaji No.1 secures a positive reception from a large number of students and the academic staff, from progressive people in the city and the liberation movements. People are pleased that the spirit and theoretical line of *Cheche* remain alive. The voices of the usual reactionary detractors on the Hill seem muted as well. Earlier, a few right wing extremists had wanted to hold a funeral procession for USARF and *Cheche*. But sensing that that would make them quite unpopular, they had refrained from doing so.

Further, not a murmur is heard from the university authorities. Mr. Msekwa, the Vice Chancellor who three months earlier had conveyed the message banning USARF and *Cheche* now does not have anything to say. The state authorities, for their part, are also quiet. Even a faint rumor of displeasure is not heard this time around. There is a background to their current aphony.

The university administration did not anticipate that a magazine in the same radical mould as *Cheche* would reappear, and so soon after the ban. Once it had conveyed the banning order from above, it had assumed that radicalism was as good as dead. But now an equally radical *MajiMaji* has appeared on the scene, and that under imprimatur of the youth wing of the ruling party. This makes them hesitant. Perhaps, unbeknownst to them, the magazine has the blessings of higher authority. But the fact is that we did not ask for permission from the TYL headquarters to produce *MajiMaji*. We assumed that the Hill TYL branch, as a bona fide student group, had, like any student group, the right to have its magazine, and went ahead to publish it. And because

TYL, the parent body, was a national organization, we did not register the magazine with the university authorities.

The state bureaucracy is in a quandary. The order to ban USARF and *Cheche* was conveyed in private. There was no official notice; no paper trail. They wanted us to pack our bags and quietly disappear. Instead, we issued *Our Last Stand*, and loudly publicized the ban at home and abroad. Both *The Standard* and *The Nationalist* had reported it as front page stories (The Standard 1970; The Nationalist 1970d). That had embarrassed and generated substantial negative publicity for Tanzania, particularly among those who supported its policies. Members of African liberation movements had expressed their sympathies to us. Why should Tanzania, they inquired, an enlightened champion of Pan-Africanism, stifle a progressive, law-abiding Pan-African student organization? Why proscribe a medium that unflinchingly promoted socialism and African liberation, the two pillars of the national policy?

Due to this unwanted negative publicity, the authorities tried to placate public opinion. The University administration issued a deceptive statement saying that the move to dismantle USARF had "been taken by the students themselves" (The Standard 1970). The accurate report of the ban in *The Standard* (under the independent editorship of Frene Ginwalla) contrasted sharply with the incoherent report of the same event in *The Nationalist*, the party newspaper (under the editorship of Benjamin Mkapa). The former accurately stated our claims, headlined the event as a ban, and reported the administration's version. But the latter gave a report that said one thing here and quite another there. It refrained from using the word "ban." Instead, the headline read "Hill Students' Front asked to cease," the implication being that the move reflected the outcome of a polite sort of request. It went on to say:

> It is understood that both steps [i.e. cessation of USARF and Cheche] were agreed upon at the Front's General Council's meeting held on Wednesday night following an earlier meeting with the Vice-Chancellor of the University of Dar es Salaam, Mr. Pius Msekwa, at which these two issues were discussed. The Nationalist (1970d).

In the first place, USARF did not have a "General Council." And, USARF certainly did not agree to anything. If you are banned by the state, you are banned, whether you agree with the move or not. Further, USARF as an organization did not have any meeting with Mr. Msekwa. The meeting in question was between Msekwa and the Hill

TYL committee. Yet, even after stating that the steps "had been agreed upon" by USARF, *The Nationalist* went on to say that "*Cheche* has been ordered to cease publication because of its name." Can you first be politely requested to die, then take the decision to kill yourself, and then be ordered to do so, and that just because of your name? If it was that innocuous a matter, why not just ask the magazine to change its name?

A letter to the editor critical of *Cheche* No. 2 in July 1970 in the ruling party paper that seemed to have official blessing had hoped "that the next few issues will contain something close to our realities and more explicitly connected with the efforts of Tanzanians to build *Ujamaa*" and avoid turning into a medium for "purposeless theory" (Mwana wa Matonya 1970). But just as it matures and starts to analyze local conditions and issues in an original manner, *Cheche* is felled by the official axe.

The Nationalist had also carried an editorial declaring that the ban did not mean that the youth should not be militant, or the government sought to discourage critical discussions of its policies. Curiously, it only mentioned USARF, avoiding talking of *Cheche*, and falsely presented the ban as an internal university matter. It had a strange conclusion:

> This [the ban] is a deliberate move intended to consolidate and re-invigorate further the TYL and enable the country's revolutionary youth to contribute more energetically to our revolution. The Nationalist (1970e).

First USARF and *Cheche* are criticized for not dealing with local issues and problems. But when they vigorously and broadly start doing so, they are blamed for not following the right channels! Surely, George Orwell would have admired this creative double talk.

A message delivered to us in person by an emissary from the State House at that time implied that the move was a way to "rationalize" (whatever that meant) the student activities on the campus (Hirji 1971a). These confusing messages and pronouncements reminded one of the embarrassment suffered by a person caught with his pants down. The world has plainly seen what you do not want it to see, and now you hastily try to camouflage the facts of life.

MajiMaji is born in this vacuous atmosphere of political uncertainty. The progressives on the Hill have taken advantage of the ensuing ambivalence to turn the tables, and quickly produce a new magazine under an authentic name but whose contents follow the same ideological spirit as that of *Cheche*. The politicians are being taken up on their word.

They now lack a convenient excuse like that of a foreign name. They do not seek further negative publicity. So for now, and in the near future, those in power will probably just let it be.

Prospects

The road ahead is foggy and unclear. On the one hand, there are prospects for expanded critical discussions on the liberation of Africa and the struggle for socialism in Tanzania in the pages of *MajiMaji*. On the other hand, it will be an uphill struggle. As the magazine is anchored within the ruling party, attempts to stifle it in one way or another, to undermine or dilute its ideological line and independence are inevitable.

Such efforts are soon underway. During the long vacation from April to June of 1971, there are proposals from the TYL main office that concern *MajiMaji*. They seem to be given in good faith, and at first sight, appear to give it a wider scope and readership. But below the surface, they portend politically and ideologically unpleasant outcomes. These proposals are (i) to convert *MajiMaji* into a national magazine, and (ii) to have it published in Swahili.

Indeed, that is also the future envisaged by the comrades. The magazine eventfully has to go beyond the Hill and spread the ideological message to the broad masses. That step should, however, be taken when we are capable of doing it ourselves on a sustainable basis and on our own terms. Accepting it now will dilute the content, inject an *Ujamaa*-worship mentality, and impose external control. The TYL branch committee discusses the matter with the editorial board. The need to resist outside control is clear. So the comrades decide to thwart the proposals in one way or another.

As a delaying tactic, the editorial board is silent at first. Later it says that most students, including TYL members, are not on the campus at this vacation time. The matter needs to be discussed with them before a decision can be taken. As the new academic term starts, the second and third issues of *MajiMaji* come out, all in English, and without involving the TYL national office.

Sensing the reluctance to implement their suggestions, the national office seeks to know why. The issue also creates divisions within the campus TYL. The mainstream, nationalist students favor the proposals while the radicals do not. This reflects a long-standing divide. The former had also disliked the earlier solid alliance between USARF and TYL. In August 1970, rumors of a coup organized by the nationalists to oust the leftist leadership of TYL had circulated.

The matter comes to a head in the annual meeting of the Hill TYL. This is also the time for election of a new branch leadership and editorial board. Henry, the outgoing chief editor of *MajiMaji*, presents a written report to make the case against the proposals from the main office. He first notes that of the hundreds of TYL branches in the nation, the Hill TYL branch is the only one that publishes a magazine. This fact has drawn praise from many people within and outside of TYL. He agrees with the need for a national political magazine in Swahili for the youth but then suggests that the TYL headquarters ought to start a separate magazine for this purpose. *MajiMaji* has to remain a university-based magazine because certain specific goals preclude it from playing a nationwide role. He explains that one major aim of *MajiMaji* is to illuminate the extent to which bourgeois ideology has penetrated the teaching of social sciences, especially at the university level. As the medium of instruction at the university and all related materials are in English, it is best that the consequent critical analyses also be in English, at least for now, and the magazine be based at the Hill.

He informs the audience that by October 1971, four issues of *MajiMaji* have appeared. Another issue will be out within a week. These achievements reflect the energy and effort expended by the editors and other activists, sometimes even to the detriment of their studies. *MajiMaji* now goes out across the nation, to six countries in Africa, and fourteen countries beyond Africa. All this, moreover, has been achieved through self-reliance and without any funds from the TYL headquarters.[4]

Henry makes his case in a strident and logical manner, though his language is quite diplomatic. His presentation gets wide support, and eventually carries the day. Thus one surreptitious attempt to dilute the radicalism at the Hill is thwarted. *MajiMaji* is out of the danger zone, at least in the short run.

This event transpired in October 1971, and I have run ahead. In that period, important events and upheavals took place at the Hill. A former USARF activist was elected to lead the students' union. For a while, the campus as a whole was radicalized because of heavy-handed, irrational bureaucratic interference in student affairs. Classes were boycotted, the Hill students and workers joined hands for the first time, and riot police were called in. In the aftermath, the university governance was

---

4   Henry Mapolu and *MajiMaji* Editorial Board (1971) *Taarifa Juu Ya Uchapishaji wa Gazeti MajiMaji, Umoja wa Vijana wa TANU, Wilaya ya Chuo Kikuu,* (copy in TYL Office File for *MajiMaji* No 1).

further democratized.[5] The issues of *MajiMaji* that came out in this period contained analytic material on rural development, the economy, education and world affairs that led to extensive debate. That saga, including the subsequent fourteen-year of the life of this magazine, is, however, reserved for another day in another work.

A Milestone

I end this chapter with personal musings. My undergraduate sojourn at UDSM reaches its destination in March 1971. Two months earlier, I had received a posting to serve as a mathematics teacher at Kibaha Secondary School, located twenty four miles from Dar es Salaam. But this changes once the final examination results come out. Now I am recruited to the Mathematics Department of UDSM as tutorial assistant. That is as I had wished. It also means that my close association with campus radicalism and *MajiMaji* can continue.

The graduation ceremony for my class is on a windy day of June 1971. The cool breeze counters the tropical sun. A large group of smiling graduates, proud relatives and happy well-wishers, somber-faced academic staff, and others in a celebratory mood gather in Nkrumah Hall to witness the Chancellor, Mwalimu Nyerere, confer the degrees. I too am in a festive mood. Yet, I do not sit with the new graduates because I have refused to don the academic gown. That feudal attire has no basis in our customs. It promotes elitism that has no place in a society striving towards socialism. Instead, I cheerfully walk among the crowd selling *MajiMaji* No.2 that is hot off the press. Henry and George, now final year students, do likewise. Later we sit down for a big meal in my room in the post-graduate students' block. George recites one funny tale after another, Henry laughs aloud, and I too am happy at this fitting ending of my exciting time as an undergraduate student at UDSM.

As I look back to the day three years ago when I ascended the Hill, I see I am not the same person. I know a slice of heavy-duty mathematics, and have been trained as a teacher. More importantly, it is what I learned outside the classroom, the endearing bonds I formed with comrades of varied races, nationalities and backgrounds, and my immersion in progressive activities that truly matter. My outlook has been transformed in a fundamental way. Now I see myself as a socialist entering the University of Life to continue learning and working with my fellow human beings to strive for justice, equality and a good life in

---

5   I refer to the onset of what has been called the Akivaga crisis. For a day-to-day, on-the-spot description and dissection of this crisis, see Hirji (1971b) and Njagi (1971).

Tanzania and beyond. Real life verily differs from student life, which I do appreciate. Only time can tell the extent to which I will be faithful to the goals I set for myself today.

11

Poetic Sparklets

"Man can find meaning in life, short and perilous as it is, only
through devoting himself to society."

- Albert Einstein -

Editorial Note: The three poems below directly relate to this book. *The Day the Rags Didn't Show Up*, by Ramadhan N Meghji, was written in 1968 after the demise of the Rag Day (Chapter 7). Submitted by Zakia Hamdani Meghji, it is published here for the first time.

The Apolitical Intellectuals, by the Guatemalan poet Otto Rene Castillo, has appeared in *Monthly Review* (June 1970), *Cheche* (September 1970, No. 3), and Castillo (1984). He crafted simple, piercing verses against injustice and oppression. In March 1967, at the tender age of 31, he was burnt to death by the US-backed and funded Guatemalan army after being brutally tortured and mutilated. This poem was often recited in the conversations of radical students, and cited in essays and articles.

A State of Withering, by Karim F Hirji, was written after Ramadhan N Meghji passed away in December 2003. A memoriam for the comrades no longer with us, most of those named in it appear in this book. It previously appeared in *Daily News*, 20 January 2004, and *Awaaz Magazine*, 6(1): July 2009. This is a slightly revised version.

The Day the Rags Didn't Show Up

Ramadhan Ntalyaga Meghji

On the hill, the University College, Dar,
The Rags Day had come
There was excitement,
A jolly festival was about to commence,
All active students awaiting
And impacting with slowness of time.

The Rags Day, a tradition born in Europe
Among sons and daughters of the privileged
One day in a year, to put on rags,
Or rather to wear patches of rags,
On elegant and dear Van Hussen} shirts
And exquisite woolen skirts or shirts

One day in a year, in jollity and hilarity
We the privileged kids
Let us initiate, let us dress down
Let us copy for a few hours
The posture, the carriage, bearing
The personality of the poor

These few hours of mock and play acting
Is done for a noble cause
'Cos around town we shall pass
The richer folks approached
And reminded of the underprivileged
Hats in hand, a collection be made
And finally the ragged-trousered philanthropists
Of one day, hand-over donations to the poor.

Later on, in the evening, back on campus
With sundowners, the booze in bars
Will flow, to celebrate
A good day's job done
A noble cause, for the poor
Life then goes on as usual
Awaiting the next year's Rags Day.

Thus a flurry of activities that day
On the hill, no classes, no lectures
The Rags Day activists busy
Organizing and arranging
Stitching patches, here and there
And the fleet of University vehicles
Ready for the parade of the year

The neutral students onwards with
Their own affairs, either book-worms
Or those consolidating their positions
With the opposite sex students, Dates and Romances
Others still asleep, nursing hangovers
Yet still others, free time for more boozing
Starting early till late.

That day a few valiant students
Preparing and readying to stop
To put to a stop, once and forever
The mockery of the poor
The few hours of enjoyment and
Patronization, of the poor
To put to a stop, these blind
Importation of foreign rituals.

That day on the car parking square
Where the procession was to start
The sons and daughters, nieces and nephews
Of the underprivileged, as well as
The enlightened and progressive middle class
Gather to confront, to sabotage
To shock educate others
On why rags, be not the solution.

Bus, tractor and car tires deflated
Barriers boldly erected
Drivers and turn-boys sensitized
Point well taken, point understood
And Rags Day procession failed to start
That's the day in Dar
The Rags didn't show up.

The car-park baptized: The Revolutionary square
A few militant radicals
Heads held high, winning the day
And a turning point, a start
To the University Hill, becoming
A center of Revolutionary, Nationalist
Pan-Africanist and Marxist ideas
But some battles won
The war a long one, and who knows
Maybe one day, the Rags will come on again.

The Apolitical Intellectuals

Otto Rene Castillo

One day
the apolitical
intellectuals
of my country
will be interrogated
by the simplest
of our people

They will be asked
what they did
when their nation died out
slowly
like a sweet fire
small and alone

No one will ask them
about their dress
their long siestas
after lunch
No one will want to know
about their sterile combat
with "the idea
of nothing"
No one will care about
their higher financial learning

They won't be questioned
on Greek mythology
or regarding their self-disgust
when someone within them
begins to die
the coward's death

They'll be asked nothing
about their absurd
justifications
born in the shadow
of the total lie

On that day
the simple men will come
those who had no place
in the books and poems
of the apolitical intellectuals
but daily delivered
their bread and milk
their tortillas and eggs
those who mended their clothes
those who drove their cars
those who cared for their dogs and gardens
and worked for them
and they'll ask:

"What did you do when the poor
suffered, when tenderness
and life
burned out in them?"

A State of Withering

Karim F Hirji

In dusty Dodoma, it began unexpectedly
Things falling apart suddenly
Nazir Virji, teaching on stubbornly
Ngugi and Brecht, his homily
A diabetic coma, effacing a dream brazenly

Politicizing the youth progressively
Brother Moronda worked actively
Ever supporting Ujamaa seriously
Yet devoured by a crash horridly

Interpreting the world perspicaciously
Rallying against injustice eloquently
Grounding with his brothers gingerly
Walter Rodney organized tenaciously
Murdered by the running dogs brutally

Puffing his exotic pipe incessantly
Jonathan Kamala theorized endlessly
Castigated neo-colonialism cantankerously
Succumbed to a malignancy gruesomely

Dethroning the Rag Day decisively
Embracing Pan-Africanism wholeheartedly
Protesting worker slaughter courageously
Andrew Shija passed away mysteriously

Mobilizing the Umma strategically
A. M. Babu led a revolution heroically
Enduring jail and exile stoically
With teeth protruding bizarrely
Promoted socialism unflinchingly
Struck down by an illness instantly

For years, fought Apartheid vigorously
Conducted ideological classes inspiringly
Sardonic political wit his specialty
Still pursuing a dream realized partially
Gora Ebrahim embraced oblivion quietly

Tortured by the state savagely
Abdulrahaman Hamdani spoke gently
Harvesting papayas in serenity
Consumed by loneliness slowly

A warm handshake without parity
Karim Essack wrote too prolifically
Bugging the reactionaries endlessly
Passed onwards laughing boisterously

Phillipe Wamba composed insightfully
An heir to Lumumba's intrepidity
Fostered the tradition of a family
A nascent promise dashed tragically

Ramadhan Meghji struggled poetically
Sneaked ideology to Hall 3 surreptitiously
Drawing for humanity poignantly
Soothed the hotheads jovially
Educated for work cooperatively
Our latest dispiriting loss unbelievably

Are they with Malcolm, Che and Ho finally
Or, listening to Fanon and Cabral eagerly
Yet we miss Ramadhan and all so dearly
Anguished tears our sole company

Not that any lived perfectly
We all exhibit that human frailty
Capitalism fractures our morality
Life, indeed, is not a dinner party

Mother Africa writhing in agony
Children in pain excruciatingly
Imperialism running amok unabashedly
Keep the candle burning brightly
Honor their sparkle, love and memory

12

Socialism Yesterday

Karim F Hirji

"[T]here is no treachery in the truth. There may be pain, but to
face honestly all possible conclusions formed by a set of facts is
the noblest route possible for a human being."
- Sherlock Holmes -

Introduction

The order to disband USARF and cease publication of *Cheche*, though conveyed by the university administration, came from the State House. Of that, there is no doubt. And in that, it infringed upon academic freedom, and the right to free speech. It was a blow against open, critical debate on socialism in Tanzania. A Pan-African student organization with progressive credentials that had not engaged in illegal activity of any form was commanded, without due process or being accorded opportunity to defend itself, to close its shop immediately. Why? And what did that action signify?

Placed in the international context, the ban was a sign of the times. Not just radicals and students but virtually all persons expressing views mildly critical of the existing order were being jailed, tortured or murdered across the world. Outspoken writers and editors faced harsh reprisal from the state; publications were outlawed. That was the life in Iran under the Shah, the Philippines under Ferdinand Marcos, Indonesia under General Suharto, Turkey, and South America. Across Africa, dissent was routinely suppressed. The police in Kenya and Malawi, thus, periodically mounted offensives against students and critics, and seized material deemed sensitive. Many repressive regimes received lavish funds, military assistance and diplomatic support from the USA. In the Western world, people protesting the war on Vietnam, fighting for civil rights or otherwise opposing the status quo, many of whom were university-based, faced reprisals. In socialist nations like China and USSR, dissenting voices were curtailed and suppressed. Only the official party line was allowed to make it into print.

Viewed in that setting, the ban on USARF and *Cheche* was like a slap on the wrist, a far cry from the harsh assault on dissent elsewhere. Mwalimu Nyerere did not behave like Mobutu Sese Seko of Congo (Zaire) who often murdered students and opponents with impunity (Legum 1972). Yet, that does not mean we should not analyze this case of direct state interference in progressive student activities in 1970. Examining the context in which took place, and seeking the reasons behind it provide us a valuable opportunity to learn from history.

The day after the ban, USARF issued a statement which asked:

> [T]his university is supposed to stimulate debate within the socialist context. Can socialism be built without sincere and rigorous discussion? USARF (1970).

Accordingly, how did the ban on USARF and *Cheche* fit within the general drive to construct a socialist society in Tanzania? Was it an anomaly or reflective of a trend? And there are more queries: What were the main features, in theory and practice, of socialism in Tanzania? Why did this effort fail? This chapter focuses on these critical matters. Other, contrasting views on these issues also exist. Here, I express my personal views with the hope that they will provide a stimulus for a fruitful debate.

Bureaucratic Capitalism

Let us begin with the salient features of the socialist experiment in Tanzania. While Mwalimu Nyerere had talked about socialism from the early days of *Uhuru*, the Arusha Declaration of 1967 marked the first serious step in that direction. The Declaration envisioned a society based on equality, service for the common good and justice for all. It advocated public ownership of the major means of production and other pillars of the economy; it sought to extricate the masses from poverty, ignorance and disease by establishing *Ujamaa* villages; and it limited the private income-generating activities of political and governmental leaders to prevent the emergence of a privileged stratum cut off from and ruling over the common man. It also stated that these goals would be achieved primarily with internal, national efforts, and not through reliance on foreign funds or support.

Banks, factories, agricultural estates, major trading firms, and other economic entities were thereafter taken over by the state. Commercial and rental buildings and, later, smaller business entities, were put under public ownership. Western powers, the local business community, and state bureaucrats were, to say the least, not in favor of these moves. Furthermore, it did not have discernible backing, at the outset, from university students.

On the other side, the Declaration was met with broad enthusiastic grass roots support. Peasants, workers and school students--unlike university students--across the nation hailed it. Many embarked on long distance marches to endorse it. These outpourings of support were not orchestrated actions but genuine reflections of the sentiments at the bottom of the social ladder. Common people hoped that their interests would finally prevail. And they expressed their willingness to play their part. In terms of the values it embodies, the Arusha Declaration is a noble document. If you have the interest of the people at heart, you cannot fail to be inspired by it. Even for the present age, it embodies a worthy overall social philosophy for Africa.

Yet, within less than a decade after it was issued virtually everything went askew. Living conditions of the people hardly changed; the word *Ujamaa* became an object of cynicism and derision. The hitherto popular support for socialism had vanished. Now only lip service was paid to the ideals of cooperation and public service. In fact, life in the 1980s was so dire that people were heard saying that colonialism was better. How and why did that happen?

This outcome was a product of a number of interrelated external and internal factors. Two key factors were the class base of TANU, and the structure and character of the state in Tanzania. TANU was a nationalist party. Apart from a few individuals, it did not have cadres knowledgeable about and committed to socialism. As with nationalist parties elsewhere, its members aspired to fill the shoes left by the colonialists, to replace the existing middle commercial strata. Their vision of how the society and economy should be organized was shaped by the legacy of colonial rule and what they gathered from the advisors of the World Bank. After 1967, most of them opportunistically mounted the band wagon of *Ujamaa*. But they were not genuine *Wajamaa*. The alignment of forces favored such hypocrites to prevail and prosper over time while the dedicated few were marginalized and became disenchanted. Thus, Abdulrahaman Babu, the only person in Mwalimu Nyerere's cabinet with a grasp of socialist economic planning was perpetually frustrated, up-staged by the pragmatist ministers who did not want to rock the boat. After a while, Babu landed in preventive detention, without any charges being leveled against him.

The petty bourgeois character of TANU was manifest in the political education it developed to promote socialism. Given in schools, offices and public gatherings as well as over the radio, it was a mish-mash of nationalistic rhetoric, anti-colonial agitation, and idealist day-dreaming. Failing to respect grass roots initiative, it did not inspire people, except when it came to exhortations against the Apartheid system in South Africa or the vestiges of colonial rule. Classes were not integrated with technical and scientific knowledge that reflected local conditions, and barely guided people in areas like health and agriculture. Mostly, it was boring, repetitive and superficial, and failed to mobilize people into effective and sustained action for long term changes in the structure, function and economic conditions of society. The 1977 merger of TANU and Afro-Shirazi Party into *Chama cha Mapinduzi* (Party of the Revolution) was, from the vantage of socialist transformation, simply a shiny ornamental cover for a moribund political reality.

Another critical factor was that even after the Arusha Declaration, the character and structure of the state remained what it essentially had been under colonial rule. It was a structure evolved to impose the rule of a few on the many, to protect capitalist commerce and private property. It was not a structure designed to enforce popular will and could not be changed by cosmetic steps like placing political commissars into the ministries, corporations and rural administration. These commissars were robotic functionaries who lacked clue or courage to advocate or carry out crucial changes. Enlarging the bureaucracy, they became a burden on public funds. Wearing Maoist attire or Kaunda suits, singing praises of *Ujamaa*, undertaking militia drills, holding political meetings, and so on, were symbolic activities that enabled TANU to pretend that things were different from what they actually were.

But it was symbolism without substance. The basic problem was that the economy was solidly integrated into the global capitalist system in ways that drained most of the generated surplus abroad. Not much remained for reinvestment. Without that, a quantitative and qualitative transformation of the domestic productive forces could not be carried out. A fundamental step required for socialist construction was to disengage the economy, even if in a gradual way, from Western domination. Its orientation had to change from one of export of raw materials and import of finished or semi-finished goods to one with strong domestic intersectoral linkages between agriculture, industry, communication, education and health. Comprehensive, integrated socialist planning was all but absent in the Declaration, other policy documents as well as in practice. Stimulation of food production, institution of a viable policy of improving health, and setting up small scale industries in rural areas, implementing locally built and managed projects for water and energy, and the like, were not attempted in a serious way. A few good initiatives in some districts showed initial progress but deteriorated into oblivion soon thereafter.

The combination of diffuse rhetoric with absence of sound socialist planning meant that Socialism and Self-Reliance in Tanzania developed a dualistic characteristic. High flown, vague policies promised one thing but the practice either manifested major deficiencies or often was quite the opposite. Articles in *Cheche* and *MajiMaji* highlighted such contradictory and limiting features of *Ujamaa*. Other books and papers have documented these anomalies as well. For example, Cliffe (1972), Cliffe and Saul (1973), Coulson (1982), Hirji (1973), Kamuzora (2010), Mapolu (1979; 1986; 1990), Packard (1972), Rodney (1975), Rweyemamu

(1973), Saul (2009), Segall (1972), Shivji (1973; 1976; 1986; 2010) and von Freyhold (1979). The main issues have been alluded to in the previous chapters. Here, we draw the key messages from this body of material:

- Western imperialists and local capitalists were decried in political speeches as economic blood suckers. Banks and major firms were nationalized. But virtually the next day, major companies from the West were engaged in a managerial or advisory capacity to run the state-owned firms. Socialism was to be built by the capitalists! While the state exercised nominal ownership, control rested with external capitalists.

- People were made to live in *Ujamaa* villages. But to do what? To produce coffee, cotton, cashew nuts, etc. for the world market, and be subjects to its vagaries and price instability as before. The returns were as paltry as in the colonial era. Agricultural extension services operated, in substance and form, as in the colonial era, dispensing chemical fertilizers and pesticides without room for local, intermediate technology-based approaches. Health education campaigns urged farmers to plant food crops, but bank loans were available only for the traditional export crops.

- Socialism was to be built through self-reliance, not foreign funds. Yet the flow of foreign grants and loans to Tanzania increased appreciably after 1967. By the middle of the 1970s, the nation was among the highest per capita recipient of foreign funds in sub-Saharan Africa. Projects we could undertake with local resources and effort (like health education campaigns on the radio) were done with funds from Scandinavian countries. By the late 1970s, the nation was effectively partitioned: Different Western "donors" including the World bank were given the responsibly to plan and undertake development projects in different regions. No genuine development materialized. Giant state farms, ambitious water supply projects, a colossal leather processing factory, so-called integrated rural development schemes, and so on, set up with massive foreign funding ended up as rotting white elephants. The culture of dependency (*omba-omba*) that so seriously plagues the nation today was firmly institutionalized in this so-called age of self-reliance.

- Economic planning was based on superficial financial indicators and projections under the guidance of and with advisors from the World Bank, the imperialist powers' bank. Other capitalist agencies were also involved. The methodology and substance of these plans were no different than what was done in capitalist Kenya.

- The energies and resources of local professionals, small businessmen, farmers and industrial sectors were not mobilized effectively. Instead, they were alienated and harmed by bureaucratic bungling and simplistic measures. Pseudo-socialist expatriates in the ministries and university had front rows seat at the decision-making table while local experts, including those with good technical and socialist credentials, had to fidget and stand in line at the door.

- Socialism in Tanzania was, according to the documents, not to be implemented by force or coercion. At the outset, numerous rural communities voluntarily set up *Ujamaa* villages, favoring farming on a cooperative basis. Yet, in many areas, poor or no planning prevailed. Rural people were told to move overnight without prior notice or consultation to undeveloped places which lacked water, health and other services that had been promised. Many were reluctant, but had to move whether they liked it or not. They faced the same bureaucratic hurdles, their proceeds were misappropriated by party and district officials. No wonder they began to oppose the policy. When the pace slowed down, force was used. Hasty, unplanned settlements often led to higher malnutrition and spread of diseases like cholera. Villagization became a chaotic exercise entailing destruction of people's houses and property. Their possessions were regularly looted by the militia forces enforcing the move. It was the same pungent colonial era wine in new bottles!

- Socialism in Tanzania was to be based on grass roots democracy. The *Mwongozo* explicitly declared, in 1971, that power was to be transferred to the people. In practice, this meant placing an elaborate, top down administrative structures in the regions to exercise strict control over the rural population that, moreover, was designed by an American consulting firm with absolutely no socialist credentials.

- The *Mwongozo* proclaimed that workers must be involved in running factories, other enterprises and institutions. When workers rose up in one factory after another to expose unfair managerial practices, they were met with armed Field Force Units, as in the colonial era. The national trade union did not uphold the rights of the workers but became a mouth piece of TANU. Most Worker's Councils became appendages, if not tools, of the bosses. Workers and their leaders who were defiant were silenced or fired.

Accordingly, the managerial and organizational practices in nationalized industries and the governmental sector continued to be top-down hierarchal in style and unit-level oriented in substance, often driven by management consultants from capitalist nations. The double standards were well recognized by the workers:

> *Efforts to inculcate socialist values many times degenerate in such situations to forms of "hortatory" socialism, which lack meaning for the worker and therefore have little appeal. One can suspect that they are viewed as disguised forms of manipulation, no different in substance from other forms of exploitation. Packard (1972).*

- The policy of *Education for Self-Reliance* was to cultivate a new generation of youth who would value practical work and service to the people. On top of the usual subjects, they were to learn and practice skills like farming, carpentry, and building construction that would give them the means of earning a living and contributing to the expansion of the rural economy. Several schools set up successful projects along these lines at the outset. But the momentum was not sustained. At the national level, the program lacked imagination and planning, and there was little guidance or concrete support from the Ministry of Education on what to do and how to do it. Local education officers rarely involved the schools in the planning of such activities but tended to adopt an authoritarian approach that did not make practical sense.

In most schools, farms, poultry rearing, and other projects did not thrive. When they did, the nutritional status or condition of the students did not necessarily improve. Students, teachers and parents alike thereby came to dislike the program just after a short while. Activities like *shamba* work were thus viewed and often implemented as a punishment.

One critical factor was that available jobs, especially the well paid jobs, continued to be based on qualifications derived from on traditional schooling. The neo-colonial economic set-up drew the so educated into urban areas where jobs or gainful occupations were relatively more available. The additional practical tasks at school were then seen as a diversion from "real education." Even colonial schools had had more practical work for African students -- so that they would remain where they belonged! Because of this disjuncture between the actual neo-colonial economic trajectory and empty socialist rhetoric, Tanzania in that era developed an education system that was deficient both by socialist and traditional standards, in effect, a system with features of the worst aspects of both these worlds.

- The national health policy did not markedly deviate from the guidelines that were laid down by the World Health Organization and the World Bank, and adopted in most African nations. These did not pay adequate attention to disease prevention, were not intersectoral in nature, and especially, not coordinated with the agriculture, water and energy sectors, and lacked a mass participatory base. Even this constrained policy was implemented in a disorganized, inefficient manner:

> *The present health policy of Tanzania is the same as that of non-socialist, developing countries; it should be different. Health is an area of society that has not been penetrated by Tanzanian socialism. Segall (1972).*

My personal experiences confirmed this state of affairs. While lecturing at UDSM from 1971 to 1974, I supervised the practical training of mathematics teachers in the secondary schools in Coast, Iringa, Kilimanjaro and Tanga regions. Comrades teaching in schools invited me to give talks on current affairs and science. These contacts and visits alerted me to the dismal state of the policy of Education for Self-Reliance. Later, I wrote an article in *MajiMaji* critically evaluating the policy, especially its implementation (Hirji 1973). That was the last straw for the bureaucrats: I had to be disciplined. Consequently, I was "decentralized" (euphemism for expelled) to Sumbawanga, the Siberia of Tanzania. The head of my department and others at the Hill complained about it, but to no avail. As a cynical right-winger expressed it: "You write about serving the people; this is your chance to be with them!"

April 1974 saw me transmuted, overnight, from an academician to a planning officer in the Rukwa region administration. My task, as I soon found out, was to serve the regional bosses, not necessarily the people. No room for any initiative existed. Most of the time, there was nothing to do in the office, with the day spent reading month-old newspapers. But I had to dutifully report to work on time and depart on time. During the two years I spent in the region, I was often able to visit *Ujamaa* villages and talk with peasants, teachers, students and workers. In village after village, the emptiness of socialist rhetoric combined with harrowing tales of bureaucratic misconduct were heard. In our planning office, systematic collection of the data on the economy, transport, water supplies, health and education was all but absent. Every year, our boss made us sit down as he drafted his annual report. We made reasonably sounding guesses about what had or had not transpired place during the past year. Economic and social statistics were conjured up. Together with similarly dubious data from other regions, they became the basis for the glowing reports on the socialist transformation in Tanzania noted in official documents and the reports of international bodies like UNESCO, WHO, and UNDP and various bilateral aid agencies.

In 1976, I joined the newly established National Institute of Transport in Dar es Salaam to lecture on transport statistics. My six years there provided me with first-hand knowledge about the transport sector in Tanzania. Many of our students came from within the sector. Every year, I spent three months visiting students attached to regional and national transport institutions and companies. The general picture was of total external dependency in financing and supplies, lack of coordination within and between the sectors in the economy and poor management and corruption. The extensive suppression of youth initiative I found was a sad spectacle. Our former and current students regularly complained, in firm after firm, that their voices and skills were marginalized while expatriate advisors, who in many cases were less qualified, were treated as demi-gods. The Ministry of Transport was afflicted with economic myopia as well; for example, instead of harmonizing the goods and passenger vehicles used for regional and city transport and setting up common workshops and manufacturing units for spare parts, foreign funders essentially decided what was done and how it was done. Transport policy reinforced the export-import structure of the economy. Promoting regional integration and trade was not the central organizing principle. Lack of popular accountability made day-to-day running of the firms grossly inefficient, and led to the bankruptcy of one entity after another.

A viable socialist policy would have had an intermediate technology based state and collective farming sector, and small-scale industries and enterprises across rural and urban areas. Such projects would be located in an internally planned economy utilizing local resources and initiative. Education and the economy would complement each other as students versed in practical skills would man these sectors, as in socialist China or Cuba. TANU, dominated by the petty bourgeoisie, however, showed itself incapable of formulating such sustainable, locally designed, and integrated economic activities, and mobilizing the people to implement them.

Many gains were transient; there for a few years when funds flowed with reversions to the *status quo* thereafter. This happened, for example, with water supply projects. Swedish funds financed deep wells in many villages. Water was extracted using motorized pumps. But when the pumps failed, money to buy spare parts was not available. Often the villagers, who had had shallow wells or stream water nearby their previous area of residence, were left worse off than before.

Mwalimu Nyerere is to be credited for putting socialism on the agenda. He was a valiant nationalist who upheld the national dignity. He was not corrupt like many African leaders. He diligently fought for African liberation. In international diplomacy, he upheld our national dignity. He did not torture or kill his political opponents or jail them in large numbers. He was an erudite philosopher and internationally respected statesman. All that is true, undeniable and eminently commendable.

But at the same time, we must not forget that the socialism implemented by him was not socialism in any shape or form. The overall record makes it clear that TANU under his leadership demonstrated a remarkable degree of incompetence, inconsistency and confusion in the attempts to implement the policy of Socialism and Self-Reliance. The policies said one thing; the practice was in a reverse direction. The nation was not steered towards equality or economic development. Instead it was mired in continued dependency, debt and poverty. In more ways than one, *Ujamaa* gave us the worst of both the worlds, a system without accountability to the masses, a system not capable of sustained development. One legacy of that era was the bitter taste for socialism left in the mouths of ordinary Tanzanians. Because of that astounding gap between words and deeds, in the 1980s, socialism became a dirty word in Tanzania.

And soon the officials circumvented the leadership code and became thoroughly corrupt. Independent initiatives of the youth, workers, peasants and professionals were quashed even when they supported socialism. Instead of a dynamic, popular drive towards socialism, the mixture of bureaucratic mediocrity and mismanagement produced the collapse of one public enterprise and institution after another, and led to the prevalence of disillusionment and cynicism. To put it more accurately, *Ujamaa* in Tanzania was actually a dysfunctional and underdeveloped form of bureaucratic capitalism.

Ujamaa in Context
In those days, working people everywhere were strongly attracted to socialism. In advanced capitalist nations, concessions won by reformist labor movements resembled socialism. The Welfare State in the UK, Canada and Europe was a product these struggles. The capitalist state initiated socialistic looking changes like nationalization and social

security to control major economic and political crises. Global trends and flawed economic policies in socialist nations similarly made them adopt measures that seemed to be oriented towards capitalism. Yet, despite these convergent trends, the two economic systems remained qualitatively different economic systems. The presence of socialist-type features within capitalism has been observed by Marx and many others thereafter. Several articles in *Cheche* and *MajiMaji* also noted that reality (Hirji 1970; Namama 1970; Semonin 1971; Shivji 1970; Vestbro and Persson 1970).

The socialist model of development, which provided spectacular economic benefits for the broad masses, as in China and Cuba, had a particular appeal in the Third World. Newly independent nations sought to distance themselves somewhat from the former (capitalist) colonizers and obtain aid from the communist camp. At the same time, the World Bank, the main funder of projects, and bilateral capitalist agencies preferred dealing with the state rather than with small scale firms in Third World nations. In that respect, they funded infrastructure development, large dams, export crops, mineral extraction, education and other activities. Colonial rule had provided poor social services to the natives. Post-colonial nations hence rapidly expanded, often under state control, free education, provision of health care, water and electric supply. These tendencies had a socialistic flavor, and when leaders of newly independent states implemented such measures, they did so with socialistic rhetoric. Such words enhanced their political legitimacy. Sekou Toure in Guinea, Gamel A Nasser in Egypt, Kwame Nkrumah in Ghana, Jawaharlal Nehru in India, Ben Bella of Algeria, Leopold Senghor in Senegal, Modibo Keita in Mali, and of course, Julius Nyerere of Tanzania were among the prominent leaders who had socialist leanings. Even the openly pro-West Kenya had many state-owned enterprises, almost free higher education and state-subsidized health care and said it was following a distinctive brand of African socialism. Leaders of the former Portuguese colonies, Mozambique and Angola, went further to state that their nations would follow the Marxist-Leninist path.

Socialism was in fashion. It was the politically preferred ideology in days after direct colonial rule ended. As a prominent historian astutely observed:

> *Ex-colonies which did not claim in some sense to be "socialist" or which did not look in some way to the Eastern model of economic development were rare birds indeed in the generation or two after 1945. Hobsbawm (1991), page 117.*

That commonplace conjunction of socialist rhetoric, state ownership and social welfare policies did not signify a fundamental break from capitalism but reflected the balance of internal and international class forces. People's forces were unified and energized by during anti-colonial struggles. Local left-wing or communist parties, though small in size, had played influential roles in that struggle. The anti-colonial movements had formed links with and secured assistance from the communist camp. Imperialism was in a defensive posture. Its strategy had to take the existing socialist alternative into account and had to make concessions which it normally would not have.

But when imperialism felt decisively threatened, it struck back with vigor. Jacobo Arbenz in Guatemala and Mohamed Mosadegh in Iran were deposed by the CIA soon after they nationalized the property of multinational companies. Patrice Lumumba in the Congo, Kwame Nkrumah in Ghana and Salvador Allende in Chile met a similar fate. However, by and large, many Third World nations were able to adopt limited socialistic-type policies, provided they remained ensconced in the international capitalist system. The diplomatic and material support these nations secured from Sweden, Norway and other social democracies also gave them further breathing room.

African nations who had declared themselves socialist or Marxist did not take energetic and consistent steps to disengage themselves from the international capitalist system. For example, "... *in their relationship with international capitalism, Ghana and Guinea were not so different from less militant regimes, and equally short-sighted*" (Saul 2009, page 51). Overall, their economic policy was driven by the World Bank. It produced short term growth but at the same time cemented their status as exploited neo-colonies. They had political independence but did not move towards economic self-determination (Nkrumah 1966; Magdoff 2003). Assistance from the communist camp at times made them somewhat less dependent. The development of capital goods industries in Egypt and India aided by the USSR were cases in point. Often even such aid entrenched the dependent status of these nations. That Angola was liberated with the help of Cuban troops, and later obtained generous Cuban and Soviet assistance, did little to prevent its subsequent slide into a grotesque model of a neo-colony.

In contrast, after the Sandinista revolution a serious attempt to disengage from the global capitalist system was undertaken in Nicaragua. The US retaliated swiftly and viciously, armed terrorist gangs to murder teachers, health care workers, and generally destroyed the economy. In a few years, that valiant attempt lay in ruins, the clock was turned back (Grossman 1985; Walker 2003).

In this context, the policy and practice of *Ujamaa* was not a substantive break from the systemic *status quo*. It was a genuine attempt to obtain a better economic deal for the people of Tanzania. It sought better terms of trade, more productive investment and more foreign aid, but essentially within the framework of the internationalist capitalist system.

The *Uhuru* railway line linking Zambia and Tanzania built with assistance from China mainly facilitated export of copper from and import of consumer goods into landlocked Zambia. It was crucial for the anti-colonial struggles, for short-term growth, and had been opposed by the World Bank. But that fact did not make it a project promoting socialism or self-sustaining development.

Some features set Tanzania apart from many nations in the pseudo-socialist mould. In early days after *Uhuru*, land scarcity was not a major problem. A large local or settler owning class did not exist. Foreign investments were not extensive. Internal and external class contradictions were less intense. Culturally, people were unified and there was a high degree of political unity. Mwalimu Nyerere was an enlightened, articulate and charismatic leader of high personal integrity whose ideas appealed to Tanzanians, Africans and liberal forces in the West. His firm commitment to total decolonization of Africa and independent foreign policy raised his standing throughout Africa and among progressive people everywhere.

Under these conditions, Mwalimu Nyerere could go somewhat further than others in his socialistic policies, and get away with them. But there was a basic line he did not cross. His nation thus remained mired within the neo-colonial framework. Consistent action to disengage from the global capitalist system was a fundamental prerequisite for building socialism. Under *Ujamaa*, this was not attempted. The abundance of militant rhetoric lacked a practical foundation, ultimately converting *Ujamaa* into a fake form of socialism. Issuing declarations does not, by itself, make a nation socialist. As John Saul aptly observed:

> [T]he ruling party has remained relatively untransformed and ineffective for mobilizing peasants and workers behind such [socialistic] program in any coherent way, and a systematic industrialization strategy along [socialist lines] is still lacking.
>
> Saul (2009), page 52.

Despite some key differences between Ghana and Tanzania, TANU had a lot to learn from the experience of the former in its attempt to build socialism. But it failed to learn that historic lesson, and thereby its own attempt collapsed due to similar shortfalls as in the former. In the quote below, I substitute "Tanzania" for "Ghana."

> .... the failure of the socialist experiment in [Tanzania] did not lie in the peculiarity of the African circumstances, and still less in the psychology of a single man. It failed because the attempt to break with [Tanzania's] colonial past was not made soon enough, and because when it was made, it was not complete enough. Fitch and Oppenheimer (1996).

Two Views

When people reflect on the era of socialism in Tanzania, two views emerge. There are those who say it failed miserably and does not deserve a second chance because we have yet to recover from its deleterious legacy. To these detractors of socialism, we ask: how can something fail when it never was there? Not even in a small way. The entity that failed was bureaucratic capitalism. What failed was the donor funded pseudo-socialism not a self-reliant economic policy. This right wing perspective fails to pose such questions for the openly pro-Western nations like Malawi, Kenya and Congo. It does not ask why, in the same period, capitalism failed equally dismally to improve the conditions of the masses? Why, in 1990, did the common person in Tanzania face identical problems as the common person in Malawi, even though Julius Nyerere was a dedicated socialist, and Hastings Kamuzu Banda, a fanatic anti-socialist? Was it socialism, or the common World Bank-oriented economic policies that failed? This view also fails to note that in those days autocratic one-party rule was commonplace in Africa and had nothing to with whether the nation called itself socialist or capitalist.

One long standing feature of politics we must take into account in such a discourse is the presence of an extremist right wing faction that tends to blow issues well out of proportion. Take a current day example: By his actions, US President Obama is a staunch ally of big business, big banks and the US war machine. Yet this fanatic faction calls him a socialist, a charge shown to be patently absurd by a cursory perusal of facts. That many people take it seriously only demonstrates the power of the dominant media to twist reality. During the Cold War, wild but influential rhetoric of this sort perpetually emanated from the US.

Mwalimu Nyerere was thus branded as a communist because he had good relations with China. This was a false label. Otherwise why would Robert McNamara, president of the World Bank and an architect of the butchery in Vietnam, support Nyerere's policies? The World Bank did not give one cent to Cuba under Fidel Castro. But, it gave loan after loan to Tanzania, and played a prominent role in planning its economy throughout the *Ujamaa* years.

The other view of Tanzanian socialism emanates from people sympathetic to socialism. It contrasts the grim reality and hopelessness of today with the room for hope opened up by *Ujamaa*. This nostalgic vision lacks empirical basis. It minimizes the major problems of that era, and focuses on one man. It ignores the central tenet that societies are to be judged on the basis of real trends and structures, not just the words and life of one person, no matter who he or she is. Even people who know better avoid, mainly for reasons of political expediency, presenting a sound analysis of the past.

In the *Ujamaa* years Tanzania was inundated with lukewarm socialists and experts from Western nations. They worked with the university, central government, rural administration and aid agencies, or visited the country. Some played a positive role, especially in the educational sphere. But they also produced a plethora of reports that often glossed over the grave problems with the national policy. The litany of flawed, inaccurate and even concocted statistics generated internally and reproduced by hallowed agencies like the WHO, UNESCO, and bilateral aid agencies added to this. To justify their aid, they peddled biased data on the gains in health, literacy, water supply, education and rural development. The dubious mythologies about socialism in Tanzania prevailing in some quarters emanate from such a background.

The vibrant debate about the actuality and viability of socialism in Tanzania in *Cheche* and *MajiMaji*, other venues at the university, and to an extent in the national newspapers in those days had steadfast promoters of *Ujamaa* at one end and those who used class analysis and a scientific perspective to analyze it at the other, and with some views in between. A bevy of local and expatriate scholars argued that after the Arusha Declaration, Tanzania had decisively disassociated itself from the effusive brands of African socialisms pervading the continent. Establishing collective villages, extensive nationalization, the leadership code, a novel educational sector, workers' participation in decision making, and restrictions on imports of luxury goods signified concrete trends in the socialist direction. Sure, there were many problems, but these were due to poor implementation and misjudgment, and were not problems of basic principles and strategy. And Mwalimu Nyerere was serious about tackling these problems one by one. Many well intentioned but lukewarm socialists tended to adopt this view.

In a talk entitled *"Ujamaa as Scientific Socialism"* in a USARF ideological class in early 1972, Walter Rodney took a similar stand (Rodney 1972b). *Ujamaa*, he argued, was a localized manifestation of the principles underlying scientific socialism. He took issue with the Marxists who declared that a society must traverse the stage of advanced capitalism before it moves to socialism. He recalled a debate among Russian Marxists nearly a century ago, and in which Marx and Engels had also weighed in. Could Russia employ its rural communal modalities as a foundation for socialism, thus bypassing the capitalist stage? Marx and Engels had not taken a clear stand on this question at the outset but later both considered it a possibility. While noting key differences between historic Russia and contemporary Tanzania, Rodney argued that Tanzania could utilize the *Ujamaa* forms to move to socialism if it also creatively utilized modern technology, drew on the experience of the other socialist nations, and set up cooperative links with them. To say that Tanzania must first attain advanced capitalism was to look at history in a dogmatic fashion, he said.

Rodney's thesis sparked off a heated discussion among the campus comrades. Other comrades critiqued it for four reasons. First, the possibility for a "non-capitalist" poor nation to directly embark on a transition to socialism was no longer an issue. The Chinese and Cuban revolutions had moved it into a concrete possibility. That it could be done was not in doubt. That historic debate was thereby, and to an extent, beside the point.

Second, as Rodney himself had noted, by early twentieth century, the capitalist mode of production in Russia, even in the rural areas, had penetrated to such an extent that the question of bypassing it had become moot. After centuries of slavery, colonial rule and neo-colonialism, Africa had correspondingly become embedded into the international capitalist system (Rodney 1969). The lives and social relations of peasants in the remotest areas had been transformed and old communal forms had for the most part disappeared. For Tanzania and Africa, the question of bypassing capitalism was thereby also moot.

The third point was more of an empirical one. At issue was not whether a socialist transition could or could not take place in Tanzania, but whether it was taking place or not. The preponderance of the facts on the ground contradicted the rosy visions projected by the officials and sympathetic scholars. Issa Shivji's seminal work in *Cheche* formed a key plank in this argument. As he and others documented, reversals from stated policy and half hearted moves were evident from the early days. Despite the rhetoric about exploitation of Africa by the West, actual moves led to greater engagement with the global capitalist system. Rodney stated that Fidel Castro had transitioned from radical nationalism to scientific socialism after coming into power. The implication was that Mwalimu Nyerere, despite his own words to the contrary, could and possibly would make that transition. But what Rodney did not spell out clearly was that while Fidel progressively moved further to the left of his earlier positions, in Tanzania, each grand pronouncement was immediately followed by a rightward compromise in practice, whether in relation to imperialism, or the local power relations.

The final point was that Rodney had not done an adequate class analysis of the situation in Tanzania. True, internal class formation in Tanzania was not as pronounced as in other places. The difference between the rich and poor was not as sharp as elsewhere. But the trends and tendencies in that direction needed to be taken into account. And, further, he had not considered the issue of state capitalism.

This was a debate among comrades committed to the same cause. Rodney, for his part, listened to the others, especially the Tanzanian comrades. When his talk was published, the title was changed to "*Tanzanian Ujamaa and scientific socialism.*" The substance, though, was essentially the same (Rodney 1972b).

Rodney, however, was not an armchair scholar. He was a committed intellectual who, in accordance with his scientific ethic, continued to learn from observation, experience, study and discourse. His views continued to evolve, especially as the actuality of "socialism" in Tanzania became more manifest. Four years later, he gave a lecture at Northwestern University in the USA on "Class Contradictions in Tanzania." His method for analyzing the situation in Tanzania as well his assessment of the possibility of attaining socialism stood in sharp contrast to his earlier views (Rodney 1975). Now his analysis was firmly grounded, and considered the divergent interests of the petty bourgeoisie, on the one hand, and the workers and peasants, on the other. He no longer speculated about possibilities but examined the actual direction of the social trajectory. He took note of the setbacks faced by workers, peasants and progressive forces, and concluded that "at the present time, the petty bourgeoisie, although small in number, is in the control of the state. It is reproducing itself. It still retains certain kinds of links with the international monopoly capitalist world" (Rodney 1975). While remaining hopeful about long term prospects, Walter Rodney was no longer among those whom he now called the "romanticizers" of *Ujamaa.*

In sum, I find that the views of Tanzania that prevail today on both sides of the political divide are biased. The rightists say that Tanzania was headed towards monolithic communism and the leftists say it had laid a good foundation for building socialism. Both views are simplistic portraits that do not represent the reality of that era. Neither a rightist dismissal nor a leftist glorification of that time serves us well since both deny us the opportunity for deeper reflection.

We need to carefully examine the past and learn from it. We need to discuss the works, documents and debates of that era in order to get a historically valid and empirically accurate view. For a start, I suggest taking a look at what Walter Rodney wrote in 1975 and what Henry Mapolu wrote in 1980 (Mapolu 1980). These works provide excellent, easily readable, perspicacious descriptions of *Ujamaa* in Tanzania. They can be followed by the critical writings noted above. When reading the more recent works like Leys and Mmari (1995) or Chachage and Cassam (2010) one should take note of the absence of a sound and integrated analytic methodology, and the selective nature of the evidence presented.

An Aberration?
The petty bourgeois leadership dominating TANU and the state apparatus not only failed to take serious and consistent measures to move towards socialism but it also was not well disposed to the facts of the matter being disclosed and discussed in public. It was also opposed to independent initiatives to move the nation onto a socialist path. Many incidents during this period demonstrated these reactionary proclivities. Take the case of the Ruvuma Development Association (RDA), a grass roots collective of villages organized along democratic lines that strove to promote integrated development of agriculture, small scale industry, education and health. This was a model that other districts could have emulated. But it was too autonomous, not in line with the top down villagization underway. Thus, " [o]n 24 September 1969 the Central Committee [of TANU] met in Dar es Salaam, under President Nyerere's chairmanship, and 21 out of its 24 members voted in favor of disbanding the RDA" (Coulson 1982). The decision was implemented in an authoritarian way with confiscation of the property of the villagers by the police and dispersal of the teachers and other cadres.

This occurred barely two months before *Cheche* No.1 came out. In July 1971, seven months after *Cheche* was banned, university students went on strike against arbitrary administrative rules and demanded the right to participate in decision making. Elite police units were sent to arrest and deport their leader. Around the same time, the editor of *The Standard* appointed by Mwalimu Nyerere to make the paper an outlet for independent, progressive debate was dismissed. Why? She had adopted her mandate too well. Months later, progressives from Zanzibar including minister Abdulrahaman Babu were detained without trial on charges that had no foundation. From 1972 onwards, the industrial sector was rocked by a series of strikes. Essentially the workers were demanding implementation of announced official policies (TANU 1971). They wanted a real say in the decision making process. Again, one after another, the strikes were quashed with intimidation and a show of force. In subsequent years, there were many small, small uprising in schools, colleges, factories and villages: the basic grievance was that the local authorities were not implementing the stated policies but peddled their own interests. Yet, almost without exception, the party and the state came out on the side of the bosses, not the people.

Mwalimu Nyerere showed undue tolerance for those in the upper echelons of the party and state bureaucracy who egregiously undermined national policies. Financial and other scandals in nationalized industries, regional administration, and central ministries were the order of the day. Caused by incompetence, shoddy management, corruption or negligence, they led to massive losses and setbacks. Yet, often these were hidden from view, and when they became public, the officials concerned were transferred from one post to another. Appropriate penalties and stern measures to substantively modify the situation were an exception, not the rule. The 1970s also saw a systematic process of removal of progressive local and expatriate staff from the University of Dar es Salaam. At times, it was done in an open manner but often it was masked.

On the political front, the one party election held every five years soon became a sham. The approved candidates often excluded those who championed the interests of people. Political sycophants were favored. Mwalimu Nyerere did not give the people of Zanzibar the needed room to determine their own destiny. in 1995, he seems to have been a party to the cover-up of the electoral irregularities in that place. With regards to the African liberation movements such as FRELIMO, SWAPO and others, Mwalimu interfered in their internal affairs, and at times jailed members of one faction in favor of another (Othman 2001; Saul 2007; 2009). In Uganda, after the overthrow of Iddi Amin, rather than respect the right of the people to freely elect their leader, he maneuvered to reinstall Milton Obote. As a result, that nation was once again plunged into chaos.

Viewed within this context, the order to ban USARF and *Cheche* was not an exceptional event. It followed the general political trends in Tanzania. The public arena was saturated with rhetoric about socialism and respect for human dignity but the real practice contradicted these words, and did not respect the right of the people to voice their views and seek their own destiny. Voices challenging this double talk could not thrive in that situation. They had to be silenced or contained. And so they were.

In August 1970, Mwalimu Nyerere gave an inspiring speech at the University of Dar es Salaam that is worth quoting at length.

> *The University must be allowed to experiment, to try new courses and new methods. The staff must be encouraged to challenge the students and the society with arguments, and to put forward new suggestions about how to deal with the problem of building a socialist Tanzania based on human equality and dignity. Further, they must be allowed, indeed expected, to challenge orthodox thinking on scientific and other aspects of knowledge ..... The staff we employ must lead in free debate based on the concept of service, on facts, and on ideas. Only by allowing this kind of freedom to our University staff will we have a University worth its name in Tanzania. For the University of Dar es Salaam will be able to serve our socialist purposes only if we accept that those whom we are paying to teach students to think, must themselves be allowed to think and speak their thoughts freely. Nyerere (1970).*

But three months later, a strong voice that challenged orthodoxy, that spoke out in favor of genuine socialist development, that stood for new and relevant substance, style and methods in education, that was independent but committed to serving the people, was silenced for spurious reasons. The political message was clear -- do not take the fine pronouncements too seriously. The contrast between words and deeds could not have been starker.

Even after 1970, you could talk and write about Marxism or criticize official policy at the university. But only within limits, and provided those voices did not go beyond the Hill into the national arena. So long as you did not venture into the broader political field to expose the limitations, failings and hypocrisy of the alleged policy of socialism and self-reliance, you were relatively safe. Elsewhere in Africa, the opposition was jailed or eliminated. In Tanzania, it was astutely contained and rendered politically ineffective. Erstwhile radicals became more petty-bourgeoisified and were assimilated into the state bureaucracy.

Without vibrant debates to develop a viable socialist policy, without attempts to convert TANU into a party firmly dedicated to socialism, without genuine mass mobilization and grass-roots economic democracy, and by reproducing the colonial state's structures of domination and control, progress towards socialism was thwarted, and neo-colonial economic domination and poverty were entrenched.

In terms of his commitment to African liberation, one may say that despite his errors, Mwalimu did more good than harm. In terms of his devotion to national unity and tranquility, one may also say that despite his mistakes, he did more good than harm. On the other hand, that verdict cannot be rendered on his alleged policy on socialism and development. In that regard, his policies, which were neo-colonial in substance and fact produced more harm than benefit to the people of Tanzania, and laid the foundation for the economic predicament Tanzania found itself in later on. Mwalimu Nyerere rallied firmly against the IMF in the 1980s, opposing the pungent dose of structural adjustment medicine it prescribed for Tanzania. But that medication was the logical end product of following, for two decades, the economic development policies laid down by the World Bank, the twin sister of the IMF (Green 1995; Svendsen 1995). If you eat high fat meat products daily, you will likely develop heart disease. When the doctor suggests painful, risky surgery for you, it is paradoxical to just blame him and forget about your own behavior that led to the disease in the first place.

13

Contemporary Capitalism

Karim F Hirji

"The hidden hand of the market will never work without a hidden fist--McDonald's cannot flourish without McDonnell Douglas, the designer of the F-15."
- Thomas Friedman -

A Different Era?

Africa has undergone profound changes since 1970. Take the case of Tanzania: Most people then never made a phone call. Today, taxi drivers, street hawkers and even domestic servants carry mobile phones. Simple consumer goods like pots and pans, apparel and shoes were in short supply. Shops nowadays are flooded with such and more products. There was one university in the nation then; today there are more than ten. A university lecturer in the past went to the library to read a journal. Today, he gets that in his office, or even at home, via the Internet. Life expectancy has gone up; infant mortality has declined. Dar es Salaam now boasts tall office towers, shopping malls, and elegant hotels -- a modern metropolis in the making.

In overall terms, most nations in Africa have now adopted multi-party democracy that functions to one degree or another. Their economies are guided by the ideology of free market and liberalism, and foreign investments are pouring fast into the continent. The word socialism has virtually been expunged from the political lexicon.

The next chapter asks whether the ideas and visions that inspired the student activism of the past are relevant today. If the world has been transformed so drastically, is reviving the old ideology not a futile venture?

This chapter shows that despite these noticeable changes, continuity persists at the structural level. Africa remains imprisoned within the excruciating grip of international capitalism. Imperialism, headed by the US, still casts the domineering shadow. Facing challenges and problems similar to those in 1970, African nations continue to function as neo-colonies within the global capitalist system. The democracy that prevails is only symbolic. The life of the ordinary African remains a life of grinding hardship, plagued as it is by profound and persistent daily insecurity. Low wages, high unemployment and underemployment, ramshackle housing, paucity of clean water, good health care and other basic services, and the high prices of food and essential goods combine to generate ill health, persistent mental anguish and a generally miserable life for his family. Yes, he does have a cell phone but he regularly also wonders where the money to pay for the next meal or malaria pills for the feverish child at home is going to come from. Despite the passage of half a century, most Africans have yet to taste the fruits of independence.

Capitalism Today

By the early 1990s, the Soviet Bloc had collapsed. Foreign investments flooded into China. Its ideologues said that capitalism had been proven beyond doubt as the only viable social system for humanity. The tentacles of capital penetrated deeper into all the corners of the globe. The fight was led by the WTO, IMF and the World Bank under the leadership of the US Treasury. In country after next, they flattened the barriers hindering the unfettered operation of multinational firms. In the aftermath, a boom in all sectors of the economy ensued. Giant firms merged into bigger business houses with the planet as their arena of action. Stock markets celebrated the gains by attaining stratospheric levels (Korten 1995).

China became the factory of the planet. India, Brazil, Indonesia, Malaysia, Mexico, the UAE appeared as the next South Korea or Taiwan. International commodity flows and financial transactions mushroomed and credit rules were eased. Consumers in the advanced economies borrowed on a majestic scale to finance a lifestyle awash with electronic trinkets, and were enveloped by sensually appealing but intellectually and morally puerile entertainment. Even in the poor nations, cheap commodities poured in like a veritable flood, and grand millennium development goals were set. The era of a decent life for all was promised. Even Africa seemed to be making a turn around.

Yet, the trend was uneven, superficial and unsustainable. The basic features of capitalism identified by Karl Marx long ago continued to manifest themselves, though in varied forms and hues. Large social and economic inequalities were generated. The multitude at the bottom remained very poor; many descended into greater poverty. The global system was fraught with economic instability, and prone to one intense crisis after another.

In the early to mid 1990s, blanket liberalization and financial speculation brought Argentina and Russia to their knees, leaving chaos and misery in their wake. Mexico, China and other nations saw expansion of sweat shop jobs, massive rural dislocation, increased emigration, escalating crime and social strife. A real estate bubble followed by speculation and capital flight fueled by Western investors in Asia turned into region wide catastrophe. More than two trillion dollars in losses ensued with bankruptcies for thousands of firms, high unemployment, a sharp decline in living standards for millions was accompanied by fire sale acquisition of Asian assets by Western firms. At the talks on dealing with the consequences of this crises, the normally diplomatic Japanese representative was so incensed by the American role in the episode that she openly called it "evil." One speculative bubble after another burst in the Western world, leaving hundreds of billions in losses for pension funds and municipal authorities. Large companies went under. People lost life savings, houses, and jobs by the tens of millions and were additionally saddled with huge debt.

Extreme inequality typifies modern capitalism. While most people live in destitution, a few maintain a fabulous existence. According to *Forbes*, there were 1125 dollar-billionaires in the world in 2008 with total assets amounting to $4.4 trillion. Based on the figures from the year 2008 in this magazine, we estimate that there are roughly 10,000 super rich and very rich people (with at least $100 million) on the planet, with their total worth around $10 trillion. They sit at the apex of the system.

In contrast, in 2007, about two billion people had income below $2 a day, and a billion had income below $1 a day. Taking the average value of the assets of the people at the bottom as $1000 per person (an optimistic figure), the total assets of 10 billion such people would amount to $10 trillion. One person at the top then equals 1,000,000 people at the bottom. This is what liberty, equality and justice under capitalism means. And, this is not a play of numbers; life at the ground level is a life of persistent toil, hunger, disease and misery. In 2008, for the first time ever, more than a billion people were afflicted by chronic hunger. On the other hand, money buys power, influence, standing and voice in governance. Such extreme inequalities convert democracy into a caricature, a front for the rule of the rich, by the rich and for the rich. This is nowhere more apparent than in the United States where the major corporations exercise such an enormous influence on all branches of the government and the political process that they can stifle even minimal moves to protect the interests of the ordinary people, or initiate minor moves to deal with global issues like climate change.

Consider India. In the 2000s, the economy grew at 6 to 8% per year and by 2007, it led the Asian nations in terms of billionaires. Yet the rates of malnutrition in some states were rising. A public nutritional support and health care program for the poor failed to make a major dent in malnutrition among the children. Food and aid are channeled into the black market by shoddy businessmen and their political cronies. India is thereby also at the top among the nations in the level of poverty and poor nutrition among children. Some states have malnutrition rates worse than that in Africa. In 2007, India had 36 dollar-billionaires and 300 million citizens living on less than $1 a day.

This scenario of extreme inequality and mass poverty exists, in varied forms, across the Third World, and quite acutely in Africa. In the rich capitalist nations like the USA, fabulous wealth also exists side by side with real desperation. While the Wall Street moguls move about in private jets and live in sumptuous villas, the twin maladies of homelessness and hunger are growing in US cities. Almost a fifth of the American children, for example, required governmental food assistance in 2009, and the rate appears to be on the upswing.[1]

Imperialism Today

Bourgeois ideologues claimed that the fall of the Soviet Union would usher in an era of global peace. That did not happen. Indeed, it could not happen, as imperialism is an inextricable facet of capitalism. There are five key reasons why the so-called peace dividend was an illusory expectation. First, military production and research, and funding for the armed forces and related industries have been, since the second world war, an integral, stable and dominant part of the US economy that provide profits to capital and well-paid employment to the people. Two, the military sector is integrated with the high technology sector, be it in computers, communication, space exploration, nano-technology, molecular biology or health research. Three, the giant multinationals that scour the globe, exploit local peoples, set up branches and economic activities in far flung places, need a strong man of last resort to come to their rescue. Four, the main American, European and Japanese capitalists need to protect their turf from each other and counter the rise and influence of new capitalist powers. Five, the US seeks decisive control of global energy, mineral and other strategic resources. These factors have led the US to maintain and control a complex web of military bases, arms exports, supplies, military training and equipment for client regimes across the globe, and institute a military support system for subsidiary powers in which it retains the final decisive say.

Instead of disarming and striving for global peace, US imperialism therefore literally ran amok once the socialist camp was in ruins. And

---

1   Among the sources depicting the various facets of the global economy, see Beaud (2001), Bello, Cunnigham and Rau (1999), Domhoff (2009), Editorial (1999), Hofman (1998), Irwin, Kim, Gershman and Millen (2002), Klein (2008), Korten (1995), Meier (1999), Sharife (2009a) and Torrie (1986). The figures on India are from BBC (2007), Wilson (2010), and *Forbes Magazine (www.forbes.com)*.

after initial hesitation, the NATO allies scurried in the foot steps of the big brother. By now, the Western economies and governments are addicted to the production for war and waging war, and even their citizens have been conditioned to consider that a normal state of affairs. Economists open-minded enough to acknowledge this despicable state of affairs politely call it military Keynesianism (Cypher 2007; Garrett-Peltier 2010). In plain terms, the fact of the giant military machine signifies a permanent need to foment conflict and fight wars to justify its existence.

In the earlier era, enemies that did not exist were invented and confronted. In 1986, Ronald Reagan declared the tiny island of Grenada, a threat to the national security of the US, claiming that it was building an air base for Soviet fighter jets. The marines were sent in to take control. Soon all claims associated with this invasion were exposed as outright lies. The civilian airport was being expanded to facilitate tourist flights with Western companies involved in the project. He branded liberated Nicaragua also a threat to US security, and armed a terrorist organization, the Contras, who killed teachers, health care workers and civilians to destabilize the new government. He labeled the Renamo brigands conducting wholesale atrocities in Mozambique as valiant Christian freedom fighters confronting the evil communists. Death squad regimes across Central and South America were armed and unleashed onto the ordinary people, all in the name of fighting communism.

The elder George Bush continued the tradition, invading Panama after blithely declaring its president, Manuel Noriega, a drug lord. The real goal was to retain control over the Panama Canal. He invaded Somalia and unleashed a war in Iraq whose real aim was to destroy the major civilian infrastructure and decimate a modern nation.

Bill Clinton continued the US military rampage in Somalia, killing thousands of innocent civilians. As the genocide in Rwanda unfolded, and the whole world saw rivers of blood flowing and corpses piling up for a hundred days, his administration and France firmly blocked an international intervention until it was too late. And when they did intervene, it was to protect the fleeing genocidal forces. In Bosnia, the US sat on the sidelines for too long, and then armed Croatian militias that conducted wholesale ethnic cleansing of the Serbs. Clinton is credited with protecting the people of Kosovo. Yet, the mass retaliation against, and exodus of the Kosovars began only after the NATO bombing started. Worst atrocities were going on East Timor and Sierra Leone at the same time. In the former, the US was complicit and in the latter, it chose to virtually do nothing. Clinton also gave extensive military assistance to Turkey in its vicious campaign against the Kurdish population that killed tens of thousands of villagers, displaced about two million and institutionalized an Apartheid-like treatment of the Kurdish people. And for eight years, his government brought out deception upon deception to fool the world that Iraq was hiding weapons of mass destruction and used them as excuses to continue harsh economic sanctions that led to the death of over half a million Iraqis. At the end of 1998, he mounted a torrential four day bombing of Iraq that included willful destruction of grain silos. He went on with almost continuous weekly bombing of Iraqi targets in the last two years of his presidency. Civilian facilities like veterinary stations were conveniently called potential biological weapons sites and bombed. At the end, the US pilots were complaining that they had run out of targets. It was a merciless and completely unjustified campaign to terrorize the people of Iraq.

The same lies were magnified under cowboy Bush. Colin Powell, his Secretary of State confidently stood with elaborate charts before the UN Security Council and presented a bogus case that Iraq had weapons of mass destruction. It was but an excuse to wage total war, decimate Iraq, cause the death of hundreds of thousands, turn about four million people into refugees, install a puppet government, and set up permanent military bases. Over two decades, the US has systematically reduced Iraq into a Western dependency in which chaos, violence, and poverty reign supreme. The control of Iraqi oil, and the Middle East, was the prize they sought and gained.

The US and its European allies now gang up on the people of Afghanistan and Pakistan in a so-called war on terror that is an excuse to fight meaningless wars abroad and institute a police state at home. Their own citizens cannot comprehend the rationale for these wars. It is a joke to say that the rag-tag Taliban poses a threat to the West. As in the past, war crimes and mass brutalities are acceptable as long as they are inflicted on people in distant lands. Iran is the next target on their list.

The international stand of the Western nations, in the economic, political and military arenas is rife with hypocrisy, double standards and outright deception. Thus the peace process in Palestine means total alienation of the land of the Palestinian people. When Israel mercilessly bombs Lebanon and Gaza, destroying thousands of lives and the entire civilian infrastructure, when it imposes a cruel blockade that restricts school supplies to the children of Gaza, they only murmur a small dissent. When their favorite dictator or president (as in Ethiopia, Egypt or Nigeria) steals elections, kills civilians, and grossly misbehaves, they are silent. When Mugabe attacks the opposition, they shout till they are hoarse. Lies, obfuscations and atrocities of the same sort continue under Mr. Obama who is a warmonger in the same imperial tradition, who prepares for war on Iran, expands drone-based illegal assassinations in Afghanistan, Pakistan, Yemen, and Somalia. He has taken initial steps to expand the US military involvement in Latin America to show the upstart governments of Venezuela, Bolivia and others in the region who is the boss. Overall, his administration continues to pursue the strategic goals of the US which are to encircle China, intimidate Russia, preserve the dollar as the global reserve currency, especially for the trade in energy, control global resources and major trade routes, and maintain undisputed planetary political and military hegemony.

Accordingly, the US almost outspends the rest of the world in the machinery for war and national security. After adjusting for inflation, the current declared US military expenditure is one-third higher than at any point after World War II (Barry 2010; Freidman and Preble 2010). Its armed forces patrol all corners of the earth, on ground and sea, underwater, and high in the skies.

> Officially, the Pentagon counts 865 [external] base sites, but this notoriously unreliable number omits all our bases in Iraq (likely over 100) and Afghanistan (60 and counting) among the other many well known and secretive bases. Vine (2010).

The US also leads the world in terms of arms exports and conducts global operations in brazen disregard for law or morality. Practicing torture, detaining people for years without trial, international kidnappings and renditions, assassinating suspects and civilians, deploying unaccountable mercenary forces, bombing civilians and civilian facilities, collective punishment, long distance murder are normal and acceptable standards of conduct even under Mr. Obama. The modern face of US imperialism is as brutal as it was during the aggression on Vietnam. In his time, Dr. Martin Luther King call America "the greatest purveyor of violence in the world." It continues to hold that record to this day.[2]

---

2   An overview of modern day imperialism is provided by Alterman (2004), Arnove (2000), Bennis and Childers (2000), Chomsky (1992a; 1992b; 1993), Foster (2006), Gabelnick (1999), Glassner (1999), Hartung (1995), Hossein-zadeh (2007), Johnson (2004a; 2004b; 2008), Madsen (1999), Mandel (2004), Nagy (2001), Parenti (1999), Perkins (2005), Tirman (1997) and Zinn (1990).

Neo-colonialism Today

The superficiality of capitalist globalization has nowhere been more evident than in Africa whose nations had no alternative but to bow down to the economic dictates of the West. At first, their economies showed signs of growth (but without development). Construction boom in the cities, expansion of the oil extraction, mining, tourism and services, the flow of "donor" funds in health and education, the growth of cell phone and computer usage, the expansion of old and new primary export products, and some local manufacturing combined with the inflow of imported commodities made it feel that a new life was afoot. A prosperous middle class (comprador petty bourgeoisie) consisting of professionals, consultants, business people, merchants, wealthy farmers, and state officials emulating the Western lifestyle grew fast, though its size in relation to the population was quite limited.

At the same time, African natural mineral and energy resources were plundered rapidly. Its cities and scenic areas became playgrounds for tourists reliant on exploited labor. Its local industries were bankrupted by cheap imports, and state assets were auctioned off to foreign firms for a pittance. The tiny social safety net was destroyed by privatization while unemployment, crime and crowded ghettos mushroomed. Rural living standards declined or stagnated while farmers and herders saw their lands being seized by foreign and local investors. African nations today are, without exception, effective neo-colonies under the yoke of the international capitalist system. Let us give two outstanding examples to illustrate the nature of this domination, Egypt and Angola.

Egypt under Hosni Mubarak is a prominent modern African neo-colony. An autocrat nurtured by the West for three decades, Mubarak presides over an all encompassing police state that keeps the population of 82 million under leash by deploying 2 million informers. State security personnel pervade universities and areas where opponents have large following. 17,000 political prisoners languish in jails, many have been there for years and years without any trial or after a summary, secretive military trial. Torture is commonplace. Symbolic elections that are marked by extensive vote rigging and intimidation of opponents attract barely a quarter of the eligible voters.

Yet, Mubarak has been treated by the West as a respectable statesman. He garnered extensive praise from the IMF for liberalizing the economy and the impressive levels of growth. As he deleted all mention of socialism in the constitution, Western and Israeli firms entered Egypt in droves. Foreign direct investment in 2006 stood at $6 billion. But the benefits accrue mostly to a tiny fabulously wealthy business class, the military brass, and the Mubarak family. While Egypt boasts one of Africa's handful of dollar-billionaires, a quarter of the working-age people are unemployed. Despite the fertile Nile basin, it depends on imports for a large portion of the food it consumes. The living standards of ordinary people remain unchanged. The high rate of inflation has affected the lifestyles of the professional stratum as well. Two years ago, food riots broke out when the government announced price increases for staple commodities.

The US has given over $1.5 billion annually to Egypt in so-called foreign aid for three decades. Much of this money is recycled to purchase arms and sophisticated weapons systems. Despite the peace treaty with Israel, Egypt has about half a million people in the armed forces, and large numbers of battle tanks, aircraft, missile batteries, and battle ships, and is slated to receive 24 advanced F-16 fighter planes from the US worth more than $2 billion dollars. Like the Shah of Iran in 1970, Egypt under Mubarak today is a key partner of Israel and the US in the oppression of the people of Palestine, and the promotion of the US foreign policy goals in the region.[3]

Angola exemplifies another modern day neo-colony. It attained freedom from medieval Portuguese colonial rule in 1975. While Apartheid South Africa and the US had backed the colonizer, Cuba and the USSR had assisted the anti-colonial forces. Even after 1975, the US continued to arm and fund UNITA, a terrorist group that destabilized the nation. Only in the past decade has egregious violence been absent from the lives of the Angolan people.

In this decade, the economy grew annually by more than 10%, the highest growth rate in sub-Saharan Africa. Vast expansion in oil production and mining were the primary factors behind that growth. Thus, by 2009, Angola produced nearly 2 million barrels of oil per day, edging out Nigeria as Africa's largest oil producer. Earnings from oil that year were nearly $16 billion, accounting for 90% of the export revenues. Despite all this new wealth and notwithstanding their immense suffering over many decades, the people of Angola have yet to reap any real benefits.

The economic activity in Angola is dominated and controlled by multi-national firms and banks from Europe, Britain, the USA, China, Brazil and other nations that have set up joint ventures with the major

---

3   For a general picture of Egypt under Mubarak consult, Margolis (2010), Sharife (2010) and Shatz (2010). See also Wikipedia (www.wikipedia.com) under topic Egypt.

state oil company, the elite in MPLA (the ruling party), the army and state bureaucracy. MPLA has more than 60 business ventures in tourism, finance, construction, media, fisheries, and commercial and rental property. It runs joint ventures with British, Portuguese and French companies in aviation, hotels, banking, breweries and other sectors. American firms operate in agriculture, and Scandinavian enterprises are in the automotive business. Norway has a substantial presence in the oil sector. Portuguese firms have partnered with the local elite to capture the multi-million dollar beverage and drinks market. British mining companies have joined state firms and high-ranking military brass to evict people from their land so as to expand diamond mines. Western banks are also involved in shadowy transactions relating to the national oil revenues. Chinese companies have also made major inroads in Angola. And, to ward off an IMF economic package, China gave a multi-billion dollar economy stabilization loan to Angola and has secured major oil supply contracts.

The US maintains good military ties with Angola, through naval visits, training programs and arms supplies, and USAID has an influential presence many sectors. Angola and Nigeria now account for nearly 20% of US crude oil imports, and that figure is expected to rise.

The Angolan economy is rife with under-the-table pillage, patronage and international corruption. External investors work hand in hand with party and government officials in ways that violate basic tenets of morality, explicit state laws and rights of the people. Capitalism has admittedly run wild. Scandals exposed in the newspapers and even court rulings are disregarded when they affect the rich and powerful. President dos Santos, in power for three decades, continues to preach the gospel of fairness, good governance, rule of law, and democracy. But, as deciphered by an Angolan activist, those words carry distinctive meanings:

The concept of social solidarity and equal opportunity applies only
to select members of the ruling elite who have been given the task
of looting the country. Marques (2010)

While the elite wallow in extreme luxury and foreign investors secure bountiful returns, two-thirds of the people live in utter poverty, earning less than 2 dollars a day. Life expectancy hovers around 44 years, and malnutrition and preventable or easily curable diseases exact an unacceptable toll in this rich nation, a smaller portion of the national budget is earmarked for education and health as compared to many other Sub-Saharan African nations.[4]

* * * * *

Such is the essential story of all African nations -- Chad or Malawi, Kenya or Tanzania, Nigeria or South Africa. A tiny local business and political class (comprador bourgeoisie) holds effective state power and sells out the national resources and state property to multinational firms and capitalists for a pittance. Some nations maintain a facade of democracy while others practice outright repression. Economic brutalization by the West has now been joined by China, India, Brazil, Korea and others. It perpetuates long-term poverty, misery and dependency, and produces one social catastrophe after another. Civil strife ensues. Nations become more divided along ethnic, regional, racial and religious lines. The West complains of corruption and lack of democracy. But they and their multinational firms keep the authoritarian corrupt leaders in power by joint ventures, military and police training, arms supplies, so-called foreign aid, and general diplomatic support. The Obama administration has budgeted over US $80 million for security assistance, arms sales and anti-terrorism programs for Africa. This is the tip of the iceberg, as it does not count the funds used under other programs, and military assistance from Europe.[5] In the long run, such assistance props up the authoritarian and pro-Western regimes in Africa.

AFRICOM, the new US military command for Africa, has been designated as the key pillar of neo-colonialism and US hegemony over the continent in the years to come. Begun under the previous administration, it is being implemented in earnest by Mr. Obama. AFRICOM formalizes and integrates military ties with African governments that have blossomed over the past two decades. The deceptive banners of fighting terrorism, humanitarian relief support, and peace-keeping are used to institute a comprehensive mechanism to keep the people and resources of Africa under Western control. While the initial attempts to build a series of large bases across Africa did not succeed, ties with local military forces have expanded through joint military exercises, weapon supplies, training of military and police officers, computerization and

---

4   More details on Angola are in Marques (2006; 2008; 2010a; 2010b), Sharife (2009b) and Reuters (2009).

5   To understand neo-colonialism, consult Bello and Kinley (1986), Chomsky and Herman (1979), Des Forges (1999), Gumede (2010), Hancock (1989), Madsen (1999), Magdoff (2003) and Nkrumah (1966). Bello (2010) gives a critical analysis of corruption.

surveillance assistance, and funds for importing armaments. The US military now has access to air bases, ports, base camps and operational sites across Africa; senior commanders pay frequent visits to African nations; and American navy ships continually patrol the coast line of Africa. By the end of 2009, the US had entered into formal military partnership of one form or another with 35 of Africa's 53 nations.

These efforts also involve NATO and European military forces. Together with the US, they are setting up the African Standby Force by funding, training, and providing equipment. This rapid intervention force will be under the effective control of outsiders. The ruling classes of Africa will have some say, but it will not be under true democratic control of the people of Africa. American special forces and air force carry out aggressive operations in Somalia and other parts of Africa. The CIA abducts suspects without regard for international law. These activities are kept from the public eye for a good reason, as Rick Rozoff explains.

> *The US is not dragging almost every nation in Africa into its military network because of altruism or concerns for the security of the continent's people. AFRICOM's function is that of every predatory military power: The threat and use of armed violence to gain economic and geopolitical advantages. Rozoff (2010).*

These developments follow the trajectory that was pursued by the US in Latin America during the second half of the last century. Military and police assistance was given in the name of promoting development and peace, and fighting extremism, communism and drug trafficking. In reality, it promoted US interests and armed death squad regimes that committed horrible atrocities, and undercut efforts to promote equitable economic development. The US armed thugs and dictators in Africa during that time, a practice that has not abated. With AFRICOM, the stage is set for US dominated militarization of Africa to be expanded and institutionalized on a grander scale.[6]

Moribund Capitalism
Nevertheless, despite and because of its rapacity, the era of globally dominant Western capitalism is drawing to a close. The global financial crisis of 2008 and 2009 exposed its major weak points. Veritable economic giants -- banks, investment houses, insurance firms, mortgage lenders, automobile manufacturers, construction firms, large retailers

---

6   Details on AFRICOM can be had from Karang (2010), Nani-Kofi (2010), Rozoff (2010), Schmidt (2010), Vandiver (2009) and Volman (2010).

in America and Europe -- faced or declared bankruptcy. Millions lost
houses and jobs; tens of thousands of small firms sank. Whole nations,
like Iceland, Greece, Portugal, Spain and even the UK face the prospect
of total or near bankruptcy. The system has been saved for now by
massive printing of money and transfer of corporate debt to the public
sphere. This has only put off the cataclysmic crisis to a later day. The
financial bourgeoisie has been saved but private and public debt remain
at levels that threaten the entire global economy.[7]

Uncontrolled, corporate driven, carbon-economy based economic
expansion for two hundred years under capitalism has presented
humanity with the prospects of catastrophic and irreversible climate
change. Most scientists expect that the accumulation of carbon dioxide
in the atmosphere to increase average global temperature, intensify
floods, droughts, hurricanes and extreme weather, create greater food,
water and energy crises, produce or intensify epidemic outbreaks and
generate social chaos. With most of humanity entangled in dire poverty,
disease and misery, future prospects are bleaker. Yet, corporate-funded
think tanks deny the urgency. Led by American politicians, they block
even minimal steps to confront it. Scientists have produced volumes of
material on building alternative energy-based economies. But concerted
global action to move in that direction is stymied as long as profit
maximization is the name of the game. If oil and auto companies oppose
rational action on climate change, Western governments follow suit; if
pharmaceutical giants stand against reorganization of health systems to
deal with health problems, public institutions toe the line; and so on.
Corporate power holds sway on the social agenda and prevents valid
ideas to confront major human problems from even being brought into
the limelight, let alone being implemented.[8]

The failure to provide adequate food -- a vital, indispensable human
need -- signifies, more than anything, the utter failure and irrelevance
of the global capitalist system. While their prevalence varies by year and
place, chronic hunger and malnutrition remain major problems affecting
people in the poor nations. In 1960, Africa was mostly self-sufficient in
food supply; today, most of its nations critically depend on food imports.

---

7   Insider accounts of the recent global financial crisis are in Arvedlund (2009),
Lowenstein (2010), Patterson (2010) and Spencer (2009). Albo, Gindin and Panitch
(2010) give a general analysis is provided though they do not pay due attention to the
role of militarization and super exploitation of the Third World peoples.

8   The science of climate change is well-explained in Archer and Rahmstoff (2010)
and Hansen (2009) while the politics behind the issue are described in Athanasiou
and Baer (2002), Berger (2000) and Oreskes and Conway (2010).

[In 2008], the number of hungry people world wide increased by 15%
to over 1 billion while U.S. food insecurity increased by 13% with
nearly 50 million people without enough food. Food First (2009).

Narrow minded experts point to lack of rainfall, poor technology, population growth and similar causes. But they do not attend to the underlying systemic cause which is that state power in poor nations is held by corrupt elite classes that work hand in hand with multinational firms to loot the nation. That is the crux of the problem. Despite recent population growth, the issue is not one of absolute scarcity of food. Sufficient food is produced world wide, and often within regions and nations as well, to adequately feed and nourish everyone. A lot of that food, however, is wasted or thrown away. Food is not distributed efficiently or is not available at affordable prices. Farm investments are driven by profit considerations. The global trade in agricultural products, and supply of farm inputs are controlled by a few giant firms. Corporate and individual farmers in rich nations receive state subsidies but those in poor nations are denied such protection under the rules imposed by the rich nations. Third World farmers have no alternative but to plant export crops whose unreliable and paltry returns barely enable them to survive. Most of the surplus revenue that remains in the poor nations is appropriated by middle men. Under this market driven scenario, simple intermediate technology-based actions and social arrangements that can effectively increase food supply and equitably distribute it cannot be broadly and consistently implemented.

When some nations face persistent drought and famine, donations by capitalist nation alleviate the immediate problem to a degree. But at the same time, the measures that follow make poor countries more dependent on external food supplies. A tragedy thus becomes an opportunity for market penetration and the international relief operations themselves generate huge profits for the corporate sector in the West. Further, a huge "aid" bureaucracy that has arisen over the years seeks to perpetuate itself and lacks the interest and ability to pursue paths that would make hungry nations self-sufficient and independent.

The recent years have seen a growing acreage of land in the Third World being diverted to produce bio-fuel crops, feed for livestock to be slaughtered for export, flowers for export, pesticide-free food for export, and so on. The end product serves foreign tourists, local elite and Western consumers while the process drives up the prices of basic foods for the local population and augments food insecurity.

The root cause of this insecurity is the food system itself, which is controlled by a handful of global monopolies. In fact, the crises comes at a time of record global profits for the world's agri-food corporations. Archer Daniel Midland, Cargill, Monsanto, General Foods, and Wal-Mart all posted profit increases in 2008 of 20% to 80%. For Mosaic, a fertilizer subsidiary of Cargill, profits increased by a stunning 1200%.Huebner (2010).

The entry of international financial speculators into the arena magnifies food insecurity. Seizure of lands owned by rural communities by local and external investors adds to the problem. Often, lands are seized for building tourist resorts, develop mining, build dams, and often, the purpose is to export food and energy for external markets. Often such evictions are conducted by the use of police forces, or other means of dubious legality.

International agribusinesses, investment banks, hedge funds, commodity traders, sovereign wealth funds, UK pension funds, foundations and individuals have been snapping up some of the world's cheapest land, in Sudan, Kenya, Nigeria, Tanzania, Malawi, Ethiopia, Congo, Zambia, Uganda, Madagascar, Zimbabwe, Mali, Sierra Leone, Ghana and elsewhere. Ethiopia alone has approved 815 foreign-financed agricultural projects since 2007. Any land investors can't buy is leased for about $1 per year per hectare. Ho (2010).

The paradox of capitalism is that the one billion chronically hungry on the planet are accompanied by an almost equal number of people who consume excess calories and are overweight. Foods and drinks with excess amounts sugar, refined carbohydrates, fat and salt pervade the shops and eating places in all nations, rich and poor. The highly processed and packaged foods are cheaper but lack essential nutrients for a balanced diet. They contribute to the growing incidence of diabetes, hypertension, heart disease, stroke, cancer and other maladies, especially in the urban areas of poor nations and the poor communities in rich nations. The extensive commercialization of the food sector, presence and influence of corporate food brands from the advanced capitalist nations, failure of governments to educate people about nutrition or regulate the food sector are the foundational causes of the problem. The lack of clean and sufficient water supplies for a significant portion of humanity is another indicator of the failure of the capitalist system.[9]

Two Choices

Almost all the governments of today are controlled by and responsive to the interests of local and international capitalists. The global media also essentially serve the same interests. Citizens everywhere are kept uninformed as to the real goings on in the inner sanctums of their national and global affairs. Democracy exists in name only. This is the principal obstacle to applying common sense, locally devised and simple solutions for resolution of food, water and other problems facing the common man today. Yes, the right type of technology, appropriate distributional and storage mechanisms, extensive public education, mechanisms to generate motivation and enthusiasm for public service and efficient administrative systems are also required. But these cannot be instituted widely and in a sustainable fashion until and unless a government that is under the control the common people and is dedicated to their interests exists. That is the basic prerequisite to human progress. So long as the power of the state and control of the major economic institutions are in the hands of the wealthy few and large corporations, everything else is simple daydreaming.

Capitalism is a failed system; that is crystal clear. It no longer possesses the vitality that made Karl Marx extol it as a historically progressive system. Today, humanity faces two choices. One leads to fascism, the marriage of corporate power with the imperial state. This will herald more wars, global unrest, collapse of the environment sustaining life on the planet, and untold suffering for the vast majority. This marriage in the West will lead to fascism; in the Third World, it will produce dictatorships. Signs of that trend are more evident now. Xenophobia and targeting of minorities is thus rampant across the globe. Europeans and Americans nowadays think all their problems stem from illegal immigration. The misery of existence in Africa is a fertile ground for the mushrooming of divisive, vicious and violent political tendencies

9   For illuminating accounts of the food problems around the world, see Baxter (2010), BBC (2007), Bethell (1993), Danaher and Riak (1995), Food First (2009), Ho (2010), Holt-Gimenez and Patel (2009), Huebner (2010), Nestle (2007), Patel (2003; 2007; 2008), Patel and Delwiche (2002), Schlosser (2005) and Shiva (2000). On the global water situation, see Barlow (2009).

without redeeming features. People resort to blind force; kill one another, rob their neighbors. Muslims take Christians as their enemies and vice versa. One ethnic group is pitted against the next. Black South Africans murder fellow Africans. Yet, underlying that is the total failure of the capitalist system to improve the lives of the majority, despite the massive wealth extracted from the African soil and labor.

The other choice is socialism which can lead to global justice, equality, harmony and collective effort to resolve national and international problems in a sustainable and equitable way. Instead of fighting for resources, land or water, people can share them. Instead of building bombs and burning fossil fuel, they can deploy sustainable, clean energy to ensure that all have sufficient food, clothing, shelter, water and good health care. Giant profit driven corporations must be dismantled and substituted by small scale local enterprises based on the cooperative way of life. Profit maximization has to be replaced by planning for human need and promoting long term sustainability as the driving forces of the economy.

However, there is no single, uniform, pre-ordained path to socialism. There is no simple solution valid for all places and nations. Each place has its own peculiarities. Minor conflicts along the way cannot be ruled out. Each nation has the right to determine its own destiny, or join a union of nations. Corporate power and the rule of the rich, however, have to be banished – that much is clear. That future can emerge only if the common people begin to take their destiny into their own hands, and come out into the streets to seize power from the parasitic and exploitative ruling classes. A new dawn for a democratic but uncompromising form of socialism looms on the horizon. Will humanity head that way or not? That is the question.

14

Socialism Tomorrow

Karim F Hirji

"There are times when you have no choice but to know. You
know even if you don't want to. You're on one side or another.
There is no alternative: pick your side."
- Claudia Pineiro -

Introduction

After getting an intimate glimpse into radical student activism at UDSM after the Arusha Declaration in this book, it is natural to wonder whether or not the ideals and theories of that era are relevant today? How do we judge the student activism of that time? Such issues have been partially dealt with in several previous chapters. In this chapter, I look at them in a systematic manner. Judging oneself always carries the risk of bias. I nonetheless venture in that direction as it also allows me to present an overall perspective. As I undertake this task, I urge the reader to judge my judgments.

The relevance of the ideas and activism of the past stems from the documentation in Chapter 13 that African peoples continue to be plundered and oppressed by capitalism and imperialism. The concrete manifestations and some basic features of these systems have no doubt changed. The ideas and activism of the past must therefore be critically examined to adapt them to the current circumstances. Below I focus on evaluation of our activism. Apart from a hint or two, I leave the issue of developing new ideas, visions and methods of struggle for a just society to the new generation of activists, principally because I am sorely unqualified to do so.

To summarize, the positive aspects of our activism lay in the moral values that impelled us, our dedication, the spirit of self-reliance, the scientific rigor we strove to attain for socio-historic analysis, the integrated world outlook we desired to attain, the scope of our reading outside the classroom, our extensive internal discussions and debate, projects like *shamba* work, adult education and stays in rural areas, and the debates and seminars on national issues we initiated in schools, at the Hill, and in the mass media. The publication of a radical socialist magazine was the centerpiece of these endeavors.

Our ideas and acts were infused with many grave deficiencies. We formed some opinions without due empirical investigation. Our formulations were often rigid and dull. Our attitudes now and then bordered on intellectual arrogance; we dismissed other views without sufficient scrutiny. In practice, we did not adequately pay attention to building broad coalitions. The tendency to supplant political and practical work with mental endeavors led over time to a gradual but marked reduction of contact with the masses in rural and urban areas. We progressively became less organized and disciplined, and more immersed into a petty bourgeois mode of life. In our personal lives, many among us strove to attain the best of both worlds. Above all, we did not invest the required will and energy into developing a mass-based, independent socialist movement.

Strengths

What I cherish foremost is the spirit that drove our activism. We were impelled by love for humanity. We felt profound sadness when we came across children in rags, or read about the millions imprisoned by poverty. Humanity for us was a single family. This was also reflected in who we were. Our ethnic, racial, class, religious, and linguistic backgrounds varied. Nevertheless, we formed close and enduring ties, sharing many things in our personal lives as well. Additionally, we were wedded to the ethic of personal integrity and respect for the truth. Not that we perfectly embodied these characteristics. Far from it. Standing at the foot of a steep hill, we but took initial steps towards the summit. Despite our faults, our journey was guided by socially responsible values, and not by petty personal goals.

These pillars of our outlook led us to pursue critical thinking that was applied without fear or favor. Our aim was to understand the nature of social reality, to learn how it had come to be, and use that knowledge for the benefit of Tanzania, Africa and humanity. In that spirit, we said we were scientific socialists. A scientific approach to history and society did not, for us, imply anything esoteric or abstruse. As Walter Rodney cogently expressed it:

> Simple honesty is a vital ingredient in Scientific Socialism
> -- honesty in the cause of man, the worker, and devotion to his
> emancipation. Rodney (1972b).

The bourgeois depiction of history and society imparted in education and the media was distorted and incomplete. It was not an honest rendition of the reality. We sought to transcended it and learn from alternative sources that had been hidden from us. Such an endeavor cannot stop at checking facts and events. It also needs to formulate broad ideas and construct theories. This is what science does, as has been aptly noted in a recent work concerning the natural sciences:

> Science amounts to simplifying the mental image we have of the
> world, allowing us to rationally interpret our environment and
> decide upon our actions. Bais (2010), page 20.

To obtain a scientific vision of reality, we read Fanon, Marx, Lenin, Mao, Che Guevara and others because of their major contributions to human emancipation and the struggle for socialism. We supplemented that with works of bourgeois and radical scholars. We gathered information about what was happening in the nation, Africa and the world. Of the key lessons we learned from these endeavors are (i) labor is the source of all wealth; (ii) modern society is divided into classes, (iii) history has been driven by class struggles, (iv) the present day economic and political system is controlled by a few capitalists and imperialists; (v) experiences gained from attempts to build socialism elsewhere were vital for building socialism in Africa, (vi) when their energies are collectively harnessed, the masses can push in momentous changes, and (vii) a successful struggle has to be guided by a valid theory. In our youthful naiveté, we at times parroted the prominent radicals of the past. Still, we were not limited by what they or others had written or done. Physicists recognize the monumental role played by Isaac Newton in uncovering the basic laws of nature. But today, while they continue to value the foundation he laid, they also acknowledge his limitations. That was our spirit as we strove to understand the social reality.

We devoured books by the dozen, discussed issues from dawn to midnight, and critiqued the bourgeois approach. Our goal was to arrive at a consistent theory based on a sound factual foundation that would serve as a guide to our actions. Again, that is not to say that we succeeded as well as we should have. Our ideas were deficient in many aspects; what we wrote had crucial limitations. Yet, these were genuine, honest attempts to improve our knowledge and understanding of the dynamics of society.

Now I can see that we profoundly underestimated the brutal tenacity and technological dynamism of modern capitalism. We did not appreciate the long term nature of the struggle to build socialism, and the profoundly deleterious influence of bourgeois culture and mass media on human behavior. At the same time, I see that we came to adopt a set of sound propositions that remain crucial for human emancipation to this day. I elaborate on these later. Another aspect of our scientific approach was the continual drive to question and improve our theories and ideas.

Mwalimu Nyerere said that if Marx had been born in Sumbawanga, he would have drafted the Arusha Declaration. We disagreed with that proposition. It was too simplistic. There is no doubt that our world outlook is molded by our social surroundings in a major way. But we can also transcend such a limitation. A thinker is revolutionary to the extent that he or she critically absorbs the visions and ideas of the time, and then formulates more profound theories. Accordingly, Marx would have applied his critical logic even from Sumbawanga. Because it espoused noble sentiments without taking adequate stock of competing social forces, because it failed to learn from the history of socialism, and because it relied on a petty-bourgeois political party to implement it, he would have called the Arusha Declaration, a version of utopian socialism. If Isaac Newton had been born in Sumbawanga, I think he would have been led to the same laws of physics.

An ingrained spirit of self-reliance was an integral facet of our activism. We had no room for dependency in any form, intellectual or otherwise. It seems that we took Mwalimu's call for self-reliance more seriously than he did. This spirit boosted our confidence in our own abilities. Especially in the social sciences, we often read and knew more than our lecturers, and did not hesitate to challenge them when it was called for. These were empirically-rooted and conceptually consistent challenges, not expressions of opposition for the sake of it. Members of USARF and TYL wrote long papers on restructuring the study programs and curricula at UDSM. Such work was done without any external funding, purely in our own time, and out of our own initiative. Imagine the current crop of students doing anything similar. Even the academic staff today disdain from undertaking simple projects on their own accord unless a financial inducement is attached!

Several facets of the educational and social environment helped us. Depth of inquiry and rigorous thought were valued. To give an example, each subject was studied for a whole year. Only the final examinations in the first and third year of undergraduate study counted for the award of the degree. This gave one an opportunity to return to the same topic months later, review it more deeply, and understand it better. High standards were maintained in most subjects, whether it was law or physics, botany or sociology. One was not all the time under the pressure of tests. That opportunity for extra-curricular reading and inquiry allowed us to broaden our knowledge and outlook. In contrast, at present the academic fields are modularized, quickly and superficially taught over a short time span, examined, and instantly forgotten.

To tackle the pitfall of over specialization, compulsory subjects like Development Studies and East African Society and Environment were offered. They balanced depth with breadth. The narrow, discipline-based view of society inculcated by traditional education was countered with an integrated societal perspective that also challenged the dominant bourgeois orientation of the social sciences.

Looking back at the rigorous and demanding academic curricula we had to follow, I wonder how we managed to participate in the spectrum of activities described in this book at the same time as taking care of our academic load and do well in the examinations. With dedication, discipline and diligence, it was possible. It is, of course, still possible. Over time these intellectually enriching features of the academic life of yesterday have dissipated. Even Development Studies has now succumbed to the allure of specialization and simplistic quantification. This trend was a global phenomenon associated with the emergence of a socially diversionary and divisive form of capitalism. Many factors, economic, educational and political, contributed to it. One of them was the increased global influence of the American system of education. Also, university education in our days was virtually free. Today, the students, especially those from modest backgrounds, struggle to survive and learn in a more hostile economic environment. That can sap one's spirit, damage one's physical and mental well-being, restrict opportunities for independent learning and contribute to academic under-achievement.

Weaknesses

We desired to serve humanity. But, over time, we lost touch with the lives and struggles of the common man. That was our major blunder. Activists at or from UDSM went on conducting progressive analysis of the African condition. But they effectively set aside Marx's key dictum that the question is not just to interpret the world but also to change it. Theoretical struggles took precedence over real struggles; the basic morality of service and sacrifice that had driven them earlier was compromised. I recall a debate we had in the early Seventies, about whether all comrades should strive for higher degrees in their academic disciplines. A few comrades teaching at the Hill had already done so. The question was whether everyone should strive to do so. The majority answered in the affirmative. In my view, it was not a politically productive step. Promotion of socialist ideas in schools and among the people, and immersion in their struggles -- activities crying out for attention -- were then displaced by endeavors for self-improvement.

Another shortcoming we sadly manifested was cultivation of undue arrogance and lack of tolerance for competing ideas. At the outset, that was a natural reaction to the hostile intellectual and political environment we faced at the Hill and beyond. The radicals were attacked by all sides, by the right-wingers and *Ujamaa* socialists. We were a tiny minority, pilloried by everyone, including the state, TANU and university officials. To survive and thrive in this atmosphere, we had to develop thick skins. Only a high degree of self-confidence enabled us to query and overcome the flawed, prejudiced mental baggage carried over from childhood, question prevailing conventional wisdom, and counter the ideological attacks we faced. I have no apologies for our vigorous response to the right-wing academics and the know-nothing bureaucrats. But I do lament the fact that even when communicating with comrades and the broad mass of students, we at times expressed ourselves in a similar fashion. More learned comrades dismissed or ridiculed the views of those who had read less. Harsh rhetoric alienated potential allies. I also wish our writing style had been simpler and more understandable, though, over time we began to correct such shortcomings.

Yet, it must be noted that here we are not talking about ordinary organized debating clubs where fine rules of decorum prevail. Across the globe, a merciless global attack, led by US imperialism, on all manifestations of socialist ideas was taking place. These attacks were ideological and physical, and included assassination of students, lecturers, trade union leaders and activists across the Third World. For example, hundreds of priests and student leaders were abducted and killed in Central and South America by US-supported regimes because they championed the interests of the peasants. Nothing of that extreme nature transpired in Tanzania, in large measure due to the enlightened leadership of Mwalimu Nyerere. Nevertheless, strong political pressures and hostility against radical socialists and Marxists were an integral and clear part of the politics of Tanzania in that era. We were called all sorts of names, and we often countered with terminology that was pointed and uncompromising.

To give a concrete example, take the case of Dr. Stephen Lucas, earlier mentioned in Chapter 3. An American, lecturer in sociology of education, he was a fine teacher, with a friendly demeanor towards students. Unlike other expatriates, he conversed reasonably well in Swahili. However, his academic approach was quite the traditional one and his lectures invoked superficial concepts like diffusion of innovation. Andre Gunder Frank's perceptive critique of sociology, or Paulo Freire's analysis of education in the Third World had no place in his intellectual repertoire (Frank 1969a; Freire 1970). Other comrades and I disagreed with the ideas he propounded. When he set a question, I would submit a twenty page essay when most students submitted two pages. I would critique his ideas, and propose alternatives. Surprisingly, he gave me high grades, saying that even though he disagreed with what I said, I deserved credit for doing extra research and for backing up what I said. His open-mindedness made me regard him one of my favorite lecturers at the Hill.

Imagine my shock thirty years later when I read an obituary on the website of the Louisiana State University (LSU) in the US with the heading "Head of International Programs, Swahili Instructor and Former CIA Agent Stephen Lucas Passes Away" (Calongne 2006). It painted him as a global traveler, who had taught in Congo, Tanzania, and France and had been with the CIA for fifteen years. He taught "Swahili language, Contemporary Africa, International Studies: Globalization and Regionalization, and Intelligence and Democracy" at LSU and was a member of the African Studies Association and the African Language Teachers Association.

As he had been in the Congo in 1964, I wonder what role he had played in the assassination of Patrice Lumumba and installation of the pro-American dictator Mobutu Sese Seko. Was he keeping tabs on progressive students and staff at UDSM? What kind of reports on USARF and *Cheche* did he submit to the CIA headquarters? Did he compile a list of "dangerous leftists" to be jailed or eliminated after a US-backed military coup, as had been done in other Third World nations like Indonesia? My friend Jonathan Kamala would say to me later on, "Karim, you and I were on a list," and I would dismiss that as paranoia. That could not happen in Tanzania, I would reply. Now I am not sure. The Dr. Lucas I had respected as a liberal teacher turned out to be one of Washington's warriors for whom academic freedom was a cloak to disguise his service to imperial interests. And there were many of them spread across the continents (Saunders 2001). The ties between the US military and security establishment and the US universities are at present as strong as, if not stronger than during the Cold War (Campbell 2010). So I suspect this sort of practice continues to this day but with changed agendas, methods and disguises.

When we spoke harshly about imperialist machinations in those days, we were not unjustified, as this unwitting expose about Dr. Lucas illuminates. We were branded as conspiracy theorists, alarmists or worse. Now that the historical record has been revealed in part, the truth turns out to have been far uglier than what we had thought (Klein 2008; Nagy 2001; Perkins 2005).

* * * * *

To return to our shortcomings: Our alienation from the struggles of the common man and the over occupation with theory climaxed in the late 1970s into what has been called the Dar es Salaam debate. Unlike the engaged, grounded and comradely exchanges of the early days, the campus leftists now hurled unprincipled vitriolic tirades against each other. In formulating a theory for African liberation, one side posited the primacy of international (finance) capital. The other said that internal contradictions were paramount. In a sense, the same key political issue had been debated earlier. But instead of mobilizing against imperialism or the state, each side became the other's main enemy. This debate, based on a false conceptual dichotomy, fomented unneeded discord and went nowhere. If there is one thing that I am quite ashamed of from those days, it is my participation in this charade at a time when we should have been in schools, factories and villages educating people, mobilizing for socialism. We were sucked into the ugly morass which demoralized and alienated many comrades because overall we lacked the courage to face the true nature of the actions that are needed to transform human society and lift the masses out of poverty, imperialist domination and bureaucratic misrule.

After graduation from the university, many comrades became teachers, and continued to educate their students about socialism. There was a degree of cooperation among them and they remained in touch with comrades at the Hill, sharing material like issues of *MajiMaji*. However, this was a short-lived phenomenon and from the late 1970s, genuine socialist activism declined, not only among ourselves but among the youth in Tanzania in general. Blatant official hypocrisy demoralized young minds and was the primary driver of the trend. Another was the fact that radicalism that had begun at the Hill had not evolved into an independent socialist movement. Some youth activists were absorbed into the opportunistic brand of activism under the umbrella of TANU (later CCM). The majority of the comrades of yesterday set aside, in practice if not in words, the ideals they had once stood for. Instead of inspiring the youth by self-sacrifice and persistent struggle, they became senior officials, wealthy tycoons, shrewd lawyers, well-paid consultants, dollar-worshiping academics, and political bosses who now served phony socialism, capitalism, and imperialism. Some joined the system overnight. Some were absorbed into it bit by bit. Some became more efficient oppressors of the people than those whom they had earlier so valiantly criticized. For my part, I spent almost two decades as an academic undertaking intricate statistical research in the heartland of imperialism. Los Angeles is as distinct from Sumbawanga as heaven is from earth. Only a few comrades, like Issa Shivji, consistently and publicly stuck to and promoted anti-imperialist and socialistic tenets.

In Context

The critical appraisal of the erstwhile comrades given above must be viewed in context. We must unequivocally note that the origin of the daunting problems faced by Tanzania in 1990 cannot be laid at the door of the radicals of 1970. The primary responsibility for that disaster twenty years in the making lies with the pseudo-socialist politicians of TANU, senior bureaucrats at all levels of the government, managers of parastatal firms, the army of foreign experts and advisors who inundated Tanzania in those days, the World Bank, the "aid" agencies, and above all, Mwalimu Nyerere. The petty bourgeois leaders directed the economy along the wrong path and managed it in an incompetent and confused way. Of course, internal and external business entities and the imperialist powers took maximum advantage of the situation to chalk up impressive gains. And, over time, they have come to attain the upper hand.

It has become fashionable to say that *Ujamaa* failed because the peasants and workers were opposed to it. That is pure nonsense. Yes, they did turn against it, but only after they witnessed the stark contrast between fine words and heavy-handed, misdirected implementation. The Hill radicals warned about the consequences of making a revolution by half-measures, and raised the possibility of a sordid debacle. Unfortunately, they were later proved to have been on the mark.

Consider, for example, the decline of the quality and scope of education at UDSM under the leadership of Pius Msekwa and Ibrahim Kaduma. These TANU functionaries were hostile to radical academic staff and students. They often blocked contract renewal for expatriate academics that had Marxist or leftist orientation. Local progressive academics were marginalized or pressured to leave the university. Obstacles were placed against radical or independent student activities. Thus, after the departure of Lionel Cliff, the new head of Development studies not only got rid of progressive graduates who had been hired as tutorial assistants but also turned the course step by step into a parody of nationalistic ideology. The new leaders failed to move the university towards a center providing intellectual guidance for national development, either along bourgeois or socialist line. Indeed, their accomplishment was a university that was neither genuinely socialist nor one upholding traditional academic standards. Instead, it became an academic morass. Later, Professor Geoffrey Mmari boldly tried to salvage the situation but was dismissed by the higher authorities for being too independent.

It is an irony of history that those who condemned the radical students for embracing a foreign ideology were precisely the people who later sold out our nation, lock stock and barrel, and for a pittance, to foreign firms and investors, and turned it into a place where the foreign "donor community" has the final say on the direction in which our nation is headed. Take the case of former President Benjamin Mkapa. As editor of *The Nationalist* in days past, he had permitted progressive views to grace its pages. The paper had a socialist, anti-imperialist orientation. However, mostly pieces that did not stray far from the official line were allowed. He published editorials and ostensible letters criticizing campus radicals for peddling a foreign ideology, and the radicals did not get an adequate space to respond. The situation was different in the nationalized *The Standard*. Frene Ginwalla, the first editor, gave critics on the left greater opportunity to write for the paper and encouraged open, unfettered debates. Her independence alienated the party and state bosses, and so she was eventually removed after writing an editorial critical of the US-backed military coup in the Sudan. Mr. Mkapa became the new editor of the renamed paper *Daily News*. Under him, however, it became a mouth piece of the state. Independent voices from the left now had a hard time getting into print. The days of vibrant, open debates on major national issues were gone.

Mr. Mkapa later became Foreign Minister, and, in 1995, the President of Tanzania. Under his reign, the neo-liberal agenda of US imperialism was fully and fervently implemented. Public services were drastically curtailed; state-owned entities like banks, transport firms, utilities, and factories were sold off to foreigners at far less than the market value; laws protecting ordinary people were reversed; contracts incredibly unfair to the nation were signed; and the dependence of the state on external guidance and funding increased. This era was marked by lavish misuse of state funds, and by one giant corruption scandal after another. Multinational firms, big bureaucrats and local businesses reaped huge rewards while public coffers were depleted. Indeed, that is essentially what Mr. Mkapa himself admitted in a recent interview.

> *We privatized everything the state had. Everything was bought up*
> *by foreign capital because we had no national capital to compete.*

> *The foreign companies almost always closed local business, which were not competitive, transforming them into distributors of foreign products and driving up unemployment. The experts of the World Bank and the IMF predicted that this would happen, but they told us: Now the influx of foreign investment will lead to the creation of new competitive and technologically current businesses that will provide the foundations for everlasting, modern development. None of this happened for us. Former President Benjamin Mkapa quoted in Savio (2009).*

It is difficult to know whether this is a confession of immense naiveté, or a convenient deflection of blame. He is silent on the issue of substantial benefits derived by local officials during the process of privatization. Mr. Mkapa's policies earned him a tonnage of accolades from Western governments and agencies. The gigantic, as yet to be fully-disclosed and resolved financial scandals under his rule, on the other hand, remain the stuff of the headlines. When Mr. Mkapa was a journalist, the pages of *Cheche* and *MajiMaji*, and even his own paper, had abounded with analytic perspectives and descriptive articles on the true nature of economic imperialism, and cautioned against the kind of naiveté expressed in the above quote.

Bashing socialism or radicals is a favorite activity bourgeois ideologues engage in so as to conceal the stupendous crimes of capitalism and its cronies. They like to project leftism as a passing fad for students, equate socialism with hypocrisy, and promote platitudes like equality contradicts human nature. We should, however, set aside such superficiality, probe under the surface and take a longer-term view. Our judgments must consider that human life rarely follows a straight line, especially when that line begins to deviate from the norm. Swimming against the tide, challenging dominant ideas, confronting those in power, or standing up against injustice always risks danger, to oneself and one's family. Other than in times of major transformation or upheaval, not more than a few souls venture into these rough domains. And even after doing so for a while, a tendency to revert into the mainstream may prevail.

As noted earlier, many UDSM leftists were reintegrated into the system. Some became fabulously wealthy, some rose in the realm of state power, and one reached the apex. Many became stooges of imperialism looking out for their own interests and betraying the masses. Despite this, it remains a fact that at one point, they had set aside personal interests to champion the rights of the people. That history cannot be erased. In doing so, they laid a foundation upon which further progress can occur. They were thereby quite distinct from the rightists and pseudo-socialists of the past who sold out their people right at the start. While individuals must account for their actions, the salutary task is to question and change the system, the capitalist system in its national and international manifestation.

One comrade who escaped that trap was Walter Rodney. At UDSM, he wrote his seminal book *How Europe Underdeveloped Africa* and published a series of papers making material contributions to African history and the anti-imperialist movement in Africa. He challenged the anti-Africa bias in Western scholarship. His popular formal classes projected a rich, interdisciplinary portrait of African history. Yet, he was not an arm-chair scholar. As noted earlier, he worked closely with radical students, supported *Cheche* and USARF in varied ways, taught and attended the Sunday classes, worked in *Ujamaa* villages, and engaged with African liberation movements. His frequent public lectures, delivered with melodic and passionate oratory, enlightened students and academic staff on the signal international issues of the day. He inspired activism and made you thirst for knowledge. Western embassies and state bureaucrats, however, often took exception to his principled, forthright stand. At times, he risked deportation. But he did not compromise. With other progressive staff, he played a frontline role in the initiatives to reorient the academic training at UDSM towards a factually robust and conceptually grounded Pan-Africanist and socialist direction.

In 1974, he returned to Guyana in order to continue the struggle on the home front. Right from the outset, the authorities were on his case. First, his appointment as Professor of History was rescinded. When he became a central figure in the Working People's Alliance, an organization aiming towards a multi-racial popular democracy in Guyana, he and other WPA activists were now and then harassed and arrested on contrived charges. Eventually, his steadfast commitment to humanity cost him his life. In June 1980, Walter Rodney lost his life from a bomb placed in his car.

In those years, repressive regimes across South America, led by that of Augusto Pinochet of Chile, ran a joint program to liquidate political opponents. They had strong backing and material support from the US. The US spy agency, the CIA, had a long history of meddling in the internal affairs of Guyana as well. When the archives of the CIA are made public, I will not at all be surprised if it comes to light that the CIA had a hand in the murder of Walter Rodney.

Rodney's ideas, formulations and practice evolved over time. But their direction remained unchanged. To the last days of his life, he remained a Marxist committed to the struggle for liberation from imperialism and attainment of socialism. (Selected writings of Walter Rodney are accessible at www.marxists.org/subject/africa/rodney-walter/index.htm).

Five Tools

Despite changes in concrete manifestation, the capitalist/imperialist system remains at the root of the dire predicament confronting Africa (see Chapter 13). In the process of critiquing this system and its ideology in our student days, we learned valuable lessons that remain relevant to this day. The resurgence of bourgeois ideology has, however, buried them from view. In this section, I lay down five tools of reasoning and analysis that students of today can utilize to develop their own perspective on human society and development. These tools, which have been alluded to earlier, are: independent thinking, meticulous scholarship, integrated perspective, attending to history, and intellectual integrity.

INTELLECTUAL INDEPENDENCE: African academia at present is, institutionally and individually, completely dependent on funds from and links with universities, think tanks, research groups, commercial entities and governmental bodies from the West. A distinctive aspect of the contemporary intellectual scene in Africa thereby is that of uncritical subservience to (Western) bourgeois theories, expressions, sources and conceptualizations, and a blanket distortion of research and scholarly priorities. Some of that is packaged with Africanist sounding labels but the underlying substance is firmly pro-capitalist. Even erstwhile radical scholars change their tune when donor dollars dangle at the door. Issues favored by the West get the bulk of the attention while the issues crucial for improvement of the lives of the people are neglected. Two prominent scientists from South Africa elucidated this conundrum in their own field:

> *The dependence on international finance has shifted the focus of South African scientists from local to global priorities. For example, important research is being done in South Africa on developing HIV vaccines yet little attention is being paid to devising approaches to reducing high rates of infection among young women, the main drivers of the HIV epidemic in the country. Karim and Karim (2010).*

Intellectual independence does not mean reinventing the wheel. It means deciding for ourselves and with objective criteria what is, from the vast array of knowledge developed by humanity, more accurate, relevant and suitable to our concrete conditions and future development. It does not mean isolation. It means engaging with the world as equals, not just as consumers of ideas produced by others. It means not blindly or automatically following the conceptualizations approved by those who fund us, but to consider other ways and examples of approaching issues as well. For example, students doing a master's degree in public health in Tanzania never learn about strategies and achievements of public health in Cuba or 1960s China, even though they were highly successful and are most relevant to our present conditions. Why not, we must ask?

Critical thinking means probing simplistic headlines, like that stating "*Tanzania listed among the emerging markets in 2010*" (Guardian Reporter 2010). Such stories make us believe that things are better than they actually are, and make no distinction between superficial growth and self-sustaining economic development. They rely on misleading financial indicators, and are slanted towards the interests of the rich and powerful, and the international investors rather than the common man. And they use facile statistical measures to hide the fact that the wealth of Africa is being extracted mostly to benefit outsiders.

STELLAR SCHOLARSHIP: Each major social issue has to be probed in depth by a comprehensive search for sources, formulations and evidence. Each matter needs to be examined with a critical eye. Cast doubts even on generally accepted propositions until you are satisfied about their validity. Question authority, no matter how esteemed. Understand that many dominant views derive from selective evidence. In the conventional discourse, important but unconventional information is often ignored. However, do not adopt a cynical viewpoint, or automatically dismiss all propositions, simply because they derive from external sources. Always base your critique on carefully thought out reasons and good evidence.

One source of simplistic thinking derives from uncritical use of common labels. For example, China is often referred to as a communist nation. However, even a cursory look at its economy reveals that it is a capitalist society through and through. The USA is called a democracy. An in-depth analysis shows that the political process, congress, judiciary, media and foreign affairs in that nation are effectively controlled by major corporations and the very rich. It is more accurate to call the USA a plutocracy (Domhoff 2009).

A large proportion of African academic output today takes the form of consultancy reports largely funded from outside. These pay good fees, but have weak mechanisms of quality control. The selection of issues is determined by the funder. What is written for local and international journals follows standard formats and ways of examining issues, rarely probes matters in depth, or from an original standpoint. Such superficiality derives in part from excessive dependence on computerization, and reflects the abysmally low standards and quality of university instruction across Africa today. There is considerable room for improvement in terms of the choice of the topic, methodology and depth of analysis in all these endeavors. Above all, African scholars must write of their own initiative, on matters chosen by them and with accurate methods that transcend the formula driven, standardized version of science.

INTEGRATED CONCEPTUALIZATION: The complexity and scope of modern knowledge necessitates specialization. But that narrow focus must be complemented with a scientifically-based holistic perspective. An integrated view is crucial for understanding, facilitates the appropriate utilization of knowledge for social needs, and converts the specialist from a cog in an unwieldy, dysfunctional machine to a potentially effective participant in understanding and transformation of the machine.

The academic training prevalent today produces specialized scholars and professionals who converse with a small group of similarly specialized colleagues. A small step outside that circle exposes their ignorance. The reductionist bourgeois mentality has taken hold to such an extent that even Development Studies -- a discipline forged in academic battles to promote an holistic and critical analysis of society, science and history -- has now succumbed to the compartmentalized approach of bourgeois social sciences.

To give another example, the dominant approach in public health is a disease by disease approach. The linkage between disease patterns, on the one hand, and the social, economic structures and development, on the other, is rarely made. When it is done, it is done in a superficial one-sided manner: low level of development is thus attributed to high prevalence of acute, infectious conditions. The more important connection in the reverse direction is forgotten. For enlightening examples of integrated approaches to public health relevant for the African condition, see Castro (2004), Horn (1969), Irwin, Kim, Gershman and Millen (2002), Katz (2008), Metzi (1988), Sidel (1993), Whiteford (2009) and Zhang (2008).

UNDERSTAND HISTORY: Knowledge of the past provides a firmer handle on the subject at hand and what lies beyond it. In public health, it is vital to know what was done earlier, where those efforts went, and for what reasons. A historical perspective is absent from most academic fields taught today. You can get a Master's degree in public health without having an idea of the global history of malaria, that is, apart from tit-bits about the discovery of this or that scientist. Even history as a discipline has reverted to tradition, and is not integrated with economics, sociology, or class analysis. A historical approach can be and needs to be built into the teaching of all subjects, be it law, economics or mathematics. History is not just for historians.

INTELLECTUAL INTEGRITY: Science seeks truth, and truth derives from honesty. We must respect the truth in our personal, professional and social lives. The future prospects for Africa critically depend on students and scholars being committed to honest scholarship in health, social sciences, law, education and other fields.

Yet, today plagiarizing is widespread, and cheating in class work and examinations frequent. Lecturers skip classes, do minimal amounts of teaching and attend to money-generating activities. Research is poorly formulated, designed, implemented, analyzed and interpreted. In addition, stuffing data with imaginary numbers and other forms of misconduct are common. People know and talk about this. But no one takes remedial steps. Whenever I look closely at research data in the projects done at my university, I am astounded at what I find beneath the surface. Even minimal ethical norms are in short supply.

* * * * *

Applying these tools on a consistent and regular basis will facilitate clear and critical thinking. African students need them not solely for an intellectual exercise. Conceptual clarity is essential for effective action. To take appropriate steps to change reality, we need to be armed with an honest and comprehensive representation of the past and the present, and of the mechanisms by which societies change from one form into another. Only that perspective allows us to appreciate that poverty is not simply a question of genetics, knowledge, technology, nature, or environment, but above all, it is a question of power, a question of social structure (Hickel 2010; Katz 2008).

On Socialism

Almost the entire communist bloc of yesterday has disappeared. Only Cuba stands defiant. People say that socialism not only failed but did so in such a stark manner that it is permanently off the human agenda. That is a factually deficient, one-sided view based on a short term perception of history. Capitalism as a system matured over centuries. Its history included major calamities like the European wars, slave trade, colonial rule, two world wars, major economic crises, famines, civil strife and imperial aggression. While capitalism has brought tangible benefits to humanity, it, as was shown in the last chapter, continues to extract a gigantic toll on human welfare.

The attempts to construct socialism in China, the Soviet Union, Korea, Eastern Europe, Vietnam and Cuba in the 20th century faced numerous ups and downs. These nations disengaged from the global capitalist system to institute an economic and social system that served the interest of the people at the bottom. There were remarkable changes and large catastrophes as they embarked on that path. The major achievements were vast and rapid improvement in the lives of ordinary people -- unleashing their creative energies -- and the formation of relatively egalitarian, tranquil social systems. (Dobb 1970; Hinton and Magdoff 2008; Raby 2009; Sweezy and Bettleheim 1971; Walker 2003)

Yet, often the rights of the people were grossly violated by the state bureaucracy. This bureaucracy eventually transformed itself into a new class of capitalists. The extensive inhumane purges under Stalin or draconian misrule under Pol Pot in Cambodia form sad chapters in that history. Persistent attacks on the political, economic and military fronts by Western imperialism also played a key role in the reintegration of these nations into the capitalist system. (Blackburn 1991; Hobsbawm 1994; Prashad 2008)

The actual history of socialism is clouded by persistent misinformation from Western media and scholars. They vastly exaggerate the problems faced under socialism and ignore worse problems of capitalism. For example, the millions who died in India due to internal violence, famines and poor health in India after independence are never ascribed to capitalism while a smaller human toll in China under Mao is always blamed on communism. They rarely acknowledge that the reason China is ahead of India today in human development stems from the solid foundation laid under communist rule (Han 2008; Tempest 1997). A comprehensive survey of the health indicators under capitalism and socialism was done by Navarro (1993). His major finding was that both in developed and underdeveloped nations, socialist forces and states tended to produce better health outcomes and indicators of social welfare than was done by capitalist forces and states. On the other hand, socialist states that reverted back to capitalism experienced significant deterioration in the public health (Castro 2004; Irwin, Kim, Gershman and Millen 2002; Nelson 1994; Notzon et al. 1998; Sidel 1993; Zhang

2008). A recent work has documented that greater equality generates better indicators of social well-being in terms of health, crime, social strife, drug use and educational indicators (Wilkinson and Pickett 2009).

Comparing socialism and capitalism, and exploring the histories of the two systems are broad issues that students and scholars in Africa need to independently explore. They need to unearth the voluminous documentation on these issues that has been buried, and make up their own minds. It is a task requiring deep study and careful reflection. In this regard, one needs to go beyond the readily available bourgeois commentaries and analyses that are often biased and factually wanting. The conceptual and methodological challenges in such an exercise have been clearly laid out in a recent article by Levins (2010). The recent attempt initiated in Latin America by Hugo Chavez to chart a new direction towards socialism has met with hostility and misinformation by the global mainstream media. Instead of simply being swayed by them, one has to look at sources that are both sympathetic towards socialism as well as independent of state authority and critical. Thus, for example, one may contrast Chavez and Harnecker (2005) on Venezuela with the more critical evaluation by Petras (2009).

What I have read and experienced in the four decades since 1970 have only confirmed to me the main lesson I learned from my early association with USARF and *Cheche*. And this lesson is that socialism is the sole sound option for humanity. In that respect, I remain in agreement with what Albert Einstein said in 1949:

> I am convinced there is only one way to eliminate these grave evils [of capitalism], namely through the establishment of a socialist economy, accompanied by an educational system which would be oriented toward social goals. In such an economy, the means of production are owned by society itself and are utilized in a planned fashion. A planned economy, which adjusts production to the needs of the community, would distribute the work to be done among all those able to work and would guarantee a livelihood to every man, woman, and child. The education of the individual, in addition to promoting his own innate abilities, would attempt to develop in him a sense of responsibility for his fellow men in place of the glorification of power and success in our present society. Einstein (1949).

The march towards socialism goes on. No doubt, it will be a prolonged one. But we have to start by treating the matter with the seriousness it deserves. Only a few voices in Tanzania today raise the issues of socialism, capitalism and imperialism. Professor Issa Shivji continues to publish, teach, and organize annual symposia and other events on such matters. Among the journalists, Mkwaia wa Kugenga, Jenerali Ulimwengu and Nizar Visram stand out in that respect (for example, Kuhenga 2008). More voices are needed, especially from the up and coming generation of journalists, students and scholars.

Mr. Zitto Kabwe, an opposition member of parliament in Tanzania, has boldly exposed incidents of official corruption, and is respected across the nation for his efforts. In a radio interview on August 28, 2009, he talked about what divided him and the chairman of his political party. He said he was a *mjamaa* (socialist) while the chairman followed the capitalist ideology. Today, it is rare for a politician to call himself or herself a socialist. Yet, the fact Mr. Kabwe continues to be in a political party which, like other parties, is wedded to the neo-liberal agenda and supported by Western governments and bourgeois organizations is perplexing. Is he serious about socialism, or was that just a public relations statement?

Africa needs political parties dedicated to socialism. They will provide a framework for progressive students and intellectuals to ally with workers and peasants. Such a move cannot occur overnight but it is a medium-term goal we need to consistently work towards.

The Challenge

Schools, colleges and universities across Africa are in a constant state of turmoil. Extensive discontent prevails, often manifested in protests and strikes. High fees, cost-sharing, inefficient disbursement of loans, low governmental allocations to education, excessive reliance on foreign funds, administrative inefficiency, misuse of funds, illegal payments to contractors and suppliers -- such problems combined with bureaucratic arrogance to generate one crisis after another. Neo-liberalism is unable to build a modern, relevant, efficient and expanded education system for Africa. Instead of driving towards education (and health and other services) being basic human rights, a class-based system in which the children of the rich and well-connected have far better prospects than others is taking root.

Student activism in Africa today focuses on diverse, intertwined problems. They have been greatly affected by neo-liberalism and state suppression. In their struggles, their immediate economic interests take the center stage. Broader issue like the type and quality of education at times come to the fore. Students also mobilize to protest against electoral fraud and other national matters. But overall, they adopt the fragmented and short-term agenda prevailing among foreign-funded non-governmental organizations that claim to champion this or that group or cause in society. If social issues are raised, it is within the framework laid down by the funders. Many talk about HIV and AIDS; a brave few expose misdeeds of foreign firms. The issue of imperialism or capitalism is rarely raised. Students are often divided along narrow ethnic lines. Pan-African solidarity is wanting. Yet, there are exceptions too. Students in Sierra Leon and Ethiopia, for example, continue to fight for social justice and against police brutality, paying a heavy price in the process (Alidou, Caffentzis and Federici 2000; Bah 2009; Diouf and Mamdani 1994; Zelig 2007).

The so-called free media are generally no better though several valiant journalists often expose issues that disturb the powerful and land them in trouble. But mostly, the media focus on petty scandals and selectively pander to issues the tycoon, funder or politician behind them espouses. In international matters, they promote the worst prejudices and selective perspective of the Western media. The modern African intellectual absorbs these mendacities uncritically and regurgitates them, often with an artificial air of pomposity.

But times are bleak; people are hungry; children are suffering; urgency pervades the air. The challenge is to build independent organizations to address the burning questions of the day in a comprehensive and scientific manner. The socio-economic system and its political superstructure as a whole have to be probed. In such endeavors, students must take the initiative here as most of their learned professors are too deeply embedded within the system to do it.

Form Pan-African organizations -- modern day USARFs -- to champion emancipation and socialism. Begin study groups and self-education classes. Learn from history, from past achievements and mistakes. Pursue well-researched and thought-out paths. Rise to your full humanistic potential and act. Here I can do no better than echo a brave Palestinian academic:

> [I]f humanity survives the next 100 years, it will have been because of those who act with dignity/self respect instead of cowardice and self-interest. Qumsiyeh (2010).

History does not just repeat itself. The alignment of social forces and material conditions in society have changed. But we can build on the past. Social groups embody memories of the past. Outcomes that can surpass our wildest dreams can be attained. No matter how discouraging the current conditions, we must set imaginative, ambitious goals. As we used to proclaim long ago, be a realist, and demand the impossible.

A Hopeful Obituary

The first issue of the Marxist journal *Monthly Review*, a magazine founded in 1949, carried a keynote paper by Albert Einstein. His article concluded thus:

> *Clarity about the aims and problems of socialism is of greatest significance in our age of transition. Since, under present circumstances, free and unhindered discussion of these problems has come under a powerful taboo, I consider the foundation of this magazine to be an important public service. Einstein (1949).*

Monthly Review has more than lived up to his expectations in the past six decades. To this day, it carries relevant, incisive analyses of capitalism, imperialism and socialism. Throughout its existence, it has been independent of any state, commercial or other authority. It also provided critical commentaries on what was happening in the socialist world. To this day, it remains a major source for insightful analyses of global issues.

At UDSM in the 1960s and 70s, this journal together with the books produced by the associated Monthly Review Press formed an indispensable resource for the progressive students and staff. Many of the books used in the ideological classes derived from this outlet. When people accused us of being foreign inspired, it would have been more accurate to brand us as following a version of American Marxism rather than following Russian or Chinese communism! Of course, the truth was that we were not beholden to any foreign authority, be it from the East or West.

Given the scholarly and international reputation of *Monthly Review*, it was especially gratifying for us to read in the editorial notes of the July-August 1971 issue of this esteemed magazine the following lines:

> *We recently received the first issue of what appears to be a new and very promising periodical MajiMaji, published by the TANU Youth League at the University of Dar es Salaam (P.O. Box 35054, Dar es Salaam, Tanzania -- subscription terms not indicated). In addition to articles focused on imperialism and socialism, this issue contains a list of 75 books which "anyone who wants to understand the problems of the contemporary world must read." We were naturally proud of the fact that of these 75 titles, no fewer than 17 were published by MR Press. Monthly Review (1971).*

The reference in question was to *MajiMaji* No. 1, which contained articles that had earlier been planned for *Cheche* No. 4, prior to the ban on the latter. This case was just one of the many examples of how the products of progressive student and staff activism at UDSM were getting international attention and recognition.

At the opening of the Kivukoni College in 1961, Mwalimu Nyerere extolled the "non-conformist in society ... who by by the irritation he causes, stops society from ceasing to think, forces it to make constant re-evaluations and adjustments." (Nyerere 1961). And when he inaugurated the University of East Africa in 1963, he cautioned against "the error of abusing the non-conformist." (Nyerere 1963). In their time, *Cheche* and USARF were the non-conformists *par excellence* in Tanzania, almost alone swimming against the tide of political hypocrisy, urging the nation to re-evaluate the implementation of the policy of Socialism and Self-Reliance, and to embark on a consistent and serious journey towards its goals. They were friends of socialism, not its enemies. But instead of being accorded the hearing and attention they deserved, the ruling elite committed the error of silencing these non-conformists.

I do not think I am off the mark if I echo Einstein's words and declare that *Cheche* and later *MajiMaji* rendered, in their times, though to a more modest degree, an important and needed public service. *Cheche*, for its part, was a bold student venture into a hitherto uncharted domain that landed on the university campus and beyond with a bang, lived a brief but fiery life, and which, too soon, ended with a bang as well.

However, despite the passage of four decades, the sparks it and its progenitor kindled have not been extinguished. The issues they raised and dealt with remain singularly pertinent to the continuing struggle for the true liberation of Africa. Since the discussion of ideas on socialism and critical analysis of capitalism and imperialism continue to be a "powerful taboo," it is time for the African youth -- in the spirit of Mwalimu Nyerere's call in 1970 to challenge orthodox thinking, and as Che Guevara would express it -- to create two, three, more *Cheches* and embark on their own path to mental liberation.

Appendix A

Tables of Contents: Cheche & MajiMaji No. 1

EDITORIAL NOTE: The contents of *MajiMaji* No. 1 were essentially those planned for *Cheche* No. 4, had the latter not been banned

....

CHECHE NO. 1: NOVEMBER 1969

CHECHE NO. 2: JULY 1970

Appendix B

DATE	EVENT
22 October 1966	Mass expulsion of students from UCD
06 February 1967	The Arusha Declaration issued.
Early 1967	Socialist Club started at UCD.
10 March 1967	Education for Self-Reliance published.
10-15 March 1967	Conference on "Role of University in Socialist Tanzania." Speakers AM Babu, W Rodney, and Hon. RM Kawawa.
18 March 1967	TYL branch opened at UCD.
November 1967	USARF founded at UCD. Chairman: Y Museveni.
16-20 November 1967	USARF Seminar on African Liberation at UCD.
09 November 1968	USARF permanently derails the Rag Day.
December 1968	USARF delegation to liberated areas of Mozambique
March 1969	Students occupy the Faculty of Law.
July 1969	Walter Rodney returns to UCD.
July 1969	New course (Development Studies) for all entering students. Head: L Cliffe.
August 1969	The Singleton Affair unfolds.
10 August 1969	USARF election: Chairman N Kasihwaki.
11 October 1969	*Cheche* born. Editors: K Hirji, H Mapolu & Z Hamdani.
12 October 1969	First Sunday Ideological class. Speakers: AG Ebrahim, C Kileo, A Mchumo.
26 November 1969	*Cheche* No. 1 published.
8-14 December 1969	Second Seminar of East and Central African Youth. Speakers: W Rodney, AG Ebrahim, C Kileo, N Mwiru.

DATE	EVENT
04 February 1970	Mwalimu Nyerere holds question and answer session with students and staff at UCD.
05 February 1970	*The Standard* is nationalized. F Ginwalla, editor.
June 1970	USARF/TYL initiate tourism debate in *The Standard*.
01 July 1970	UCD becomes UDSM: P Msekwa, Vice Chancellor.
11 July 1970	*Cheche* No. 2 published.
29 August 1970	Mwalimu Nyerere gives UDSM inauguration address.
03 September 1970	*Cheche* Special Issue, *Tanzania: The Silent Class Struggle* by IG Shivji.
September 1970	USARF/TYL members stay at and work for 3 weeks in Dodoma *Ujamaa* villages.
October 1970	USARF/TYL issue report on *Ujamaa* villages.
October 1970	*Cheche* No. 3 published.
15 October 1970	USARF election. N Kasihwaki, Chairman.
09 November 1970	USARF & *Cheche* banned.
12 November 1970	USARF issues *Our Last Stand*.
13 November 1970	Front page reports of USARF & *Cheche* ban in *The Standard* and *The Nationalist*.
January 1971	*MajiMaji* No. 1 published. Editors: H Mapolu, M Njagi, G Hajivayanis, N Kasihwaki, W Kavishe.

Appendix C

Program of 1969 Youth Seminar

EDITORIAL NOTE: The seminar was organized and hosted by the UCD TYL branch. This program is a slightly edited and reformatted version of the original. The opening speech was given by Vice President Rashidi Kawawa. The seminar proceedings were to be produced as the second issue of *Cheche*. But, due to the circumstances discussed in Chapter 4, this was not done.

THE SECOND SEMINAR OF EAST AND CENTRAL AFRICAN YOUTH

Theme: The African Revolution *Purpose, Problems, Prospects and Strategies*

University College, Dar es Salaam, Assembly Hall

	MONDAY, 8TH DECEMBER 1969
9:00 am	Opening Speech by Mwalimu JK Nyerere
12:30–2:00 pm	Lunch Break
2:30 pm	Addresses by Leaders of Delegations, Election of Seminar Chairman and Chairmen of Various Committees
8:30 pm	Entertainment
	TUESDAY, 9TH DECEMBER 1969
8:30 am	Walter Rodney: The Ideology of the African Revolution
10:00 am	Committee Sessions
12:30–2:00 pm	Lunch Break
2:30 pm	Plenary Session: Committee Reports
8:30 pm	Films Show
	WEDNESDAY, 10TH DECEMBER 1969
8:30 am	Ahmed Gora Ebrahim: Colonialism in Africa
10:00 am	Committee Sessions
12:30–2:00 pm	Lunch Break
2:30 pm	Plenary Session

	THURSDAY, 11TH DECEMBER 1969
8:30 am	Visit to Ruvu National Service Camp and Ujamaa Village

	FRIDAY, 12TH DECEMBER 1969
8:30 am	Charles Kileo: Neocolonialism and the Problem of Building Socialism in Africa
10:00 am	Committee Sessions
12:30–2:00 pm	Lunch Break
2:30 pm	Plenary Session: Committee Reports
8:30 pm	Entertainment

	SATURDAY, 13TH DECEMBER 1969
8:30 am	Ngombale Mwiru: Youth and the Consolidation and Defense of the African Revolution
10:00 am	Committee Sessions
12:30–2:00 pm	Lunch Break
2:30 pm	Plenary Session: Committee Reports
8:30 pm	Film Show

	SUNDAY, 14TH DECEMBER 1969
8:30 am	General Discussion and Resolution
4:00 pm	Closing of Seminar: Minister of National Education, C Y Mgonja

Appendix D

The First Syllabus for USARF Ideological Classes –1969

"There can be no revolutionary party without a revolutionary theory."
- V.I. Lenin -

EDITORIAL NOTE: This is a slightly edited version of the syllabus for the first set of Sunday ideological classes run by USARF. Karim F Hirji was assigned the responsibility for producing the syllabus.
....

In drafting this tentative scheme for ideological classes I have been guided, above all, by the imperative for all comrades to gain a scientific and systematic understanding of the world, past and present, to enable them to discern the mechanism of social development, and to equip them with an integral world outlook. A revolutionary must possess a methodology for analyzing concrete situations (as opposed to ossified dogmas) if he or she aspires to change the world for the better. The extreme complexity of the contemporary situation entails a clear appreciation of reality if our actions are to serve a progressive goal.

Acquisition of clarity of thought is not a child's game. It requires intensive reading and vigorous debate to be combined with revolutionary practice. That is the challenge which History has placed before us.

Part I: Philosophical & Methodological Foundations (2 lectures)

Topics: Idealism vs. materialism; philosophical concepts of matter; modes of existence of matter and consciousness; materialist dialectics; dialectics and modern science; theory of knowledge.

Readings
1. Mir Publisher, *Fundamentals of Marxism-Leninism* (Chap. 1,2,3.)
2. Mao Tse Tung, *On Contradictions*
3. VI Lenin, *Three Sources and Three Component Parts of Marxism*
4. F Engels, *Theses on Ludwig Feuerbach*
5. F Engels, *Dialectics of Nature*
6. K Marx and F Engels, *The German Ideology*
7. J Lindsay, *Marxism and Contemporary Science*
8. R Garaudy, *Karl Marx: The Evolution of His Thought*

Part II: Materialist Conception of History (2 lectures)

a. Theoretical Topics: Application of dialectics to human history; class struggle; the individual and masses in history; the State.

b. Application Topics: Brief survey of evolution; human history from the Paleolithic age to the present day and historical materialism; rise and growth of capitalism and socialism.

Readings

1. Mir Publisher, *Fundamentals of Marxism-Leninism* (Chap 4,5,6,7.)
2. F Engels, *The Origins of the Family, Private Property and the State*
3. F Engels, *Socialism: Scientific and Utopian*
4. G Plekhanov, *The Role of Individual in History*
5. RH Tawney, *Religion and the Rise of Capitalism*
6. H Gordon Childe, *What Happened in History?*
7. P Sweezy, *Theory of Capitalist Development*
8. E Williams, *Capitalism and Slavery*
9. M Dobb, *Studies in the Development of Capitalism*

Part III: Political Economy: Basic Concepts (1 lecture)

Topics: Contradictions of capitalist economies; commodity production; theory of surplus value; economic crisis of capital accumulation; the concept of economic surplus; surplus accumulation.

Readings

1. Mir Publisher, *Fundamentals of Marxism-Leninism* (Chap 8.)
2. J Eaton, *Political Economy*
3. P.I. Nikitin, *Fundamentals of Political Economy*
4. P Baran, *Political Economy of Growth*
5. O Lange, *Political Economy*
6. A Seidman, *An Economics Textbook for Africa*
7. K Marx, Value, *Price and Profit*
8. K Marx, Wage, *Labor and Capital*

Part IV: Underdevelopment and Monopoly Capitalism (3 lectures)

Topics: Analysis of contemporary world situation; monopolistic corporations; international patterns of exploitation; the underdeveloped regions; neocolonialism; problems of socialist development.

Readings

1. P Baran & P Sweezy, *Monopoly Capital*
2. P Baran, *Political Economy of Growth*
3. K Nkrumah, *Neo-Colonialism: The Last Stage of Imperialism*

4. VI Lenin, *Imperialism: The Highest Stage of Capitalism*
5. J Woddis, *Introduction to Neocolonialism*
6. J de Castro, *The Geography of Hunger*
7. P Jalee, *The Pillage of the Third World*

Part V: Current Political and Economic Issues

Topics and reading list to be announced.

*   *   *   *   *

The following books are a must reading for all comrades. They will facilitate the formulation of an overall perspective on relevant issues.

Readings
1. F Fanon, *The Wretched of the Earth*
2. P Baran, *Political Economy of Growth*
3. P Baran & P Sweezy, *Monopoly Capital*
4. K Nkrumah, *Neocolonialism: The Last Stage of Imperialism*
5. F Engels, *Socialism: Scientific and Utopian*

Karim Hirji
November 1969

Appendix E

Our Last Stand

Our Last Stand
USARF Has Been Banned!!!
Cheche is Dead!!!!

EDITORIAL NOTE: This is a linguistically edited and reformatted version of the statement issued on 12 November 1970 by the University Students African Revolutionary Front of the University of Dar es Salaam in response to the banning of USARF and *Cheche* by the government. The statement was written by Karim F Hirji and Naijuka Kasihwaki.

A Bleak Day
Last Monday, 9 November 1970, was a bleak day for us. The campus TYL committee was hurriedly summoned in the evening to the Vice Chancellor's office. The following information was conveyed to us: USARF should wind up its activities and *Cheche* should cease further publication. We were told that this was a directive from the State House. And the reasons given were:

(i) USARF is a redundant organization since TYL is supposed to have a monopoly of political activities on the Hill. USARF has committed the cardinal sin of meddling in Tanzanian politics by its mordant commentaries on various issues. That USARF does not represent any national body, here or elsewhere, is another reason for discontinuing its existence.

(ii) *Cheche* has to cease publication since its name is derived from *Iskra*, the Leninist revolutionary journal. So, we were told, *Cheche* tended to give the impression that Tanzania was building "Russian socialism" and not "true Tanzanian socialism." TANU and TYL have always been ideologically self-reliant, hence such borrowing from "foreign ideologies" could not be tolerated.

It is not our intention to dispute the above allegations. We neither have the ability nor the wish to do so. We write to bury USARF and its joint child *Cheche*, and not to praise them, least of all to glorify them. As to the successes achieved by us, and the faults committed, or the correctness or otherwise of our ideas and aims, we dare not comment. No man shall be his own judge. In the course of our lifetime, we have been branded "extremists," "fanatics," "arm-chair theoreticians," "opportunists," and all the degrading labels one can think of. Of course, these charges emanated from honorable and respected people. Though on some occasions, one could hear exclamations, even from our antagonists, regarding our tenacity and perseverance. But that is beside the point. Below we outline in brief the history of our operations – in order that all be our judges – and judge us from facts, not rumors.

A Short History

The University Students African Revolutionary Front (USARF) was born in the month of November 1967. It began with the Socialist Club which was organized immediately after the proclamation of the Arusha Declaration. The Club came out to initiate, organize and conduct socialist debate. It was an initiative of both the progressive students and staff. It is significant to note that this was possible after the Arusha Declaration.

The Socialist Club, right from its inception, had its limitations. It could at best organize debates. It became all the more obvious that socialist debate must have a purpose. USARF was conceived with the view of translating the socialist debate into socialist revolutionary action.

This demanded membership. It was open to all students prepared to take up the challenge. USARF membership has at one time or another included students from Zimbabwe, Kenya, Uganda, Malawi, Malawi, Sudan, Ethiopia and Tanzania. Full membership has always been open to students only; some members of staff have been allowed associate membership though.

USARF set out to accomplish the following tasks:

a. To work unceasingly for the promotion of a revolutionary spirit within the University, Tanzania, Africa and the World in general.

b. To contribute to the success of various Liberation Movements and to work hand-in-hand with progressive forces here and elsewhere.

c. To drive home the urgent need for African solidarity as the only means of getting real independence for Africa and of safeguarding that independence.

d. To keep a constant vigil against imperialist ideology and propaganda by every possible means.

e. To stand firmly within the ranks of the workers and peasants of Tanzania, Africa and the World in their fight against imperialism and for socialism

Various methods were used to affect these aims:

a. The Front has been an agency for the dissemination of revolutionary ideas at the Hill designed to foster the cause of Liberation Movements and anti-imperialist forces the world over.

b. The Front has organized public talks and discussions with regard to the cause, nature and progress of Liberation Movements and other anti-imperialist forces in Africa, Asia and Latin America.

c. The Front devised means and ways of raising funds to aid the cause of the liberation struggle in Africa.

d. The Front kept contact with anti-imperialist forces of the world and exchanged experiences and views with them.

The history of USARF has been revolutionary. In October 1968, it helped sabotage the Rag Day poppycock, a reactionary caravan ride organized by the elite ostensibly to show their sympathy with the poor. On this occasion they appear as philanthropists, philanthropism being a euphemism for those who plunder by the ton and give by the ounce. USARF stopped the university students from cladding themselves into laughing stocks, and imitating the poor by deflating the tires of their buses. The press, especially *The Standard*, then under the grip of Western imperialism, dubbed USARF as irresponsible. This action brought USARF to the front lines, and it has never gone back.

Five USARF members visited the liberated areas of Mozambique in December 1968. They witnessed the progress being made by FRELIMO. Their visit convinced them of the necessity for more revolutionary propaganda to counter the reactionary propaganda that usually sang the same cacophonous song about the inability and problems of the liberation movements. This visit also made USARF members appreciate the problems in Mozambique, and they wrote a paper which included suggestions as to how to overcome some of the problems.

Until recently the USA has tried to control and gather information through various means by using the Faculty of Law. What is commonly referred to as the Faculty of Law crisis was a culmination of honest misgivings against US machinations by the progressive students from this and other faculties. It was triggered off by a new curriculum which wanted to introduce, among other things, military law. The law students organized by USARF rejected this bait, and they went further to form a Vigilance Committee, charged with the duty of seeing that such insidious and perfidious activities would not be allowed to crop up again.

The Political "Science" Department is a mellow group for US traitorous activities as is the Faculty of Law. In August 1969, one American character by the name of Singleton, a visiting lecturer, made snide remarks on both Frantz Fanon and the African Revolution. USARF organized a panel discussion on both Fanon and the African Revolution, and after a perceptive study of imperialist strategy, students contributed money which was sent to the (OAU) Liberation Committee to buy bullets for liberation movements.

One of the major revolutionary functions of USARF was to (i) inform the students and the public the strategy and tactics of imperialism, (ii) to oppose imperialist manipulations; and its attention was mainly drawn to Southern Africa. The British Conservative Government came into power proclaiming their intention of resuming selling arms to South Africa. All progressive African countries have pointed out what this means both to their countries but particularly to the oppressed South Africans. USARF organized fundraising activities, and also went around collecting clothing. Our collection was handed to the Liberation Committee.

Before the inception of the University of Dar es Salaam, a Visitation Committee was appointed to make recommendations on the structure and contents of the new University. USARF, in cooperation with TYL and the TANU Study Circle, forwarded proposals on nearly all aspects of the University. Specifically, our recommendations on the student organization were endorsed by the Committee. Furthermore, in one of the audiences granted to us by the President last June, we proposed the changes in the University Bill to raise the student representation on the Council from two to five. This was carried through and the amendment was affected by the parliament immediately.

Again, towards the end of 1968, one student from the campus was taken to court for involving himself in a brawl with one of the Hall Managers. It was USARF that arranged his successful defense by getting a free lawyer from Uganda.

Official Hostility

We have elected to highlight those incidents we could refer to as central turbulent spots. The theme recurring in these incidents is imperialism coming through such imperceptible means as political science lectures or crude ways like the Rag Day or the British Government's desire to sell arms to South Africa in order to "contain Communism."

USARF did much to stimulate and awaken both the students and the general public from a crippling intellectual slumber. It initiated, through the press, debates on Karadha, a subsidiary of the National Bank of Commerce, which offered – and offers – loans to bureaucrats for buying luxuries. The argument which was never answered was and still is that this is an indulgence into conspicuous consumption, a preserve of the leisure class. Debates were initiated on tourism in Tanzania, *ujamaa* villages, TANU (whether it can carry out a socialistic revolution with its "come-one-come-all" composition), and many other issues. USARF has also given the students and the public the opportunity to listen to revolutionaries like Stockley Carmichael, Robert Williams, C.L.R. James, A.G. Ebrahim, the late Dr. Eduardo Mondlane, Cheddi Jagan, Minister A.M. Babu, and many others.

Perhaps it would be correct to say that it was the tourism debate that started the systematic strangling of the revolution at the Hill of which the banning of USARF and *Cheche* are but a culmination. It started with an exchange of views between us and the Minister responsible for the "industry." The exchange was a fiasco as the Minister seemed incapable of understanding either the economics of the "industry," or the ideological implications. We therefore put our views in the press, triggering a useful debate that however earned us a multitude of enemies. Threats against us were to be heard even in the parliament.

For more than a year, USARF has organized ideological classes. This year's program included such areas of study as Marxist Philosophy and Methodology and the Problems of Underdevelopment and Socialism. President Nyerere's works have always been regarded as required reading. USARF has for instance through its joint organ *Cheche* published a review of one of his works: *Nyerere on Socialism*.

USARF has jointly with TYL been publishing a magazine *Cheche* that has now been banned as well. *Cheche*, which recalls Lenin's *Iskra* and Nkrumah's *The Spark*, has contributed to the socialist debate in Tanzania, Africa and World context. But it did not at any time pretended to duplicate *Iskra* or *The Spark*. The name was suggested and accepted because of the high position in human history that Leninism occupies. Those of us who had the opportunity to read *Cheche* know how engaging it has been, both intellectually and in terms of socialist commitment.

USARF has also, hand-in-hand with TYL, engaged itself in manual work. During the cashew nut season, it picked cashew nuts, sold them, and the proceeds therefrom found their way into coffers of the Liberation Movements. We have accompanied TYL comrades to Bagamoyo to work in Yombo *ujamaa* village.

We were with them in Dodoma too. USARF has all the time participated in the Tanzanian revolutionary process. But this is precisely the reason for it being banned. As a last gesture, we are donating USARF funds to the African liberation struggle.

Ideas Live On

USARF was conceived as and lived as a militant political movement. It has stood firmly for the materialization of true socialism. By its very nature it was bound to participate in and comment on the socialist experiment in Tanzania, to play its part in building socialism. Is that deplorable? If it is a question of TYL having a monopoly over political affairs, do not DUSAUN, WUS, etc. have political affiliations? Are there not many other organizations with dubious ideological orientations on the campus?

Agreed that it is a crime to assimilate foreign socialist ideologies but quite acceptable to be drenched from head to feet in foreign bourgeois ideology. Agreed it is a crime to vehemently uphold the interests of the masses when one sees them being flaunted but quite legitimate to flatter the bureaucrats and petty bourgeoisie for being nominal members of *ujamaa* villages. Agreed it is a crime to be honest, in spite of threats to one's own skin, than be sycophants concerned about expanding the waistline. In brief, it is accepted that it is a crime to think further than the system allows. That is being utopian and adventurist!

The Echo with its hilarious columns on fun, fags, fashion and females is quite relevant to building socialism in Tanzania. But *Cheche*, despite its incisive analyses, is "destructive and irrelevant." In the course of its one year life, *Cheche* has gained tremendous and wide reputation. We have received congratulatory messages from nearly all Liberation Movements in Africa. We were in contact with comradely organizations in places as far as China, the Middle East, Scandinavia, the USA, etc. It may be recalled that after the second issue came out, certain circles accused us of not being down-to-earth, of not bothering about the problems of Tanzania, of not being original. The publication that was to follow, *Tanzania: The Silent Class Struggle* by one of our members caught them unawares and exploded many myths. Once again we were accused of being an alarmist and destructive group. So many people in so many places have anxiously looked forward to each issue of *Cheche*. We take this opportunity to thank them for their encouragement. We are particularly grateful to those who had committed themselves to contributing articles in the future issues of *Cheche*.

Going to *ujamaa* villages, working and learning with people, and forcefully airing their grievances is "none of our business" but the hypocritical bread-and-butter politics of DUSO are to be applauded. A small dedicated group is not conducive for Tanzanian socialism but the large bunch of apathetic students comprise "the true revolutionaries." It is not anyone's job to analyze investment policies of NDC, the TTC, or the NBC for these are being advised by competent and experienced American consultants!

We ask a simple question. Can a magazine be banned just because of its name? Cheche no doubt means the same thing as Iskra. But then how original is The Standard, The Nationalist, or The Echo? Or is it the contents of Cheche that are pricking someone's conscience? If what Cheche publishes are fabrications, then why not disprove them with facts and figures? After all, this University is supposed to stimulate debate within the socialist context. Can socialism be built without sincere and vigorous discussion? Are there as many varieties of socialism as there are nations? If people will think we are building "Russian Socialism" because of the name Cheche, then will they not also think we are building "American Socialism" since our nationalized institutions get advice from American management consultancy agencies! Or perhaps we are building "British Socialism" since Kivukoni College – the party school – is modeled after Ruskin College. If we want to be totally self-reliant, then why not invent Tanzanian political science, sociology, economics, physics, and mathematics? The Catholic Church, among other bodies, has spread slanderous rumors about ujamaa villages and socialism in general all over Tanzania's countryside. But we can stomach that!

We do not have answers to these questions. Yet we do not doubt the wisdom prompting our ban. But one thing must be remembered. Organizations can be banned, individuals can be liquidated, but ideas live on.

REVOLUTIONARY IDEAS NEVER DIE.
THAT IS OUR FINAL STAND.

* * * * *

THE UNIVERSITY STUDENTS AFRICAN REVOLUTIONARY FRONT
University of Dar es Salaam, Tanzania (12/11/1970).

Contributor Profiles

George G Hajivayanis is a holder of a BA (Hons) in Sociology and Political Science (University of Dar es Salaam, 1972), MA in Sociology (University of Dar es Salaam, 1974) and PhD in Sociology (University of Paris at Sorbonne, 1993). He is fluent in English, Kiswahili and French, and converses adequately in several Tanzanian dialects and Arabic. As a student at UDSM, he was a member of USARF and an editor of *MajiMaji*.

He has lectured at the Institute of Development Management at Mzumbe, Institute of Regional Planning in Dodoma, Sokoine University of Agriculture of Morogoro, National University of Lesotho, Lesotho and University of the North in South Africa. In 1997, he attained the rank of Associate Professor. His research has dealt with agricultural issues, politics and nationalism. Among his key publications are: Hajivayanis (1974; 1995; 2000), and Hajivayanis and Ferguson (1991).

Karim F Hirji: is holder of BSc (First Class) in Mathematics and Education (University of Dar es Salaam, 1971), MSc in Operations Research (University of London, 1972), and SM (1982) and DSc (1986) in Biostatistics from Harvard University. As a student at UDSM, he was a USARF activist and an editor of *Cheche*.

Currently he is a Professor of Biostatistics at Muhimbili University of Health and Allied Sciences in Dar es Salaam. Previously he taught at the University of Dar es Salaam, National Institute of Transport, Tanzania, University of California at Los Angeles, and University of California, San Francisco. He is a recognized authority on methods for analysis of small sample discrete data, the author of the only book on the subject (Hirji 2006), and a recipient of the Snedecor Prize for Best Publication in Biometry from the American Statistical Association and the International Biometrics Society. He has published extensively in areas of statistical methodology, applied biomedical research, and the history and practice of education in Tanzania.

His current research relates to quality assessment of clinical trials, analysis of clinical trial data, teaching methods for biostatistics, and ethics of health research. He is writing a case-studies based textbook on medical statistics.

Christopher C Liundi holds BA (Political Science and Education, 1974) from the University of Dar es Salaam. Before joining UDSM, he worked at the TYL Headquarters as a liaison for TYL branches at higher educational institutions. As a student at UDSM, he was a TYL activist, chairman of the Hill TYL branch, and member of the editorial board of *MajiMaji*.

After graduation, he worked with TANU. Later, he joined the Tanzanian foreign service and rose to be the Permanent Delegate to the Organization of African Unity, the Permanent Delegate to UNESCO, and Ambassador to France for Tanzania. Ambassador Liundi is associated with Radio Uhuru, a major broadcaster in Tanzania, and participates in national affairs. He was an invitee at the Oslo Forum 2009, a gathering of prominent African personalities.

Henry Mapolu holds BA (Sociology, 1972) and MA (Sociology, 1974) degrees, both from the University of Dar es Salaam. As a student at UDSM, he was a USARF/TYL activist and member of the editorial boards of *Cheche* and *MajiMaji*. He played a critical role in enabling the birth of the latter magazine after the demise of the former.

After graduation he joined the Sociology Department of UDSM reaching the post of lecturer in 1977. The following year, he made the transition from academia to industry by joining the Friendship Textile Mill as a Worker Education Officer and Training Officer. Among other things, he instituted a series of innovative educational programs for the more than 5,000 employees at the Mill and produced numerous educational pamphlets. From 1982 to 1993, he was a Consultant at the East and Southern Africa Management Institute in Arusha. He left this position to co-found a private management consulting firm, REDMA, which he runs to this day. His company has taken assignments from clients in Tanzania, Malawi, Zambia and Namibia that have focused on organizational development, human resource management and training technology.

In the 1970s, he authored a series of path-breaking papers on workers and management in Tanzania. Two of these were reproduced in the classic work Mapolu (1979). He also did stellar research on *Ujamaa* villages and peasantry under imperialism. Two representative works are Mapolu (1985; 1990).

Ramadhan N Meghji held BA (Economics, 1971) and MA (Development Studies, 1975) degrees, both from the University of Dar es Salaam. As a student at UDSM, he was a USARF/TYL activist and was the designated designer and artist for *Cheche*.

After graduation in 1971, he joined the National Agriculture Marketing Board in Dar es Salaam. From 1972 to 2003, he taught at the Cooperative College, Moshi. He became the Head of the Department of Research and Consultancy. By 2003, he had attained the rank of Professor. He co-authored a book on women and cooperatives, Meghji, Meghji and Kwayu (1985), and wrote papers on the structure and function of cooperatives. In his spare time, he wrote many poems. He passed away in December 2003.

Zakia Hamdani Meghji holds BA (History, Linguistics and Education, 1971) and MA (Economic History, 1977), both from the University of Dar es Salaam. Her MA dissertation was on the status of women workers in industries in Moshi. As a student at UDSM, she was a TYL/USARF activist and member of the editorial board of *Cheche*.

She first taught at the Cooperative College in Moshi. Later she joined the International Cooperative Alliance, where for ten years she conducted programs and training in ten African countries on women and cooperatives. Hon. Zakia Hamdani Meghji (MP) has been a member of the Parliament of Tanzania since 1985 and has held ministerial level portfolios in health, natural resources and tourism, and finance. Presently, she remains an active parliamentarian, and is widowed with five children and eight grandchildren. She is a coauthor of a book on women and cooperatives, Meghji, Meghji and Kwayu (1985).

Yoweri K Museveni holds BA (Political Science, 1970) from the University of Dar es Salaam. As a student, he was a founding member and chairman of USARF from 1967 to 1969. Currently, and for over two decades, His Excellency Yoweri K Museveni has been the President of the Republic of Uganda. The biography of President Museveni is available at the official web site of the Government of Uganda.

Bibliography

Albo G, Gindin S and Panitch L (2010) *In and Out of Crisis: The Global Financial Meltdown and Left Alternatives*, PM Press, Oakland, CA.

Ali T (2005) *Street Fighting Years: An Autobiography of the Sixties*, Verso, New York.

Alidou O, Caffentzis G and Federici S (editors) (2000) *A Thousand Flowers: Social Struggles Against Structural Adjustments in African Universities*, Africa World Press, Trenton, NJ.

Alterman E (2004)*When Presidents Lie*,Viking, New York.

Al-Zaidi M (2009) My flowers to Bush, the occupier: The story of my shoe, *McClatchy Newspapers*, 15 September 2009 (translated by Sahar Issa).

Amara HA and Founou-Tchuigoua B (editors) (1990) *African Agriculture: The Critical Choices*, United Nations University Press and Zed Books, London and New Jersey.

Archer D and Rahmstorf S (2010) *The Climate Crisis: An Introductory Guide to Climate Change*, Cambridge University Press, Cambridge, UK.

Arhin K (1993) *The Life and Work of Kwame Nkrumah*, Africa World Press, Trenton, NJ.

Arnove A (Editor) (2000) *Iraq Under Siege: The Deadly Impact of Sanctions and War*, South End Press, Cambridge, MA.

Arrighi G (1968) Revolution for the social sciences, in IN Resnick (editor) (1968):211–220.

Arvedlund E (2009) *Madoff: The Man Who Stole $65 Billion*, Penguin Books, London.

Athanasiou T and Barr P (2002) *Dead Heat: Global Justice and Global Warming*, Seven Stories Press, New York.

Bais S (2010) *In Praise of Science*, The MIT Press, Cambridge, MA.

Bah K (2009) Memories of war in Sierra Leone: The August 18th uprising, *Pambazuka News*, 3 September 2009 (www.pambazuka.org/en/category/54860).

Baran PA and Sweezy PM (1968) *Monopoly Capital*, Monthly Review Press, New York.

Barlow M (2009) *Blue Covenant: The Global Water Crisis and the Coming Battle for the Right to Water*, New Press, New York.

Barry T (2010) Synergy in security: The rise of the National Security Complex, *Dollars & Sense*, 19 March 2010.

Baxter J (2010) Protecting investors, but what about the people? Dissecting the contradictions of agricultural investment in Sierra Leone, *Pambazuka News*, Issue 480, 6 May 2010 (www.pambazuka.org/en/category/features/64224).

BBC (2007) Child nutrition campaign "fails," *BBC News*, 16 January 2007 (http://news.bbc.co.uk/south_asia/6268487.stm).

Beaud M (2001) *A History of Capitalism: 1500–2000*, Monthly Review Books, New York.

Bello W (2010) Does corruption create poverty, *Foreign Policy in Focus*, 22 April 2010 (www.commondreams.org/55225).

Bello W, Cunningham S and Rau B (1999) *Dark Victory: The United States and Global Poverty*, Food First Books, San Francisco.

Bello W and Kinley D (1986) *Development Debacle: The World Bank in the Philippines*, Institute for Food and Development Policy, San Francisco.

Bennis P and Childers E (2000) *Calling the Shots: How Washington Dominates Today's United Nations*, revised edition, Interlink Publishing Group, New York.

Berger JJ (2000) *Beating the Heat: Why and How We Must Combat Global Warming*, Berkeley Hills Books, Berkeley, CA.

Bethell T (1993) Exporting famine, *The American Spectator*, December 1993:16–18.

Blackburn R (editor) (1991) *After the Fall: The Failure of Communism and the Future of Socialism*, Verso, London & New York.

Bleifuss J and Freeman S (2006) *Was the 2004 Presidential Election Stolen?* Seven Stories Press, New York.

Blum W (2009) *Killing Hope: U.S. Military and CIA Interventions Since World War II* (updated edition), Common Courage Press, Monroe, Maine, USA.

Borjesson K (editor) (2004) *Into the Buzzsaw: Leading Journalists Expose the Myth of a Free Press*, Prometheus Books, New York.

Cabral A (1966) The weapon of theory, *Cheche*, July 1969, No. 2:25–38.

Calongne K (2006) Head of international programs, Swahili instructor and former CIA agent Stephen Lucas passes away, Louisiana State University, (www.lsu.edu/lsutoday/060616/).

Castillo OR (1984) *Tomorrow Triumphant: Selected Poems of Otto Rene Castillo*, Night Horn Books, San Francisco.

Castro A (2004) *Unhealthy Health Policy: A Critical Anthropological Examination*, Altamira Press, New York.

Chachage C and Cassam A (editors) (2010) *Africa's Liberation: The Legacy of Nyerere*, Pambazuka Press, London.

Chavez H and Haranecker T (2005) *Understanding the Venezuelan Revolution*, Monthly Review Press, New York.

Childe WG (1960) *What Happened in History*, Penguin Books, UK.

Chomsky N (1992a) *Deterring Democracy*, Hill and Wang, New York.

Chomsky N (1992b) *What Uncle Sam Really Wants*, Odonian Press, Berkeley.

Chomsky N (1993) *Year 501: The Conquest Continues*, South End Press, Boston, 1993.

Chomsky N and Herman ES (1979) *The Washington Connection and Third World Fascism*, South End Press, Brooklyn, MA.

Cliffe L (1972) Planning rural development, in J Rweyemamu, J Loxely, J Wicken and C Nyirabu (editors) (1972):93–118.

Cliffe L and Saul JS (editors) (1973) *Socialism in Tanzania: A Reader*, Volumes I & II, East African Literature Bureau, Nairobi.

Coulson A (1982) *Tanzania: A Political Economy*, Clarendon Press, Oxford.

Cox OC (1964) *Capitalism as a System*, Monthly Review Press, New York.

Cypher JM (2007) From military Kenynesianism to global neoliberal militarism, *Monthly Review*, June 2007, 59(2) (www.monthlyreview.org).

Danaher K (1994) *50 Years Is Enough: The Case Against the World Bank and the International Monetary Fund*, South End Press, Brooklyn, MA.

Danaher K and Riak A (1995) Myths of African hunger, *Food First Backgrounder*, Spring 1995.

Des Forges A (1999) *Leave None To Tell the Story: Genocide in Rwanda*, Human Rights Watch, New York.

Diouf M and Mamdani M (editors) (1994) *Academic Freedom in Africa*, CODESRIA, Dakar.

Dobb M (1970) *Socialist Planning: Some Problems*, Lawrence & Wishart, London.

Domhoff GW (2009) *Who Rules America? Challenges to Corporate and Class Domination*, 6th edition, McGraw-Hill, New York.

Donahue JM (1986) *The Nicaraguan Revolution in Health: From Somoza to the Sandinistas*, Bergin and Garvey, New York.

Editorial (1999) Robbing Russia, *The Nation*, 4 October 1999:4–5.

Einstein A (1949) Why socialism? *Monthly Review*, May 1949, 1:1–10.

Fanon F (1965) *The Wretched of the Earth*, Grove Press, London.

Fanon F (1967) *Black Skins, White Masks*, Grove Press, London.

Feinsilver JM (1993) *Healing the Masses: Cuban Health Politics at Home and Abroad*, University of California Press, Los Angeles.

Fitch B and Oppenheimer M (1966) *Ghana: End of an Illusion*, Monthly Review Press, New York.

Foner P (editor) (1984) *Clara Zetkin: Selected Writings* (translation by Kai Schoenhals), International Publishers, New York.

Food First (2009) Hunger grows in America and around the world: Do government leaders care? *Food First News & Views*, Winter 2009, 31(115):1–2 (www.foodfirst.org).

Foster JB (2006) *Naked Imperialism: The US Pursuit of Global Dominance*, Monthly Review Press, New York.

Frank AG (1969a) *Sociology of Development and the Underdevelopment of Sociology*, Zenit Reprint, New York.

Frank AG (1969b) *The Development of Underdevelopment*, Bobbs-Merrill, New York.

Freidman B and Preble C (2010) Who are we defending? *Los Angeles Times*, 14 June 2010.

Friedman TL (2000) *The Lexus and the Olive Tree: Understanding Globalization*, Anchor Books, New York.

Freire P (1970) *Pedagogy of the Oppressed*, Seabury Press, New York.

Gabelnick T (1999) Turkey: Arms and human rights, *Foreign Policy in Focus*, May 1999 (www.fpif.org).

Gadea H (2008) *My Life With Che: The Making of a Revolutionary*, Palgrave Macmillan, New York.

Garrett-Peltier H (2010) Why military Keynesianism is NOT the solution, *Dollars & Sense*, 5 March 2010 (www.commondreams.org/53525).

GK (1970) Review: Cheche No. 2, *The Nationalist*, 25 July 1970.

Glassner B (1999) *The Culture of Fear*, Basic Books, New York.

Green RH (1995) Vision of human-centered development: A study in moral economy, in C Legum and G Mmari (editors) (1995):80–107.

Grossman K (1985) *Nicaragua: America's New Vietnam*, Permanent Press, New York.

Guardian Reporter (2010) Tanzania listed among emerging markets in 2010, *The Guardian* (Tanzania), 3 February 2010.

Gumede W (2010) Wealth for Africa, not from Africa, *Pambazuka News*, Issue 447, 10 September 2009 (www.pambazuka.org/en/category/features/58601).

Hajivayanis G (1974) Prisons in Tanzania, *Eastern African Law Review*, 7:227–253.

Hajivayanis G (1995) *Ardhi ni Uhai*, OXFAM and International Institute for Development, UK.

Hajivayanis G (2000) Pemba nationalism and the struggle for the state in Zanzibar, *Developing Alternatives*, 1:3–21.

Hajivayanis G (2010) Revolutionary hot air, *Chemchemi* (University of Dar es Salaam), April 2010, No. 3:42–45.

Hajivayanis G and Ferguson E (1991) The development of a colonial working class, in A Sheriffe and E Ferguson (editors) (1991):186–219.

Han D (2008) *The Unknown Cultural Revolution: Life and Change in a Chinese Village*, Monthly Review Press, New York.

Hancock G (1989) *Lords of Poverty*, The Atlantic Monthly Press, New York & Mandarin Paperbacks, London.

Hansen J (2009) *Storms of My Grandchildren: The Truth About the Coming Climate Catastrophe and Our Last Chance to Save Humanity*, Bloomsbury Press, New York.

Hari J (2009) Lies, damned lies…and the double-speak I would expunge, *The Independent*, 2 September 2009 (www.independent.co.uk).

Harris B (1968) An ideological institute for Tanzania? in IN Resnick (editor) (1968):153–162.

Hartung WD (1995) *And Weapons for All*, Harper Perennial, New York.

Herman ES and Chomsky N (1988) *Manufacturing Consent*, Pantheon Books, New York.

Herren H (2010) Supporting a true agricultural revolution, *Pambazuka News*, 13 May 2010, Issue 481 (www.pambazuka.org/en/category/comment/64419).

Hickel J (2010) Africa, geology, and the march of the development technocrats, *Pambazuka News*, 16 February 2010 (www.pambazuka.org).

Hinton W (1970) *Iron Oxen*, Random House, New York.

Hinton W and Magdoff F (2008) *Fanshen: A Documentary of Revolution in a Chinese Village*, Monthly Review Press, New York.

Hirji KF (1970) Salient implications of "The Silent Class Struggle," *Cheche*, No. 3:23–34.

Hirji KF (1971a) Militancy at the Hill, *MajiMaji*, No. 2:6–13.

Hirji KF (1971b) Crisis on the campus: Diagnosis and implications, *MajiMaji*, No 3:7–11.

Hirji KF (1973) School education and underdevelopment in Tanzania, *MajiMaji*, No. 12:1–23.

Hirji KF (1990) Academic pursuits under the link, *CODESRIA Bulletin* (Senegal), No. 2:9–16.(Updated version in CB Mwaria, S Federici and J McLaren (editors) (2000), Chapter 6.)

Hirji KF (2006) *Exact Analysis of Discrete Data*, Chapman & Hall/CRC Press, Boca Raton.

Hirji KF (2009a) Liberating Africa with laughter: Ahmed Gora Ebrahim at the University of Dar es Salaam, *Awaaz Magazine*, 6(1):26–27.

Hirji KF (2009b) Books, bytes and higher miseducation, *Chemchemi* (University of Dar es Salaam), April 2009, Issue 1:13–20, with rejoinder by Justinian Galabawa, *ChemChemi*, Issue 1:20–22.

Ho M-W (2010) "Land rush" as threats to food security intensify, *Pambazuka News*, 13 May 2010, Issue 481 (www.pambazuka.org/en/category/comment/64403).

Hobsbawm E (1991) Goodbye to all that, in R Blackburn (editor) (1991).

Hobsbawm E (1994) *The Age of Extremes: A History of the World*, 1914–1991, Pantheon Books, New York.

Holsti KJ (1967) *International Politics - A Framework for Analysis*, Prentice–Hall, Inc., New Jersey.

Hofman D (1998) Only elite benefit in "people's capitalism," *Guardian Weekly*, 25 January 1998.

Holt-Gimenez E and Patel R (2009) *Food Rebellions: Crisis and the Hunger for Justice*, Food First Books, San Francisco.

Horn JS (1969) *Away With All Pests: An English Surgeon in People's China: 1954–1969*, Monthly Review Press, New York.

Hossein-zadeh I (2007) Parasitic imperialism: The economics of war profiteering, *Global Research*, 14 July 2007 (www.globalresearch.ca/6330).

Huebner A (2010) How agri-food corporations make the world hungry (http://farmlandgrab.org/11027).

Iliffe J (1979) *A Modern History of Tanganyika*, Cambridge University Press, Cambridge, UK.

Irwin A, Kim JY, Gershman J and Millen JV (2002) *Dying For Growth: Global Inequality and the Health of the Poor*, Common Courage Press, Monroe, Maine, USA.

Jalee P (1968) *The Pillage of the Third World*, Monthly Review Press, New York.

Johnson CA (2004a) *Blowback: The Costs and Consequences of American Empire*, 2nd edition, Holt Paperbacks, New York.

Johnson CA (2004b) *The Sorrows of Empire: Militarism, Secrecy and the End of the Republic*, Holt Paperbacks, New York.

Johnson CA (2008) *Nemesis: The Last Days of the American Empire*, Holt Paperbacks, New York.

Kamenju G (1973) In defense of a socialist concept of universities, in L Cliffe and JS Saul (editors) (1973), Volume 2:283–288.

Kamuzora F (2010) Nyerere's vision of economic development, in C Chachage and A Cassam (editors) (2010):93–104.

Kaniki MHY (1980) *Tanzania Under Colonial Rule*, Longmans, London.

Kanywanyi JL (2006) The University of Dar es Salaam: From a single brick to a "skyscraper": October 25, 1961 to 2006, *The Dar Graduate: Journal of the University of Dar es Salaam Convocation*, 6:1–27.

Karang B (2010) AFRICOM and the US's hidden battle for Africa, *Pambazuka News*, 6 May 2010, Issue 480 (www.pambazuka.org/en/category/features/64223).

Karim SS and Karim QA (2010) AIDS research must link to local policy, *Nature*, 11 February 2010, 463:733–734.

Katz A (2008) Editorial: "New global health:" A reversal of logic, history, and principles, *Social Medicine*, 3(1):1–3.

King LR (1994) *The Beekeeper's Apprentice*, Picador, New York.

Klein N (2008) *The Shock Doctrine: The Rise of Disaster Capitalism*, Picador, London.

Korten D (2001) *When Corporations Rule the World*, 2nd edition, Berrett-Koehler Publishers, New York.

Kreisler H (2010) *Political Awakenings: Conversations with History*, The New Press, New York & London.

Kuhenga M (2008) Why socialism is superior: Cuba's example, *The Citizen* (Tanzania), 29 September 2008.

Legum C (1972) *Africa: The Year of the Students*, Rex Collings Ltd., London.

Legum C and Mmari G (editors) (1995) *Mwalimu: The Influence of Nyerere*, Mkuki na Nyota, Dar es Salaam.

Levins R (2010) How to visit a socialist country, *Monthly Review*, April 2010, 61(11) (www.monthlyreview.org).

Leys C (1975) *Underdevelopment in Kenya: The Political Economy of Neo-Colonialism, 1964–1971*, University of California Press, New York.

Lowenstein R (2010) *The End of Wall Street*, The Penguin Press, New York.

Madsen W (1999) *Genocide and Covert Operations in Africa: 1993–1999*, Edwin Mellen Press, Lewinstone, New York.

Magdoff H (2003) *Imperialism Without Colonies*, Monthly Review Press, New York.

Mamdani M (1978) *Politics and Class Formation in Uganda*, Monthly Review Press, New York.

Mandel M (2004) *How America Gets Away With Murder: Illegal Wars, Collateral Damage and Crimes Against Humanity*, Pluto Press, London.

Mapolu H (editor) (1979) *Workers and Management in Tanzania*, Tanzania Publishing House, Dar es Salaam.

Mapolu H (1986) The state and the peasantry, in IG Shivji (editor) (1986):107–131.

Mapolu H (1990) Tanzania: Imperialism, the state and the peasantry, in HA Amara and B Founou-Tchuigoua (editors) (1990), Chapter 8.

Margolis E (2010) Egypt a ticking time bomb, *Toronto Sun*, 25 April 2010 (www.commondreams.org/55312).

Marques R (2008a) The power of oil and the state of democracy in Angola, *Pambazuka News*, 2 November 2006, Issue 276 (www.pambazuka.org/en/category/comment/38118).

Marques R (2008b) Harvesting hunger in Angola's diamond fields, *Pambazuka News*, 28 July 2008, Issue 391 (www.pambazuka.org/en/category/books/49779).

Marques R (2010a) Unicer: Brewing corruption in Angola, *Pambazuka News*, 25 February 2010, Issue 471 (www.pambazuka.org/en/category/features/62544).

Marques R (2010b) MPLA Ltd: The business interests of Angola's ruling elite, *Pambazuka News*, 11 February 2010, Issue 469 (www.pambazuka.org/en/category/features/62194).

McChesney RW (1997) *Corporate Media and the Threat to Democracy*, Seven Stories Press, New York.

Meghji ZH, Meghji RN and Kwayu C (1985) *The Woman Co-operator and Development Experiences from Eastern, Central and Southern Africa*, Maarifa Publishers Ltd, Nairobi.

Meier A (1999) Russia in the Red: Undone by capitalism, Moscow drifts towards chaos, *Harper's Magazine*, June 1999:63–72.

Metzi F (1988) *The People's Remedy: The Struggle for Health Care in El Salvador's War of Liberation*, Monthly Review Press, New York.

Monthly Review (1971) Editorial notes, *Monthly Review*, July/August 1971: 357.

Museveni Y (1969) Why we should take up rifles, *Cheche*, November 1969, No. 1:32–36.

Museveni Y (1970a) My three years in Tanzania, *Cheche*, July 1970, No. 2:12–14.

Museveni Y (1970b) On "The Silent Class Struggle," *Cheche*, September 1970, No. 3:35–38.

Mwana wa Matonya (1970) Cheche can do more (letter to editor), *The Nationalist*, 31 July 1970.

Mwaria CB, Federici S and McLaren J (editors) (2000) *Africa Visions: Literary Images, Political Change and Social Struggle in Contemporary Africa*, Praeger Press: Westport, Connecticut.

Nagy TJ (2001) The secret behind the sanctions: How the U.S. intentionally destroyed Iraq's water supply, *The Progressive*, September 2001.

Namama AS (1970) Does nationalization help stamp out exploitation? *Cheche*, September 1970, No. 3:19–22.

Nani-Kofi E (2010) US militarisation: The tragedy of Somalia, *Pambazuka News*, 27 May 2010, Issue 483 (www.pambazuka.org/en/category/features/64754)

Navarro V (1993) Has socialism failed? An analysis of health indicators under capitalism and socialism, *Science and Society*, 57:6–30.

Nelson L (1994) Free markets peril Vietnam's health, *Los Angeles Times*, 25 January 1994.

Nestle M (2007) *Food Politics: How the Food Industry Influences Nutrition and Health* (revised edition), University of California Press, Los Angeles, 2007.

Njagi M (1971) The upheaval against bureaucratic arrogance, *MajiMaji*, No. 3:1–6.

Nkrumah K (1966) *Neo-Colonialism: The Last Stage of Imperialism*, International Publishers, London.

Notzon FC, Komarov YM, Ermakov SP, Sempos CT, Marks JS and Sempos EV (1998) Causes of declining life expectancy in Russia, *Journal of the American Medical Association*, 279:793–800.

Nyerere JK (1961) Groping forward: The opening of Kivukoni College, in JK Nyerere (1966a):119–123.

Nyerere JK (1963) Inauguration of the University of East Africa, in JK Nyerere (1966a):218–221.

Nyerere JK (1966a) *Freedom and Unity: A Selection of Writings and Speeches, 1952–1965*, Oxford University Press, Dar es Salaam & Oxford.

Nyerere JK (1966b) The role of universities, in JK Nyerere (1966a):179–186.

Nyerere JK (1967) *Education for Self-Reliance*, in JK Nyerere (1968a):267–290.

Nyerere JK (1968a) *Freedom and Socialism: A Selection of Writings and Speeches, 1965–1967*, Oxford University Press, Dar es Salaam & Oxford.

Nyerere JK (1968b) Implementation of rural socialism, in JK Nyerere (1973):5–11.

Nyerere JK (1968c) *Ujamaa: Essays on Socialism*, Oxford University Press, Dar es Salaam & Oxford.

Nyerere JK (1970) Relevance and Dar es Salaam University, in JK Nyerere (1973): 192–203.

Nyerere JK (1973) *Freedom and Development: A Selection of Writings and Speeches, 1968–1973*, Oxford University Press, Dar es Salaam & Oxford.

Oreskes N and Conway EM (2010) *Merchants of Doubt: How a Handful of Scientists Obscured the Truth on Issues from Tobacco Smoke to Global Warming*, Bloomsbury

Press, New York.

Othman H (editor) (1980) *The State in Tanzania: Who Controls It and Whose Interests Does It Serve?* Dar es Salaam University Press, Dar es Salaam.

Othman H (editor) (2001) *Babu: I Saw the Future and It Works*, E&D Limited, Dar es Salaam.

Othman H (2010) Mwalimu Julius Nyerere: An intellectual in power, in C Chachage and A Cassam (editors) (2010):28–43.

Packard PC (1972) Management and control of parastatal organizations, in J Rweyemamu, J Loxley, J Wicken and C Nyirabu (editors) (1972):73–91.

Panaf (1974) *Kwame Nkrumah*, Panaf Books, London.

Parenti C (1999) *Lockdown America: Police and Prisons in the Age of Crisis*, Verso, London and New York.

Patel R and Delwiche A (2002) The profits of famine: Southern Africa's long decade of hunger, *Food First Backgrounder*, 8(4):1–8.

Patel R (2003) Bad farm policies starve millions: The "export model of agriculture" is a globally destructive force, *Los Angeles Times*, 26 December 2003.

Patel R (2007) *Stuffed and Starved: The Hidden Battle for the World Food System*, Melville House Publishing, New York.

Patel R (2008) The food crisis is over (if we want it), *San Francisco Chronicle*, 19 June 2008.

Patterson S (2010) *The Quants: How a New Breed of Math Whizzes Conquered Wall Street and Nearly Destroyed It*, Crown Business, New York.

Perkins J (2005) *Confessions of an Economic Hit Man*, Plume, New York.

Peter C and Mvungi S (1986) The state and the student struggles, in IG Shivji (editor) (1986):157–198.

Petras J (2009) Latin America's Twenty-First century socialism in historical perspective, *Axis of Logic*, 11 October 2009 (http://axisoflogic.com).

Pineiro C (2009) *Thursday Night Widows*, Bitter Lemon Press, London.

Prashad V (2008) *The Darker Nations: A People's History of the Third World*, New Press, New York.

Public Agenda (2010) New scramble for Africa's minerals: The untold story, *The Guardian* (Tanzania), 26 July 2010.

Qumsiyeh M (2010) Of cowardice, dignity and solidarity, *Common Dreams*, 2 June 2010 (www.commondreams.org/56788)

Raby D (2009) Why Cuba still matters, *Monthly Review*, January 2009 (www.monthlyreview.prg).

Reuters (2009) Angola mulling a Norway-style oil fund: report, *Reuters News*, 27 November 2009 (http://af.reuters.com/articleId=AFJOE5AQ08C20091127).

Resnick IN (editor) (1968) *Tanzania: Revolution by Education*, Longmans of Tanzania Limited, Arusha.

Rodney W (1967) Declaration: Implementation problems, *The Nationalist*, 19 August 1967.

Rodney W (1968) Education and Tanzanian socialism, in IN Resnick (editor) (1968):71–84.

Rodney W (1969a) African labour under capitalism and imperialism, *Cheche*, November 1969, No. 1:4–12.

Rodney W (1969b) Ideology of African revolution: Paper presented at the 2nd Seminar of East and Central African Youth, *The Nationalist*, 11 December 1969.

Rodney W (1969c) Letter to editor: Dr. Rodney clarifies, *The Nationalist*, 17 December 1969.

Rodney W (1971) Some implications of the question of disengagement from imperialism, *MajiMaji*, January 1971, No. 1:3–8.

Rodney W (1972a) *How Europe Underdeveloped Africa*, Bogle L'Ouveture and Tanzania Publishing House, Dar es Salaam.

Rodney W (1972b) Tanzanian *Ujamaa* and scientific socialism, *African Review*, 1(4):61–76 (www.marxists.org/subject/africa/rodney_walter).

Rodney W (1975) Class contradictions in Tanzania, in H Othman (editor) (1980):18–41 (www.marxists.org/subject/africa/rodney_walter).

Rosendahl M (1998) *Inside the Revolution: Everyday Life in Socialist Cuba*, Cornell University Press, Ithaka.

Rozoff R (2010) New colonialism: Pentagon carves Africa into military zones, *Pambazuka News*, 20 May 2010, Issue 482 (www.pambazuka.org/en/category/comment/64564)

Rweyemamu JF (1973) *Underdevelopment and Industrialization in Tanzania: A Study of Perverse Capitalist Industrial Development*, Oxford University Press, Nairobi.

Rweyemamu JF, Loxley J, Wicken J and Nyirabu C (editors) (1972) *Towards Socialist Planning: Tanzania Studies No. 1*, Tanzania Publishing House, Dar es Salaam.

Sanders E (2008) Ethiopia war gets little attention, *Los Angeles Times*, 23 March 2008 (www.latimes.com/news/nationworld/world).

Saul JS (1968) High level manpower for socialism, in IN Resnick (editor) (1968):93–105.

Saul JS (1971) Who is the immediate enemy? *MajiMaji*, January 1971, No. 1:9–15.

Saul JS (1973) Radicalism and the Hill, in L Cliffe and JS Saul (editors) (1973), Volume II:289–292.

Saul JS (2007) *The Next Liberation Struggle: Capitalism, Socialism, and Democracy in Southern Africa*, Merlin Press, London.

Saul JS (2009) *Revolutionary Traveller: Freeze-Frames from a Life*, Arbeiter Ring Publishing, Winnipeg, Canada.

Saunders FS (2001) *The Cultural Cold War: The CIA and the World of Arts and Letters*, New Press, New York.

Savio R (2009) The sudden demise of neoliberal economics, *Business Mirror* (Philippines) 19 August 2009 (http://businessmirror.com.ph/home/

opinion/14843) (from I Shivji (2009) Barua ya wazi kwa Mhe. Benjamin William Mkapa, Rais mstaafu, *Mwananchi*, 27 October 2009).

Schaff A (1968) *A Philosophy of Man*, Bell Publishing Company, UK.

Schlosser E (2005) *Fast Food Nation: The Dark Side of the All-American Meal*, Haper Perennial, New York.

Schmidt M (2010) The new American imperialism in Africa, *Pambazuka News*, 4 February 2010, Issue 468 (www.pambazuka.org/en/category/features/62008).

Segall M (1972) The politics of health in Tanzania, in J Rweyemamu, J Loxley, J Wicken and C Nyirabu (editors) (1972):149–165.

Semonin P (1971) Nationalization & management in Zambia, *MajiMaji*, January 1971, No. 1:16–24.

Sharife K (2009a) Tanzania's pot of gold: Not much revenue at the end of the rainbow, *Pambazuka News*, 1 October 2009, Issue 450 (www.pambazuka.org/en/category/features/59142).

Sharife K (2009b) The battle for Angola's oil, *Foreign Policy in Focus* (www.fpif.org/articles/the_battle_for_Angola's_oil).

Sharife K (2010) Egypt: Between a pyramid and the Empire State Building, *Pambazuka News*, 3 June 2010, Issue 484 (www.pambazuka.org/en/category/features/64926).

Shatz A (2010) Mubarak's last breath, *London Review of Books*, 27 May 2010 (www.lrb.co.uk/v32/n10/).

Sheriffe A and Ferguson E (editors) (1991) *Zanzibar Under Colonial Rule*, James Currey and Heinemann, Nairobi, Kenya.

Shiva V (2000) *Stolen Harvest: The Hijacking of the Global Food Supply*, South End Press, Brookline, MA.

Shivji IG (1970) *The Silent Class Struggle, Cheche*, September 1970, Special Issue.

Shivji IG (editor) (1973) *Tourism and Socialist Development*, Tanzania Publishing House, Dar es Salaam.

Shivji IG (1976) *Class Struggles in Tanzania*, Heinemann, London.

Shivji IG (editor) (1986) *The State and the Working People in Tanzania*, CODESRIA, Dakar, Senegal.

Shivji IG (1993a) Rodney and radicalism at the Hill, 1966–1974, in IG Shivji (1993c):32–44.

Shivji IG (1993b) What is left of the left intellectual at the Hill, in IG Shivji (1993c): 200–209.

Shivji IG (1993c) *Intellectuals at the Hill: Essays and Talks 1960–1993*, Dar es Salaam University Press, Dar es Salaam.

Shivji IG (2010) The village in Mwalimu's thought and practice, in C Chachage and A Cassam (editors) (2010):120–133.

Singleton FS and Shingler J (1968) *Africa in Perspective*, Hayden Book Company, Inc., New York.

Sidel VW (1993) Lessons from China: Equity and economics in rural health care (editorial), *American Journal of Public Health*, 83:1665–1666.

Spencer A (2009) *Tower of Thieves*, Brick Tower Press, New York.

Svendsen KE (1995) Development strategy & crisis manamgement, in C Legum and G Mmmari (editors) (1995):108–124.

Sweezy PM and Bettleheim C (1971) *On the Transition to Socialism*, Monthly Review Press, New York.

TANU (1967) *The Arusha Declaration and TANU's Policy of Socialism and Self-Reliance*, TANU Publicity Section, Dar es Salaam.

TANU (1971) *Mwongozo: TANU Guidelines*, National Printing Company, Dar es Salaam.

Tempest R (1997) How China beat India in success race, *Los Angeles Times*, 10 August 1997.

The Citizen Reporter (2009) Peace Corps set for duty in 19 districts, *The Citizen* (Tanzania), 26 November 2009.

The Nationalist (1967a) Turn College into socialist institution: Babu calls for complete transformation at "the Hill", *The Nationalist*, 13 March 1967.

The Nationalist (1967b) University must produce socialist people, *The Nationalist*, 13 March 1967.

The Nationalist (1967c) Varsity to undergo structural changes, *The Nationalist*, 14 March 1967.

The Nationalist (1967d) Stress on socialism at the University, *The Nationalist*, 15 March 1967.

The Nationalist (1967e) Expel U.S. Peace Corps: TYL resolves, *The Nationalist*, 2 October 1967.

The Nationalist (1967f) Seminar on African Freedom Struggle: USARF panel discussion on "The Strategy, Conduct and Tactics of the African Liberation Movements," *The Nationalist*, 16 November 1967.

The Nationalist (1967g) Teach revolution at Varsity call: Rodney at the USARF Conference, *The Nationalist*, 20 November 1967.

The Nationalist (1967h) Students resolve on E.A. affairs, *The Nationalist*, 28 December 1968.

The Nationalist (1969a) Students reject new curriculum, *The Nationalist*, 5 March 1969.

The Nationalist (1969b) Law students stage protest, *The Nationalist*, 14 March 1969.

The Nationalist (1969c) Dar college authority speaks out, *The Nationalist*, 15 April 1969.

The Nationalist (1969d) Students challenge lecturer, *The Nationalist*, 31 July 1969.

The Nationalist (1969e) University Visitation meets, *The Nationalist*, 6 August 1969.

The Nationalist (1969f) Sack lecturer - students demand, *The Nationalist*, 8 August 1969.

The Nationalist (1969g) Youth condemn U.S. imperialism: Rally held to honor Vietnamese hero, *The Nationalist*, 17 October 1969.

The Nationalist (1969h) Visitation report presented, *The Nationalist*, 4 November 1969.

The Nationalist (1969i) African revolution "must be accepted," *The Nationalist*, 10 December 1969.

The Nationalist (1969j) No liberation "without armed struggle," *The Nationalist*, 11 December 1969.

The Nationalist (1969k) Editorial: Revolutionary hot air, *The Nationalist*, 13 December 1969.

The Nationalist (1969l) Work with masses, youth urged, *The Nationalist*, 15 December 1969.

The Nationalist (1969m) Hill students denounce U.S. imperialism, *The Nationalist*, 22 July 1969.

The Nationalist (1969n) Dar Students' Front snubs liberal Americans, *The Nationalist*, 17 November 1969.

The Nationalist (1970a) The Hill examined: Just what is the balance of forces at the Hill? *The Nationalist*, 13 February 1970.

The Nationalist (1970b) Msekwa to head Dar Varsity, *The Nationalist*, 22 June 1970.

The Nationalist (1970c) Independent Varsity of Dar born today, *The Nationalist*, 1 July 1970.

The Nationalist (1970d) Hill Students' Front asked to cease, *The Nationalist*, 13 November 1970.

The Nationalist (1970e) Editorial: Students' Front, *The Nationalist*, 14 November 1970.

The Standard (1970) Ban claim by USARF, *The Standard*, 13 November 1970.

Tirman J (1997) *Spoils of War: The Human Cost of America's Arms Trade*, The Free Press, New York.

Torrie J (editor) (1986) *Banking on Poverty: The Impact of the IMF and World Bank*, Institute for Food and Development Policy, San Francisco.

Toussaint E (2007) *The World Bank: A Critical Primer*, Pluto Press, London.

Tressel R (2009) *The Ragged Trousered Philanthropists* (new edition), Oxford University Press, Oxford.

USARF (1969) *A Paper Presented to the Visitation Committee Prepared by the University African Revolutionary Front (USARF)*, mimeographed document, 26 August 1969 (signed for USARF by K Mwakasungura).

USARF (1970) *Our Last Stand*, mimeographed USARF statement, 12 November 1970, University of Dar es Salaam.

Vandiver J (2009) AFRICOM building center: Knowledge development team is expected to be fully staffed within 6 months, Stars and Stripes, *European Edition*, 15 June 2009.

Vestbro DU & Persson G (1970) How socialist is Sweden? *Cheche*, July 1970, No. 2:16–22.

Vine D (2010) Too many overseas bases, *Foreign Policy in Focus*, 26 February 2009 (www.commondreams.org/38710).

CHECHE: REMINISCENCES OF A RADICAL MAGAZINE

Volman D (2010) Obama expands military involvement in Africa, *Inter Press Service*, 2 April 2010 (www.commondreams.org/54566).

von Freyhold M (1979) *Ujamaa Villages in Tanzania: Analysis of a Social Experiment*, Monthly Review Press, New York.

Walker TM (2003) *Nicaragua: Living in the Shadow of the Eagle*, Westview Press, New York.

Whiteford LM (2009) *Primary Health Care in Cuba: The Other Revolution*, Rowman & Littlefield Publishers, New York.

Wilkinson R and Pickett K (2009) *The Spirit Level: Why Greater Equality Makes Societies Stronger*, Bloomsbury Press, New York.

Wilson E (2010) Billions pour in for India's insulated superclass, *The Observer*, 9 May 2010 (www.guardian.co.uk/business/2010/may/09/india_billionaires_shashi_ravi_ruia).

Woddis J (1968) *Introduction to Neo-colonialism*, International Publishers, London.

Zelig L (2007) *Revolt and Protest: Student Politics and Activism in Subrahan Africa*, Tauris Academic Studies, London.

Zetkin C (1896) Only in conjunction with the proletarian woman will socialism be victorious, speech at the Party Congress of the Social Democratic Party of Germany, Gotha, 16 October 1896, Berlin, in P Foner (editor) (1984) (www.marxists.org).

Zhang D (2008) China's barefoot doctors: past, present, and future, *Lancet*, 372:1865–1867.

Zinn H (1990) *Declarations of Independence: Cross–Examining American Ideology*, Harper Perenial, New York.

Sources for Preface and Chapter Quotations

Preface: Al-Zaidi (2009). On 14 December 2008, Iraqi journalist Muntadhar al-Zaidi (Muntazir Az-Zaydi) hurled both his shoes at US President George W Bush during a press conference and and shouted in Arabic, "This is a farewell kiss, you dog! This is from the widows, the orphans and those who were killed in Iraq!"

Chapter 1: Nyerere (1966a), page 72.

Chapter 2: TANU (1967).

Chapter 3: Oronto Douglas is a Nigerian human rights activist and lawyer who defended Ken Saro-Wiwa. Quoted in Kreisler (2010):88–98 (Interview with Oronto Douglas, 5 May 2001).

Chapter 4: Hari (2009).

Chapter 5: Don Hector Camara was a Brazilian priest and liberation theologian. This quote was extracted from a poster. The original source is unknown.

Chapter 6: This quote is from a serialized article by Chenge wa Chenge entitled "Who is a socialist?" that appeared in *The Nationalist* in 1969 or 1970. The exact date is not known.

Chapter 7: Zetkin (1896). Clara Zetkin was a militant socialist and feminist active in the German social democratic movement.

Chapter 8: Ernesto Che Guevara wrote these words in a letter to his children sometime before his death in 1967. The letter is reproduced in Gadea (2008):231–232.

Chapter 9: Amilcar Cabral was a revoutionary Marxist who led the struggle against Portuguese colonial rule in Guinea Bissau and Cape Verde Islands. The quote is taken from Cabral (1966).

Chapter 10: Source: Kreisler (2010):88–98 (Interview with Oronto Douglas, 5 May 2001).

Chapter 11: Einstein (1949).

Chapter 12: A fictional Sherlock Holmes depicted in King (1994), page 56.

Chapter 13: Friedman (2000). Milton Friedman is a champion of corporate globalization.

Chapter 14: From a fictional dialogue in Pineiro (2009), page 273.